ROMANTIC PASSAGES

IN

SOUTHWESTERN HISTORY;

INCLUDING

ORATIONS, SKETCHES, AND ESSAYS.

BY A. B. MEEK,

Author of "The Red Eagle," "Songs and Poems of the South," etc.

SECOND EDITION.

MOBILE:
S. H. GOETZEL & CO., 33 DAUPHIN STREET.
NEW YORK:—117 FULTON STREET.
1857.

FRENCH & WHEAT,
Printers and Stereotypers
No. 18 Ann Street New York.

PREFACE.

THE maxim of Crebillon—*not as we will, but as the winds will,*—receives many a verification in literary performance. It has been so with this volume. The author originally proposed publishing an extended collection of his miscellaneous orations, sketches, and essays, and arranged the materials for that purpose, but they were found too voluminous for embodiment in the proposed limits. Yielding, therefore, to the behests of necesssity, he placed aside the larger portion of his productions, and selected such as might fairly fall within the purview of the title, suggested by his publishers, "Romantic Passages in Southwestern History." The contents of the volume are chiefly of this kind, though two of the orations, and some of the reflections in others, are of a more general literary character, and scarcely pertinent to the specific appellation of the book. They will all be found, however, it is believed,—from the stand-points of their view, and the tendency of their speculations,—to bear, reflectively at least, upon the phases and fortunes of the section of our country, to which the more strictly historic papers apply. It should also be stated that though the term "Romantic" is used, it is intended to indicate rather the peculiar character of the incidents, the manner of their arrangement, and the coloring of the style, than any want of authenticity in the facts narrated. These were gleaned, through years of labor and research, in a comparatively untrodden field, and implicit reliance may be placed upon the good faith of every historic statement.

About half this volume has been published before, in isolated portions, in pamphlets or periodicals. The author has been grattified that his researches in Southwestern History have been recognised as valuable, by Bancroft, Theodore Irving, Simms, and Pickett, in their more capacious and dignified performances. This has induced him to revive his articles as they were originally produced, with the addition of other and more copious sketches, elucidating our early history. These were written, for incidental purposes, while preparing a more elaborate work yet to be published, but they may serve, in their present form, to gratify the general reader better than in a more staid and regular connection.

With these explanations, the author submits this volume, as an humble guide-book to an almost uncultured territory, in which the Historian, the Novelist, and the Poet may find the richest materials and incentives for the highest exercise of their respective vocations.

CONTENTS.

ORATIONS.

SKETCHES AND ESSAYS.

THE PILGRIMAGE OF DE SOTO, *Continued:*

ORATIONS.

THE SOUTHWEST;

ITS HISTORY, CHARACTER AND PROSPECTS:

AN ORATION

BEFORE THE

Erosophic Society of the University of Alabama,

DECEMBER 7, 1839.

ORATION.

GENTLEMEN OF THE EROSOPHIC SOCIETY:

AROUND this altar, consecrated to the Muses, you have again assembled to celebrate the festivities of Literature. From the avocations of private life, you have called me to act an important part in the ceremonies of the time. Bossuet, the first of French pulpit orators, tells us that it was his invariable custom, when preparing for the delivery of a public address, to replenish his mind, by a close study of the productions of the master spirit of ancient learning—and that, for such occasions, he always re-illuminated "his lamp at the torch of Homer." If this was the practice of one of the chief of that galaxy of intellectual luminaries, which diffused the mild and humanizing graces of literature over the turbulent reign of Louis the Fourteenth,—how much more does it behove an humble individual, in arising to address an American audience—an audience peculiarly suited by their manners and customs, their political and literary institutions, and by all their habits of thought, to criticise and appreciate what may be said,—and many of whom are fresh from the investigation of the inimitable models of classic lore,—how much more does it behove, I say, such an individual, under such circumstances, to prepare his mind, with the utmost circumspection and care. With a due sense of this high obligation, Gentlemen, I should have answered your very complimentary request to pronounce your Anniversary Discourse, with a prompt but a grateful refusal, had I not been urged by other, and, to me, more interesting considerations. There are, in my mind, a thousand remembrances clustering around this spot, which will ever be treasured and dear. Here the most blissful period of my life was passed; and, as I now look back, through the vista of years, to that brief moonlight track upon the waters of youth, its incidents pass before me, like the creations of a dream, and the feelings it produces are akin to the holiest raptures of poetry. Such are the emotions, always, excited by a return to the intellectual home of our boyhood, and the hope of their renewal is one of the principal reasons that has brought me before you to-day.

But, Gentlemen, I should ill requite the confidence you have reposed in me, and should do violence to my own feelings, if, upon this occasion, I were merely to attempt to amuse you with rhapsodies of sentiment, or to scatter in your path the luxuriant roses that bloom in the Edens of Fancy. We live in a practical age, and are met for practical purposes. The long course of education which you are pursuing, and which to some of you, so far as its collegiate character is concerned, will soon cease,—though, to the loving heart, its occupations may appear more like elysian raptures than the dull realities of life,—and though flowers may hang upon every branch, and grateful fruits delight the taste—is intended but as a preparation and a training for the positions you are to occupy in life,—but to enable you to discharge the duties which will devolve upon you, with honor to yourselves and with benefit to your country. It should be the great moral lesson of your tuition that those duties will be aggregated and enforced by the advantages you receive.

The Society, within whose circle we are now met, is purely practical in its objects. As Lovers of Wisdom, you do not seek merely for those gratifications that die in the enjoyment,—or for incidents to variegate the tedium of study. Yours is no "Beefsteak Club," or "King of Clubs,"—such as the dissipated literati of Europe have been wont to encourage, solely to stimulate the lassitude of the senses. Intellectual and moral improvement—improvement of those faculties which are to be the bones and sinews of mental manhood—these are your views. Eloquence and Logic—that logic which can always unerringly tell right from wrong, through all ramifications and mysticism—and that eloquence which can present the deductions of the intellect or the emotions of the heart, in a manner at once clear, cogent and pleasing—are surely objects worthy the attention of any man, however utilitarian, whose desire is to be anything more than a mere machine in life.

A superficial spectator of the proceedings of this Anniversary might regard them but as the constituents of some transient pageant. Not so: if I have read aright the motives which have brought us hither. Not so: unless I greatly misappreciate the effects of such celebrations. They look to something beyond the mere rhetoric and ceremonial of the time. They are to exercise no unimportant influence, as they are to furnish a permanent remembrance for your future lives. The pomps and the processions,—the motley crowd, with the sage faces of manhood and the smiling eyes of beauty—what is said by the eloquent representative of your sister society—and even what is uttered by your own unworthy speaker, are to be blended together, and are to pass to some extent, in more than one instance, into the composition of that strange piece of mosaic work—the human mind.

These considerations, Gentlemen, warn me that it is my duty to endeavor to make the part assigned me in the festivity, productive of some practical good. With this purpose in view,—with the recollection that I am called to speak in the high cause of Letters and Morals,—with a due consideration of the intellectual employments in which you have been, hitherto, engaged—of those, which, are hereafter, to occupy your attention, and of that theatre, upon which it is your destiny to move, not as mere automata in a show, but as intellectual and moral agents, around each of whom a circle of influence is to be diffused, broader or narrower, according to your own self-formed characters,—it has appeared to me that there is no subject which presents such immediate and powerful claims upon your attention—the strong claims of practical usefulness and philosophic dignity, combined at the same time with novelty and entertainment,—as some reflections upon the History, Character, and Prospects of the Southwest—that particular portion of the Union, in which it has pleased a beneficent Providence, to cast your lots, and to the improvement of whose institutions, and the developement of whose resources, it will be your duty, no matter what professions you may pursue in life, severally to contribute your parts. It is a subject too in which the audience here assembled to witness your celebration, have as great an interest as you, whether considered as merely intelligent or as operative beings. To this subject I, therefore, respectfully invite your attention, and, if in its treatment I should appear dull and, tedious, I beg you charitably to think, in the quaint language of Selden, in his preface to Drayton's Poly-Olbion, "that it is not so much the fault of him that speaketh, or of the subject he handleth, as of that proclivitie of the human temper, to be aweary of that which is instructive, because it seemeth dry, by addressing the coolnesse of the reason, rather than the fervoure of the fancie."

When the rapt prophet of olden time was led by the hand of Divinity, to the summit of the sacred mountain, and, before his wonder-stricken eyes, the rich territories of the Promised Land, with all its scenes of magnificence and beauty, its tall forests undulating to the breezes of a golden summer, its inviting vallies, with their intersecting streams and embosomed lakes,—the blue engirdling mountains on the one hand, and the flashing sea upon the other—all spread out like some great breathing picture—the scene presented, and the emotions produced, apart from the holiness of their origin, could not have been widely different, or more inspiring, than would have met the eye and moved the heart of an intelligent spectator, if he could, an hundred years ago, have been placed upon some eminence overlooking the whole Southwest; and all its magnificence, its fertility, its serene beauty, its conveniences for the purposes of civilized man, have been presented to his mind's eye at once. Our entire country has been characterized as possessing natural advantages superior to any other part of the world. Bishop Berkeley, in that celebrated poem, in which he foretells the greatness of these "happy climes," bases his prophecy upon such advantages, and tells us that, here

> "The force of art, by nature, seems outdone,
> And fancied beauties by the true!"

But it is upon our section of the Union that these blessings are most amply bestowed. Beginning upon the eastern border of our State, and proceeding west to the farthest line of Louisiana, we pass over perhaps the most beautiful and fertile region that the sun looks upon in his diurnal travel. Its territories are everywhere, and in every direction, irrigated and linked together by noble and navigable rivers, which serve not merely to fructify the soil, but to convey its productions to safe and commodious harbors. Through its western portion, that mighty stream, called in the figurative language of the aborigines of this country, The Father of Waters, after passing through almost every latitude, and demanding, from regions well-nigh as remote from each other "as Indus from the pole," the tribute of their fountains,—discharges its accumulated waters, like a flowing ocean, into the Mediterranean of America.

This whole region is marked by a fertility of soil almost unparalleled. Most of those productions of agriculture, which mainly minister to the wants of man, here find a genial home. But it is chiefly in the production of two of the greatest staples of commerce which, by the by, give to the Southwest one of its strongest features of peculiarity, that this mighty region is distinguished: the Sugar Cane, on the one hand, which furnishes a necessary beverage, and one of the greatest luxuries of life, for countless thousands,—and the Cotton Plant, on the other, which has perhaps contributed more than any other article of agriculture, to advance the cause of civilization, to facilitate and strengthen the pacific intercourse of nations, to afford employment and subsistence to the destitute, to recompense industry with opulence, and to alleviate the ills which are the inheritance of humanity.

When we add to these things, the blessings of a climate which is always genial and agreeable, whether viewed in the regal splendor of its summer days, or the milder manifestations of its moonlight evenings; which is subject to little of that oppressiveness that belongs to those lands which lie directly beneath the path of the sun, and to none of the chilling rigors of northern latitudes, and when we remember, that with the exception of a few points upon the seaboard, "the wing of life's best angel, Health, is ever on the breeze,"—we have a correct idea of the physical characteristics of that section of the Union in which we reside.

The name of the Southwest, with a certain sectionality of character corresponding thereto, is given to this portion of the Confederacy—embracing the States of Alabama, Mississippi and Louisiana—from this pervading similarity of physical condition; from its geographical position upon the Gulf of Mexico, into which all its waters discharge themselves; from the pursuits of its population, with their resulting moral and intellectual peculiarities; and to some extent, from the unity and unique character of its early history. To some considerations upon the character of that History, let me now, Gentlemen, direct your attention.

The early annals of almost every country, particularly of the States of antiquity, is involved in impenetrable obscurity. To account for their origin, they are compelled to resort to the dim lights of some bewildered tradition, or, as in the case of that mightiest demonstration of political power of the olden world—"the Demon City," as she has been called by Herder—to create some wild fiction, which comes well nigh blending the incipients of their greatness with the depravity of a brutal connection. In vain has the luminous pencil of Livy, or the glowing pictures of the scholar of Halicarnassus, over whose immortal production the nine Muses are said specially to have presided, endeavored to throw around their primeval condition the colorings of historic truth. All is vague uncertainty or distorting gloom. Not so with the early history of the American States. Their foundations were wrought in the broad light of an illuminated age, and their story has passed with all its truthful lineaments, into the possession of "the preserving page." And yet to this general and enobling certainty there is one important exception. I mean the early history of those States encircling the northern shores of the Gulf of Mexico. Differing widely from the character of the European adventurers who first discovered and took possession of this territory; the memorials of whose settlements, progress, enterprises and intercourse with the natives, commercial, military and religious, are scattered through the rare and antiquated volumes of two foreign languages; and possessing but little sympathy for a race so diverse from their own, in manners, customs and institutions, and who, it is believed, have exercised no influence upon the character and destiny of our country; the people of the United States have silently assented to the behests of their historians, and have permitted these things to be forgotten. Even that population, which now fill the places once held by the French and the Spanish, know little or nothing of their history, and ever and anon, as they stumble over some of the relics of these vanished dwellers of our territories, the cry of *eureka* is raised; the "curiosity" becomes a nine-days' wonder; and is perhaps, in the end, transmitted to the Museum of your University, as a specimen of Indian art. To dissipate this ignorance scarcely anything has been done. A few general facts, as in the pages of Bancroft and Ramsey, have been collected and given to the world, and that is all. The whole history of the Southwest remains to be written. And whoever shall go to the work philosophically,—who shall delve, amid their quaint and musty tomes, for the records of French and Spanish colonization and settlement; and shall collect and embody the scattered materials for such a history; apart from conferring a permanent benefit upon the literature of his country, will possess the honor of being like Coleridge's Ancient Mariner, when entering the Pacific, well nigh

"——— The first that ever burst
Into that silent sea!"

Having frequently, Gentlemen, in the course of a miscellaneous reading,—under the belief that there is no merely theoretical knowledge, which it is more creditable to a man to possess, than the history of his own country, and with the conviction that, if—as Lord Bolingbroke has told us—"History is Philosophy teaching by example," that philosophy can be best learned from those pages which show us man in his most individual capacity, and under the most novel and striking phases of existence; directed my attention to this but partially explored field of Southwestern history; I may be enabled to point out, for your future investigation and improvement, some of its more prominent and interesting features. The present occasion, however, will permit us but to take a hurried and superficial glance at the subject. Such a glance will suffice to show its peculiar and romantic character, and the rich fund of historic materials which lie all unappropriated and daily perishing. For the sake of order and conciseness, we will pursue the natural divisions of the subject into general periods.

I. Two hundred and ninety-nine years ago,—near a century before the Pilgrims had landed at Plymouth, or the Cavaliers at Jamestown, and within fifty years of the discovery of the continent by Columbus,—upon an extensive plain, near the junction of two of our principal rivers, in the very heart of this State, might have been seen collected two large and hostile armies. One of them is composed of the native dwellers in the surrounding forests, to the number of ten thousand, painted and plumed and armed, according to their immemorial customs. The other, though smaller in number, presents the more regular appearance, and powerfnl implements of European warfare. They are engaged in deadly battle. For hours they fight hand to hand, with all the fury of demons. At length the savage hordes are driven back by the more systematic valor of their opponents. They fly for refuge to a city which appears in the back ground of the picture. Here they are pursued; the walls broken down; and amidst the flames of their dwellings—the shrieks of their women and children—the fury of their assailants —this mighty army is unsparingly destroyed.

Is this a picture of fancy? The historic page tells us that in the year 1539, Hernando de Soto, a Cavalier of Spain, after landing in Florida, with an army of one thousand select soldiers, proceeded north through the territory of Georgia; entered Alabama at its north eastern extremity; descended along the banks of the Coosa, to its junction with the Tallapoosa; crossed the latter stream; proceeded west along the banks of the Alabama; crossed it about fifty miles above its junction with the Tombeckbe, and there, on the 18th of October, 1540, fought the battle of Mobile with the natives, headed by their Chieftain Tuscaloosa. For the length of its continuance, the desperate character of the contest, the horrors of its details, and the numbers slain upon both sides, this was by far the most bloody battle ever fought upon the soil of the United States. After remaining several weeks near Mobile, De Soto proceeded to the north, crossed the Black Warrior not far south of the spot at which we are now assembled, and continued his course into the State of Mississippi, where he spent the winter. With the natives he fought many other desperate battles. Subsequently he discovered the Mississippi river, and made several extensive expeditions into the regions beyond it. Throughout the whole of this strange pilgrimage, to which he was incited by motives of avarice, combined with the love of conquest, he encountered dangers and endured difficulties which have no parallel save in the annals of Mexican and Peruvian conquest. At length, overcome by fatigue, dissappointed in his hopes, his forces half destroyed by perpetual battles, famine and disease—he died of a broken heart, and was buried in the middle of that mighty stream which he had been the first white man to cross. Thus, in the language of the most philosophic of American historians, "the discoverer of the Mississippi slept beneath its waters. He had crossed the greater part of the continent in search of gold, and found nothing so remarkable as his burial place!"

This romantic expedition furnishes, in its details, one of the most interesting chapters in American history; and, in its whole inception, progress and denouement, appears more like a creation of fancy than a series of events in actual life. The authenticity and correctness of the accounts concerning it, are, however, well established; and we are justified in considering it the prologue, as well as the first period, of Southwestern History.

II. By this Expedition,—which is known in her annals as "The Conquest of Florida"—Spain considered that she had acquired a right to the whole North American Continent. Her attempts to take possession of it were, however, few and far between. They were principally confined to the settlement of East Florida, and were interrupted by the interference of France, whose emissaries, in the long period from 1562 to 1698—which we shall denominate the second era of Southwestern History,—had explored the Mississippi River, taken possession of the country under the name of Louisiana, and had pushed their way as missionaries and traders among most of the native tribes of the interior. In the latter part of this period, occurred the celebrated expedition of Lasalle, into the territory now the Republic of Texas, by virtue of which, our government long subsequently laid claim to the soil, based upon the French right, as far as the Rio del Norté. The correspondence, which ensued between Mr. Adams, our then Secretary of State, and M. De Onis, the Spanish minister, gives the general outline of this ill-starred expedition, which in its details was well nigh as romantic as that of De Soto. The incidents of this period constitute an important part of Southwestern history, but as they have been generally recorded, we need not farther allude to them, than to say that in 1693, Spain took possession of West Florida, laid the foundation of Pensacola, and established a brisk trade with the Alabamon and Chickasaw Indians.

III. The third general division of Southwestern History extends from 1698 to 1768, a period of seventy years. It is the era of French colonization and settlements; and, while it is the most interesting and important, is that portion of our history of which least is known. The materials for a correct account, although they exist in the rare volumes of a foreign tongue, are, however, abundant and accessible. From them it appears that this period is naturally subdivided into four parts:

1. The first extends from 1698 to 1713. During this time, Iberville, an officer of the King of France, un-

der the direction of his monarch, who was anxious to reduce Louisiana into possession, bought out a colony of some three hundred individuals, and, in 1699, made settlements upon Dauphin Island, in the present limits of Alabama, and at the Bay of Biloxi, now in the State of Mississippi. He immediately commenced an intercourse with the natives of the interior—who consisted, he found, of numerous tribes calling themselves, Alibamons, Choctaws, Mobiles, Chickasaws, &c.; and who had already been visited by traders and missionaries, from the Spaniards in Florida, and the English in Carolina. After building a fort upon the Mississippi River, he returned to France, leaving his brother, Bienville, Governor of the colony. He, in 1702, built a fort upon Mobile Bay, a few miles below the site of our present flourishing emporium, and removed to it the head-quarters of the colony—where it remained until 1711, when in consequence of an inundation in the spring, it was removed to the present site of the city, and Fort Louis, whose ruins are yet to be seen, was built. Throughout the whole of this period, the colonists were engaged in violent wars with the neighboring tribes,—particularly the Alibamons; and, in the latter part of it, with the English of Carolina,—the parent countries at that time being at war. They suffered frequently from disease; and in 1705, the dread visitant, which has recently made such terrible havoc upon the same devoted spot, made its first appearance in the colony, and carried off *thirty-five* of the inhabitants. Nevertheless, the colonists carried on a considerable trade with the natives, in peltries and furs, which they sent to France. To agriculture they paid little or no attention. The population of the colony, which at the close of this period resided principally at Mobile and on Dauphin Island, amounted to three hundred and eighty individuals.

2. The second subdivision of the period of French colonization and government in the Southwest, embraces but four years, but is full of interesting adventure. In 1713, the officers of Crozat, a rich merchant of Paris, to whom the King had given a charter of the Colony, took possession; and Lamotte Cadillac became Governor. Under this charter, the population was greatly increased by emigration from France, and military posts were established along the banks of the Mississippi and in the interior. In 1714, a military establishment, called Fort Toulouse, with a colonial settlement, was made upon the head waters of the Alabama, at the junction of the Coosa and Tallapoosa, near which Fort Jackson was erected in 1812, by the American troops. Some of the evidences of this settlement may yet be found, though they who built, like the native tribe who assisted—then called "the Alibamons"—have long since passed away. Several other establishments were, about the same time, made in the interior of this State and of Mississippi. An old map locates one upon the Tombeckbe, another upon the head waters of the Yazoo, and a third upon the Tennessee, then called the Cherokee river.

Crozat, disappointed in his hopes of profit from commerce with the Indians, and harassed by the continual wars which he was compelled to carry on with them, particularly against the Chickasaws—in 1717 surrendered his charter to the King. He left the colony but little improved, save by the increase of population, which now amounted to near *eight hundred* inhabitants.

3. From 1718 to 1732—a period of fourteen years—the colony was under the government of a chartered association called the "Western Company," and Bienville was reinstated as Governor, much to the delight of the inhabitants. This period is marked by a great increase of population; an extension of settlements into Louisiana and Mississippi; the foundation of New Orleans; a violent war with the Spanish in West Florida; the capture of Pensacola; an attack by the Spaniards upon Dauphin Island and Mobile; the division of the country into nine ecclesiastical districts, for the purposes of the Roman Catholic religion, which was exclusively established; the dissemination of priests and friars among all the Indian tribes; the first serious attention to agriculture, by the colonists, in the cultivation of indigo, rice and tobacco; the introduction of large numbers of slaves brought from the coast of Africa; numerous bloody wars among the Indian tribes; a combination of several of these tribes against the colonists; and finally, the terrible and relentless destruction of the once powerful and almost semi-civilized tribe of the Natchez, by Perrier, who in 1726 had succeeded Bienville as Governor. We can but thus barely allude to all these important incidents. One or two events of a less general character may serve to show the condition and spirit of affairs in the colony.

In 1722, the colony at Fort Toulouse, upon the head waters of the Alabama, was disturbed by a mutiny among the soldiers. Twenty-six rose in arms against Marchand, the commander, and forcing their way out of the fort, departed for the English settlements in Carolina. Villemont, the second in command, immediately collected a large force of the Alibamon Indians, and, with them and the balance of the troops, pursued the fugitives. They were overtaken near the Chattahooche river, and, after a brief but bloody engagement, were, with the exception of eight prisoners, mercilessly massacred. These prisoners were taken back to the Fort, and thence to Mobile, where they were publicly executed. One of them, belonging to a corps of hired Swiss, was put to death according to their bloody military rules. He was placed alive in a coffin, and his body was sawed in two with a cross-cut saw.

Another incident which occurred during this period, casts a softening shadow of romance over the rude life of the colonists, and would afford, in connection with the time, the groundwork for a highly imaginative novel.

Among a company of German colonists, who arrived at Mobile, in 1721, there came a female adventurer, of great personal beauty, high accomplishments, and evidently possessed of much wealth. It was generally believed, as she herself represented, that she was the daughter of the Duke of Wolfenbuttle, and the wife of the Czarowitz Alexius Peter, the only son of Peter the Great, and that being cruelly treated by her husband, she had fled from him, for refuge in these far colonies, while he represented that she was dead. This belief was confirmed by the Chevalier d'Aubant, who having seen the princess at St. Petersburgh, recognized her features in the new comer; and, upon the strength of his opinion, formed a matrimonial alliance with the repudiated wife. After many years' residence in the colony, with all the style of a court,—the Chevalier went to Paris with his princess. Here, for some time, her story obtained general credit, and it was not till after the death of her husband, that she was discovered to be an impostor. It was now proved that the pretended arch-duchess was only an humble female, who, having been attached to the wardrobe of the princess of Russia, had robbed her of large quantities of jewelry and gold, and had fled to America. By a similarity of appearance with her mistress, she imposed upon the credulity of a young officer, who lived in splendor upor her ill-gotten wealth, and died in blissful ignorance of the truth of her history.

The "Western Company" in 1732, surrendered their charter to the king. A few years previously they had removed the seat of government to New Orleans, though the principal business was yet transacted at Mobile. The population of the colony now amounted to over *five thousand* white inhabitants and *two thousand* slaves.

4. The fourth and last period of French government in the Southwest extends from 1732 to 1768, when France became dispossessed of every inch of ground in North America. The most interesting inci-

dent of the first part of this era, is an expedition made against the Chickasaw Indians, by Bienville, who had been re-appointed Governor by the King. These Indians had made many hostile depredations upon the settlements around Mobile, and upon the Mississippi, and had refused to deliver up a party of the Natchez, who, after the massacre, had taken refuge among them. Determining to punish their audacity, and to quell them for all future time, Bienville, in the spring of 1736, left Mobile with an army of fifteen hundred troops, with all the implements and provisions of war. The greater part of the forces ascended the river upon its western bank. The baggage, artillery and provisions were transported in boats. On the twentieth of April, he reached a fort, which he had caused to be built a short time before, on the west bank of the Tombeckbe river, two hundred and fifty miles above Mobile, and to which the appellation of "Fort Tombeckbe" had been given. Here he was joined by twelve hundred Choctaw warriors, who had been engaged for the expedition. With this formidable army, he was twenty days ascending the Tombeckbe, to the point at which Cotton Gin Port now stands. Here, finding his artillery difficult of transportation, and deeming it unnecessary, he erected a temporary fortification, in which he placed it with a company of soldiers. The village, in which the Chickasaws were collected, was distant twenty miles. This Bienville reached on the morning of the twenty-sixth of May, and immediately invested. It was found to be entirely surrounded by strong pallisades, constructed of large trees, and was filled by an immense number of warriors. From several English flags, displayed over the village, evidence was given that the Chickasaws were headed by traders from Carolina. An immediate assault was made upon the fortifications, by the whole army ; but they were found impregnable. Though the most desperate valor was exhibited by the troops, and though they made repeated attempts to storm particular points, which seemed most exposed, they were continually repulsed with great loss. The well directed fire of the besieged mowed down the assailants, and, amidst their war-cries and firing, they jeered them with impotency and cowardice. After continuing his efforts until the close of the day, and finding them all ineffectual, Bienville, with thirty killed—among whom were four of his principal officers—and over seventy badly wounded, commenced a hasty retreat. This he continued for three miles, and encamped for the night. The next day he returned to his fortifications upon the Tombeckbe. His Choctaw allies here abandoned him; and, embarking his troops upon his boats, he floated down the river to Mobile. Before embarking however, he threw his cannon into the Tombeckbe. Some of these were found a few years since, near Cotton Gin, and were said by the pseudo-literati of Mississippi—who, in their wisdom, perhaps had never heard of Bienville,—to be relics of De Soto's expedition !

This unfortunate campaign, in its whole conduct and termination, partakes largely of the spirit of romance. One, who, like your speaker, has ascended the sinuous windings of the Tombeckbe, or traveled through the quiet forests and blooming prairies of upper Mississippi, can scarcely realize that their peaceful solitudes have ever been broken by scenes like these. And yet, if some day, as he is riding through those regions, he will throw his bridle upon the neck of his horse, and look around him, he will find vistages of the Frenchman's Visit visible in more places than one.

After Bienville's return from this expedition, he applied himself, for some years, to the improvement of the colony, in agriculture and commerce with the West Indies. In 1740 however, he prepared another and a more powerful expedition against the Chickasaws. With it he ascended the Mississippi river and the Yazoo, and succeeded in bringing them to terms. He then resigned the Governorship of the Colony, and returned to France.

The remainder of this period of French history, is replete with interesting details. Suffice it to say, that under the government, first, of the Marquis of Vaudreuil, and then, of General Kelerec, the colony continued to flourish to an extent, previously unprecedented: the cultivation of the sugar cane was commenced in 1751; and some attention paid even to those arts which refine and embellish life.

France being worsted in the war, which she had been carrying on with England, by a secret treaty in 1762, ceded all her possessions west of the Mississippi, with New Orleans, to the crown of Spain; and in the next year all the balance to the King of England. She thus became dispossessed of all her right to the soil of North America; though she continued in possession of Western Louisiana, until 1768, when the Spanish officers took possession.

IV. The fourth general division of Southwestern History may be said to extend through a period of thirty-nine years—from 1764 to 1803—when Louisiana passed into the possession of the United States. Of this period I have time barely to say that it is divided into three distinct parts: the one extending to 1783, and embracing the British Government in West Florida, and over the whole of that part of the present States of Alabama and Mississippi, south of the thirty-third degree of north latitude;—another comprising the Spanish government of Louisiana during the whole period, and of West Florida from 1782; and the third, commencing in 1783, of the United States, over all the country east of the Mississippi, and north of the thirty-first degree of latitude. This era is teeming with rich historic materials, whether we look to those events which go to the building of States, or to those lesser things which serve to illustrate man in his individual and social capacity. I cannot linger with them but must proceed to the fifth period of our history.

V. This extends from 1803 to 1819—when the last of the States, now composing the Southwest, passed into the Federal sisterhood. It is, perhaps, as far as we are concerned, the most interesting era of our history: embracing, as it does, the first settlement of this vast region by the pioneers of the population who now possess it,—the thrilling incidents of the "Last War," with the powerful Indian tribes of our State—

with the Spaniards in West Florida, and with the British before Mobile and New Orleans; and the establishment of those municipal institutions, under whose benign protection we live, and in the blessed light of whose influence we are this day assembled. An examination of this period will show us, what I believe is most generally overlooked, that the foundations of our own State particularly, were not effected by the tranquil course of peaceful emigration, but were wrought and consecrated through a bitter sacrament of blood. Such an examination is not now permitted. The materials for a correct history of their time have never been collected. You will find them in the scattered records of our country, and among the perishing traditions of our older inhabitants. In the Western States they have set us an example, in regard to this matter, which we should patriotically imitate. What Flint, Hall, Drake, Marshall, Butler, and many others have done for the States bordering upon the Ohio—at the same time that they have pursued honest and reputable vocations—among which the present temper of these Hesperian longitudes, in the superlative possession of that species of wisdom which belonged to the friends of Job, does not seem to consider exclusively literary occupations,—will not some of you, Gentlemen, in your hours of recreation in after life from more practical purposes, perform for the Southwest?

Only two circumstances in this period, will your time permit me to mention. Printing—which always marks an epoch in the history of a State—was commenced in Mississippi, by the publication of a newspaper at Natchez, in 1809. The first paper ever printed in Alabama, was, the "Madison Gazette," started in Huntsville in 1812. Another was begun at St. Stephens, in 1816, by Thomas Eastin. It was not inappropriately called "The Halcyon,"—and like its fabled prototype, no doubt, had much influence in softening the rude turbulence of the times.

The other circumstance, to which I allude, constitutes an interesting chapter in the history of our own State; and, as it has never been written, and is, in all its features, tinctured with the attractiveness of romance, I will briefly present it to your view. I mean the history of the FRENCH COLONY, which settled in Marengo, in 1817.

The overthrow of Napoleon was followed by the expatriation of many thousands of those who had been the most conspicuous maintainers of his colossal power. Of these a large number came to the United States. Among them were generals, who had won laurels in the proudest fields of European valor, and assisted in the dethronement and coronation of monarchs over millions of subjects; and ladies who had figured in the voluptuous drawing rooms of St. Cloud, and glittered in the smiles and favor of Josephine and of Marie Antoinette. With the irrepressible enthusiasm of their nation, they thought to find, in the quietude and peace of our boundless forests, an Arcadian exchange for the aristocratical establishments and gilded saloons of Paris. They wished to dwell together, and to form a miniature republic of their own, subject however to the same laws as other citizens of the Union. Accordingly they petitioned Congress, to grant them a portion of the public domain in the Southwest. This was done by an act of March the, 3d, 1817, granting to them four townships of land, to be selected by them somewhere in the territory of Alabama. The conditions of the grant were that the emigrants should cultivate the Vine upon one acre in each quarter section, and the Olive upon another other ; and at the end of fourteen years should pay the General Government two dollars an acre, for a fee-simple title to the land. Among the grantees were Marshal Grouchy, the hero of Linden, and the present Minister of War for France; General Lefebvre Desnouettes, Lieutenant General, who had distinguished himself in all the great battles of Napoleon; General Count Clausel, General Count Real, the two Generals L'Allemand, and Generals Vandamme, Lakanal, Penniers, and Garnier de Saintes; with a number of other subordinate officers, whose names are among the composing stars of that galaxy of greatness which encircled the "Sun of the Sleepless!" Under the direction of these men, the location of the colony was made upon the Tombeckbe river, in what is now the county of Marengo. During the year, emigrants, to near the number of four hundred, arrived, and took possession of the soil—which was portioned among them by lottery. They however did not disperse to any great extent though the country, but principally settled down in two villages ; the one called Demopolis, upon the site where the village with the same name now stands; and the other called Eaglesville, situated upon the Black Warrior river, a short distance above Demopolis. In this latter village several of the distinguished men I have named resided. Upon the Colony they bestowed the name of Marengo, which is still preserved in the county. Other relics of their nomenclature,—drawn, similarly, from battles in which some of them had been distinguished —are to be found in the villages of Linden and Arcola. In the spring, after their emigration, they proceeded to the cultivation of the soil, and were soon settled down in the occupations of agricultural life.

A more singular spectacle than the one thus presented is rarely to be found in the leaves of history. It is true that Cincinnatus, when he had saved Rome from the irruptions of her foes, returned to the plough he had abandoned. But here we have instances of men, who had been actors in scenes, which, in military magnifiicence, far transcended the wildest imaginings of the Roman—turning from the theater of their former triumphs, and exchanging the sword for the plough-share, and the spear for the pruning hook. In moral dignity, indeed, the advantage is all in favor of the ancient—for these are driven from their country by compulsion,—but in other respects the parallel is not unequal. Who, that would have looked upon Marshal Grouchy, or General Lefebvre, as, dressed in their plain rustic habiliments,—the straw hat, the homespun coat, the brogan shoes—they drove the plough in the open field, or wielded the axe in the new-ground clearing, would, if unacquainted with their history, have dreamed that those farmer-looking men had sat in the councils of monarchs, and had headed mighty armies in the fields of the sternest strife the world has ever seen? "Do you know, Sir"—said a citizen to a traveller, who in 1819, was passing the road from Arcola to Eaglesville,—"Do you know, Sir, who is that fine looking man, who just ferried you across the creek?" "No! Who is he!"—was the reply. "That Sir," said the citizen, "is the Officer who commanded Napoleon's advanced guard when he returned from Elba!" This was Col. Raoul, now a General in France.

Great as in this contrast, it was perhaps greater with the female part of the colonists. Here, dwelling in cabins, and engaged in humble attention to the spinning wheel and the loom, or handling the weeding-hoe, and the rake, in their little gardens, were matrons and maidens, who had been born to proud titles and high estates, and who had moved as stars of particular adoration, amid the fashion and refinement and imperial display of the Court of Versailles. And yet,—to their honor be it said—notwithstanding the rustic and ill-proportioned circumstances around them,—they did not appear dispirited or miserable. Nothing of "angels ruined," was visible in their condition. They were contented—smiling—happy. As cultivated women always may, they diffused around them, and over the restless feelings of their sterner relatives, the softening graces of the heart, and that intellectual glow which, as Spenser has said of the retired beauty of an English girl,

"Makes a sunshine in the shady place

But not the least amusing as well as singular circumstances, to which these French colonists were exposed, arose from their connection with the adjacent American inhabitants. Who can think of the celebrated officers I have named, being drilled and mustered by one of our ordinary militia captains, and not feel emotions of the supremely ridiculous? And yet such, I am credibly informed, was frequently the case! Many amusing incidents resulted from their ignorance of our language. One, not unworthy of preservation, was this: An officer of the colony became engaged in a fight with a citizen of one of our villages. They used only the weapons which nature had given them. The Frenchman, getting the worst of the battle, desired to surrender according to the ordinary signal in such cases. But he could not think of the word "Enough!" The only phrase he could recall, which he had ever heard upon such occasions, was the word "Hurra!" This he continued to shout, until the byestanders, guessing his meaning, removed his antagonist.

For two or three years, the colonists appeared prosperous and happy, and seemed likely to realize those visions of the pastoral state,—so sweetly sung by the Mantuan bard, and which they had caught from the pages of Chateaubriand and Rousseau. But "achange came o'er the spirit of their dream." The country was found unsuited to the cultivation of the Vine and the Olive. The restless spirits of the leaders, which had been formed and tutored to act a part in those games which loosen thrones and crack the sinews of whole nations, could not be content with the quiet circumference of their backwoods home, in an age of startling incidents, when war was afoot, and the far vibrations of its stormy music, were heard, like the Macedonian invitation, in their sylvan solitudes. Inducements were held out to some of them by the struggling States of South America: and the ferryman left his flat, and the ploughman his furrow, for posts of honor in the army of Bolivar. For some, the decrees of their banishment were revoked, and they returned to "la belle France,"—for which, in their exile, they had felt all the *maladie du pays*, to preside in her senates, or to head her armies. Seeing their leaders thus leaving them, the emigrants, in large numbers, disposed of their lands, and either returned to their native country or sought more congenial homes in our Southwestern cities. The rights of the soil passed into the hands of a few: Congress, at intervals, exempted them from the requisitions of the grant, and ultimately included them in the provisions of the general pre-emption law of 1833. The Colony thus passed away; and though there are many of the original families, at least of their descendants, yet residing in the county, a stranger would in vain look among the black lands and the broad cotton fields of Marengo, for the simple patches upon which the Duke of Dantzic, or Count Clausel attempted to cultivate the Olive and the Vine.

This, is a superficial glance at the French Colony in Alabama; and to my mind it presents a picture that is tinted with all the hues of poetry. Well has the Evil-Genius of modern song exclaimed, 'Truth is strange—stranger than fiction!' Not in the living conceptions of the Wizard of Waverly—nor in the wilder creations of a Goethe or a Boccaccio, have I found aught—with a semblance of probability about it—which could compare with this singular chapter in Southwestern history. Nowhere, but in our own annals can its parallel be found.

And here, Gentlemen, it might seem proper that we should conclude our glance at these "lights and shadows" of Southwestern history. Your attention has already been detained too long with this part of our Discourse. But there is one branch of our history —which, as it pervades the whole, and gives its most marked coloring to each seperate period,—cannot be omitted in an attempt to portray the character of that history,—which it has been my object, upon this occasion, to do, rather than to give you a mere recital of its principal events. I allude to the history of the Indian Tribes, who, until recently, resided within our borders. The time will not allow me to enter into its examination; but a few general facts, collected from the lights furnished us by the expedition of De Soto, the intercourse of the French settlers in Louisiana, and the subsequent acquaintance of the English and Americans, may be stated.

There can be no doubt that the tribes who inhabited the Southwest, thirty years ago, were the same who were in possesion of it three hundred years before,—and had occupied, throughout the time, the same relative geographical positions. At the period of their first discovery, they were much more numerous than at any subsequent date, though they have always been amongst the most powerful of the North American tribes. They have ever been distinguished for great ferocity of spirit, and have constantly waged among themselves, violent and bloody wars. In their institutions, manners, customs and languages, they had not materially changed since their first discovery. Although there are many tribes mentioned by various writers, as having resided in this region—I speak of that part east of the Mississippi,—yet they were all subdivisions of five general tribes,—viz: The Creeks, the Cherokees, the Choctaws, the Chickasaws, and the Natchez. This latter tribe was, in 1726, as we have stated, totally destroyed by the French, and five hundred of them sold into slavery in the West Indies. The remainig four tribes comprised all the other Indians resident in this extensive region. The Coosas, and the Tallisees ot De Soto, and the Alibamons, Muscogees, and Tallapoosas of the French and Spanish writers, were all merged in the Creek confederacy: and the Tuscaluza Indians of 1540, and the Mobile, Tensaw and Biloxi tribes of 1700, were but Choctaws under a different name.

Of the numerous and terrible wars, by which the intercourse of these tribes with the whites has ever been marked, and which consequently gives to our history one of its strongest features of peculiarity—it is impossible now even to make mention. They diffuse along all the lines of our progress the shadows and stains of blood : from the battle of Chicaca, three centuries ago, to the burning of St. Rosalie, two centuries after, from the butchery of Fort Loudon upon the Tennessee, in 1760, to the Massacre of Fort Mimms upon the Tombeckbe, in 1812.

The historian who shall record these things, in connection with the peculiar characteristics of the several tribes, in a manner at all proportioned to the subject, will, it seems to me, furnish as interesting and instructive a volume as has ever been written. There is room for the wildest romantic descriptions, as well as the most profound philosophical research. Vapid and unmeaning declamations will do no good. We want established facts and reasonable deductions. We want a picture of the institutions, religious, political and social; of the manners and customs, military and pacific; of the languages, in their form and construction— of these several tribes. But he, who would give us such a picture, must begin the task soon. The evidences of these things are daily becoming more indistinct. "Like the leaves of the sycamore, when the wind of winter is blowing,"—to use the fine simile of a Choctaw orator,—"the Indians are passing away, and the white people will soon know no more of them, than they do of those deep caves out of which they had their origin!" These tribes have already passed from our soil. It therefore behooves us to be the more active to collect the memorials of their history. It will be, not merely the sketches of a singular people, but will possess the additional value of being inseperably interwoven with our own history, from its earliest era down almost to the present day.

I have now, Gentlemen, concluded such a view of the History of our section of the Union, as I deemed not inappropriate for the present occasion. In the investigation, I am conscious that I have been dull and tedious, and yet, I feel satisfied that you will be better pleased with what I have said, than if I had detained you with the mere effervescence of rhetoric and fancy—with those wind-blown extravagances, which rise upon the surface of thought—the glittering existences of a minute, and then pass away, justifying you in exclaiming, with Macbeth,

> " Earth hath its bubbles as the waters have,
> And these are of them !"

There are many lessons which such a survey of our history forces upon the mind. Not the least of these is the duty of our educated citizens, to develope and collect its materials. This duty will fall with its strongest obligations, upon you, Gentlemen, who have been born and educated within our borders. Although you may never become exclusively devoted to Letters, you will yet have frequent opportunities to discharge this duty—a duty which will be as interesting and agreeable, as it will be honorable to yourselves. By so doing you will best repay to the State, the favors which she has bestowed upon you, in the establishment of high institutions of learning; and will diffuse around you, like the beautiful magnolia trees of our southern forests, a hallowing fragrance, and the influence of an example, which will beautify and adorn the community in which you may reside.

But, Gentlemen, perhaps the first and most interesting duty of a young man, in entering upon life, is to understand properly, the character of the community in which he is to live. With this belief, it was my intention to have addressed you, to-day, principally upon some of the mental and moral characteristics of that section of the Union of which you are citizens, and into whose bosom you are shortly to go as the apostles of her first Literary Institution. My remembrance of collegiate life tells me, that the student is usually better versed in the social economy of the ancient time and States, than in that of his own period and country. He can tell you more of the manners and customs, the sentiments and feelings, the institutions and intercourse, of "the world's grey fathers," than he can of his own immediate society. Many a young man passes through a University, and comes out into life, with the music of Demosthenes ringing in his ears, the morals of Seneca impressed upon his heart, and the philosophy of Epictetus learned by rote, who cannot tell what is the actual character of his own country—what is the condition and impulses of the people about him,—and what are the causes, remote and immediate, which produce that condition, and form and fashion that character. Such a youth I should describe in the language of Pope:

> "A bookful blockhead, ignorantly read,
> With loads of learned lumber in his head!"

If ancient philosophy is at all valuable, it is principally so, because it may be applied to the illustration and improvement of our own times,—because it can guide us in the understanding and formation of our own manners and institutions. It should be a hand-maid and not a usurper—an index and not a goal! Our own age—our own country—our own society—this should be the ultimate—indeed the pervading—view and object of all our acquirements. This, only, makes philosophy practical—this, only, draws the distinction between true learning, and the *Questiones Quodlibeticæ* of the Middle Ages,—beween the valuable instructions of a Stewart and a Say, and the wild theories of a Thomas Aquinas or a Duns Scotus.

It is scarcely necessary, then, to repeat, Gentlemen, that one of the subjects most worthy of your calm and philosophical attention, is the Moral and Intellectual Character of the Southwest. With this estimation, I had intended, as I have already said, to have addressed you at some length upon this topic: but the extent, to which you have been detained with the first part of our Discourse, precludes the possibility of such a view. I must content myself with general allusions to some of the principal features of the subject. Such a course, if it subserves no other end, will at least be directory to the vast field of research and reflection, which opens on the mind.

The character of a country is the aggregated characters of its individual citizens. If these are, in the main, intelligent, virtuous, liberal, industrious, hospitable, and refined, such may be said to be the general character of their community. In proportion as individuals of different qualities enter into the composition of society—so it becomes, in its general tone, less pure and elevated. Thus it will be seen that to judge exactly of the character of a country, we should know the characteristics of its several inhabitants. But it is impossible in a community of any extent, to form an opinion in this way. Resort must be had to other and more convenient methods. The best of these is to examine those general causes which operate to produce and modify the character of every community. This is the plan we propose to pursue in examining the Moral and Intellectual Character of the Southwest. Her peculiarities only, are those to which we will allude. That these peculiarities are numerous, and very prominent, we are daily reminded by the Press in other sections of the Union. Foreign travelers constantly speak of the people of the Southwest as possessing many distinctive traits. Whenever a resident of the other States—particularly from New England—comes among us, he finds many phases and features of society, which are to him not only novel but wonderful: and at the same time he affords to us a specimen of a community varying essentially in its tone, its temper, its feelings, and even, to some extent, in its pronunciation, from our own. This difference ought not to be a source of wonder to a reflecting mind. Even a superficial notice of the history of the human race, shows us that man, in his intellectual and moral attributes, is ever modified by the circumstances around him. It is therefore not more surprising that the extremes of our confederacy should vary in their social, than in their physical, conditions, if we consider that the one is an old and the other a new community. That the peculiarities, which exist in our case, and which are not always creditable to us ; which indeed have given us a character abroad, strangely blending many of the highest virtues with the ruder vices of social life—can be traced, in the main, to circumstances inevitably incident to our condition, I think clearly capable of demonstration. It is a proud consolation, too, that those causes, which have produced the ruder and less ennobling features of our character, are, by the progress of time and the operation of better influences, already passing from existence. Let us now take a glance at some of these causes.

An individual, who wished properly to understand the character of a community, should examine first, how, and of what materials, that community was formed. This is particularly right where it is recent in its origin. Now, in the case of the Southwest, let us see how its society was formed, and what are its component parts. But a few years ago, the greater portion of this vast region—of whose beauties and capacities for the purposes of social man, I have already spoken, —was an uncultivated wilderness, untenanted save by ignorant and ferocious barbarians. The tide of civilized population, however, some thirty years since, began to sweep through its forests. Its progress, at first, was slow and resisted by the primitive inhabitants. The white men consequently, who sought homes in its bosom, like the pioneers of every new country, were adventurous and daring spirits, and the manner of life, which they were forced to lead, was, in a great measure, lawless, self-dependent, and semi-barbarous. But, in a little while, the flow of population became more broad and rapid. Glowing accounts of the natural advantages of the region, attracted emigrants from every section of the Union. The Carolinian, the Georgian, the Virginian, the inhabitants of the Middle and Western States, and the New Englander, all poured, with their families, into this vast and fertile field, with unprecedented rapidity. They came—in the phrase of the day—for the purpose of making fortunes; and were accordingly "business men." Without much reference to each other, they settled down, wherever convenience or the hope of profit seemed to advise; and went to the laudable business of making laws and fortunes. If to this we add a considerable amount of foreign emigration, we have a correct idea of how the Southwestern States, particularly Mississippi and Alabama, were filled with their present population. From such materials, under such circumstances, what kind of a character is it rational to suppose that such a community would possess? The purposes for which they have emigrated warrant that they will, generally, be industrious and practical. They have not left their homes to seek the pleasures and embellishments of life. Profit—that profit which comes from laborious exertion—is their main object. Those virtues which follow in the train of industry—like sparkles in the wake of a ship—frugality, economy, honesty—must be theirs. Hospitality—the chief of social virtues—is taught them by the necessities of their situation. The same cause teaches them self-reliance—and independence of spirit is its consequence. Intercourse, under such circumstances, must be free, unceremonious, and liberal.

All being upon an equality, there can be nothing like aristocracy in society

These excellences are, however, qualified by attendant evils. Roughness of manner; an improper haughtiness of spirit, producing frequently violence and crime; a disregard of the laws and of any restraint; neglect of the charities and courtesies of social life, as effeminate and unbecoming; and a general deterioration of the moral feelings, are, in a new and backwoods community, most usually, the shadows of the virtues I have named. And yet, in the Southwest, their development has been greatly prevented by the goodness and variety of the materials out of which its society was composed. The emigrants, coming from every section of the Union, brought with them, and placed in conflict, that pride of home, with its improvements, and that desire to excel which belongs to the inhabitants of the several States. A competition for excellence, being thus produced, tends to suppress the vices, and to develope and keep alive the virtues, of the community. In such a state of society, it is not to be expected that literature or the fine arts should have a home. These, while they improve the whole structure, are but its embellishments. The architecture of society must be first strong and useful: the Doric and the Gothic are its emblematic orders! Refinement and elegance belong to more advanced stages: and it is then that the graceful Ionic, and the ornate Corinthian—fit metaphors of the beautifying branches of learning—blend their sweet proportions with the more solid parts of the edifice. To speak less figuratively, new communities pay more attention to those parts of knowledge which supply and relieve their wants; which are purely practical in their nature; than to those branches which please the fancy or gratify the heart. Such has been the course and character of the Southwest: and it is clearly referable, I think, to the general causes, I have indicated.

The character, thus drawn, applies more properly to the Southwest, as it was ten years ago, than is at present: but as it is the one yet entertained abroad, to a great extent, I have thought proper to show it, and its producing causes. The evils of a very early state of society have measurably passed from among us. Their effects to some extent yet linger, but are daily diminishing, while the beneficial effects of emigration exist in their full force. One of these, secondary however in importance, is the purity and correctness with which the English language is spoken among us. I believe there is no part of the world,—not even London—in which our mother tongue is pronounced with more accuracy than in the Southwest. No where are there fewer provincialisms. This results from the great and continual admixture of population, from all parts of the Union. Each one acts as a check and a corrective upon his neighbor; and thus the " well of English" is kept pure and undefiled.

Another good and enduring operation which this, our primitive state, has had upon our character, is its effect upon the yeomanry of our land. It has generated an honest, hardy, and patriotic population, who may be fitly described in the language Halleck has applied to the people of Connecticut:

"A stubborn race, flattering and fearing none—
They love their land because it is their own,
And scorn to give aught other reason why;
Would shake hands with a king upon his throne,
And think it kindness to his majesty!'

This leads us directly to the consideration of another general cause, which has had an important operation, in forming the character the Southwest has hitherto maintained; and which must have a preponderating influence, in all future time, upon its mental and moral development and direction. I refer to the Agricultural pursuits of its inhabitants. Such is the physical conformation of our region; such its advantages over the rest of the world for the production of the great staples of commerce and manufactures; and such its geographical, and, I may add, in a kindred sense, its mercantile position; that it must always be looked to and employed as a "growing country." Of the political results of this inevitable condition I shall now say nothing; but in it I see the secret of much of our past, and the assurance of our future, character. Agricultural communities have always been distinguished by peculiarities resulting from their pursuits. Virgil, in that inimitable poem—inimitable for its combination of the simple with the sublime, the pathetic with the humorous, the commonplace with the dignified, and which he was seven years in writing and polishing—I mean the Georgics—has given us a beautiful portraiture of the occupations of the husbandman, and their effects upon his character. The same subject was previously not less sweetly delineated by the Ascrœan bard, Hesiod, in his *Opera et Dies*, and the lessons of agriculture blended with moral reflections worthy of a Plato or a Pythagoras. Hafiz, the Persian, at a later day, and in a far different country, sang the same sweet anthem, in tones not unworthy of his predecessors.

But the beneficial effects of agricultural pursuits upon the mind and morals are not the mere raptures of fancy. It is true that poetry throws a dazzling veil over many imprefections, and shows us only the sunny side of the picture ; yet it holds to reason that that occupation, which attaches a man to the soil, which gives him a definite idea of property and home, which shows him the bountiful rewards of patient industry and economy, which leads him not into the fever and struggle of vexatious and envious life, must spread around him a calm atmosphere of good feelings, and cause the genial and ennobling virtues to spring up in his heart, like the flowers and the plants in the rich fields of his own cultivation. At the same time the operation upon the mental faculties is healthful and improving. Regular exercise is not more beneficial to the body than it is to the intellectual capabilities. *Mens sana in sano corpore* is a maxim attested by the experience of all ages. And yet it is but candid to confess that, while the pursuits of the farmer thus tend to enlarge his intellect—to make it muscular, active, and healthful—capable of prolonged and energetic exertion—they have no direct influence to make him desire or seek for extensive acquirements in learning. Practical information—that kind of knowledge which enables him to comprehend and carry on his own business—is all that he feels to be absolutely necessary. And, yet, we may remark, that if the farmer properly appreciated his own condition, he would find that the whole range of natural science would be of immense advantage to him in his occupation.

That such has been the influence of agricultural pursuits upon the inhabitants of the Southwest, I firmly believe. Their situation in a new and unopened region has, indeed, prevented a full exhibition of these beneficial effects; but the good spirit has been at work, through all their difficulties, and though silent and perhaps unnoticed as the atmosphere we breathe, yet nevertheless like it, has shed a soft and humanizing spell over the rudeness of the times. That it is not an extravagant fancy to augur well from this cause, for our character in future, I am more strongly convinced. It is true that the general diffusion of our population throughout the country, necessarily incident to the nature of their pursuits, will prevent the establishment of many large cities, which seem to be requisite always for the cultivation of the higher refinements and fashions of life. But this in itself may be regarded rather as a blessing than an evil. With those elegancies and improvements, attendant upon the collection of individuals in large masses, ever come many vices which more than counterbalance the good. Some cities will indeed arise upon our sea-coast for the purposes of commerce: but the general mass of our population, as it will be agricultural, will consequently be scattered throughout the country. Is it therefore unreasonable to suppose that they will, in the main, be characterized by those virtues which are incidental to an agricultural community—by industry, generosity, independence of spirit, hospitality, patriotism, and generally diffused and practical intelligence, if not by a refined and elevated literature? Such men make the best citizens in time of peace, and the best soldiers in war. Such men are the surest guarantee of the permanency and virtue of our republican institutions. Plain and unostentatious, they have no desire, as they have no respect, for the glittering baubles and empty metaphors of monarchial institutions. Domestic in their dispositions, firm and patriotic, they are not wafted about by those excitements in politics and trade, which have so often lashed into tempest the crowded and fevered populations of Manchester and Paris. They are not only the bones and sinews of a good community; they are its veins, its arteries, which conduct the regular and healthful currents of pure vitality through the whole body politic.

Such, Gentlemen, I believe, is a correct view of the nature and influence of the pursuits, which, at present engage, and must occupy in future, the attention of the great mass of our population—composed as it is, not of the dwellers in our towns and villages—not of planters who rule over large numbers of slaves,—but of the humble and industrious, who are scattered everywhere, among our hills and valleys, reaping, according to the primal ordinance, the fruits and treasures of the earth. It may seem that I have overrated the number and importance of this class of our society; but any one who will travel through the interior of our country; who will follow the "neighborhood roads," as they are termed, through all their humble windings; who will go to our muster-grounds, our election precincts, our county meeting houses, and occasionally to a Methodist Camp meeting, or a Baptist Association, and will then ask himself where the seventeen hundred thousand white inhabitants dwell, who at present swell the census of the Southwest,—will find that the class, ot which I have spoken, constitute at least a moiety of our actual population. And are not these to be regarded, in estimating the present and prospective character of our country?

Associated with this subject, and contituting another general influence, indeed the principal one—upon Southwestern character, is that division of society which exists throughout the South, and which is denominated our Peculiar Domestic Institution. The present occasion would be inappropriate to enter into the discussion of a topic, which has been discreetly voted a sealed subject among us. I shall therefore only remark, upon its general merits, that I am always ready to maintain, at proper times and places, that it is an Institution, in itself, naturally, morally, and politically right and beneficial. As regards its Intellectual and Moral effects, it may not be improper to say a few words. Much of that character which is peculiar to our section of the Union is traceable to this Institution. By producing two broad and distinct classes in society, it has generated, upon the part of our white inhabitants, a spirit of superiority and self-esteem, a certain aristocracy of feeling, and a proud chivalry of character, which do not elsewhere so generally exist. This has always been known as an effect of such Institutions. Lycurgus introduced the Helots into Sparta to accomplish this end. He believed that the Lacedemonians could not cherish and appreciate properly the social and political virtues, and that that spirit of equality so essential to republican governments could not exist, unless the menial and more laborious duties were discharged by a seperate and inferior class. The beneficial effect upon Spartan character is a matter of history. Bryan Edwards, in his History of the West Indies, tells us that a similar influence is exercised, by this Institution, upon the white inhabitants of those islands. He says that "the leading feature of their character is an independent spirit, and a display of conscious equality throughout all ranks and conditions. The poorest white person seems to consider himself nearly upon a level with the conditon of the richest; and, emboldened by this idea, he approaches his employer with extended hand, and a freedom which, in the countries of Europe, is seldom displayed by men in the lower orders of life to their superiors." In our own country, the same truth, so congenial to republicanism, is still more strongly attested,—and in its train follow many of the higher virtues. Magnanimity, liberality, a spirit of justice, disdain for anything like meanness or parsimony of disposition, a love of excellence, are all characteristics of the Southron.

The facilities and incentives afforded by this Institution, for intellectual improvement, are great and gratifying. The necessity for bodily labor being to a great extent removed from a large part of our citizens, they can devote their full time to the culture of the mind. The spirit which it excites, being one content with no secondary rank in excellence, prompts to the attainment of knowledge in its highest departments. In a few years, owing to the operation of this institution upon our unparalleled natural advantages, we shall be the richest people beneath the bend of the rainbow, and then the arts and the sciences, which always follow in the train of wealth, will flourish to an extent hitherto unknown on this side of the Atlantic.

I might go on and enumerate a thousand other advantages which have arisen, and which will arise, from this Institution, in a moral and intellectual way, but I feel that I am dealing with a subject, of which we had better think than speak. I will leave it therefore, with the simple remark, that it is worthy of your calm and philosophical examination,—and that such an examination will prove to you that this, our Peculiar Institution, is not only right upon principles of morality, but that it is fraught with an influence upon the whole character of our section of the Union, of the most gratifying kind.

If I were here to conclude my enumeration of the general causes, which have tended to produce Southwestern Character, and their results, I should be accused of drawing a flattering and incorrect picture for the sake of sectional gratulation. It is but honest to admit that there are many faults which have not been mentioned. De Tocqueville—perhaps the most sensible foreigner who has ever visited the United States—in speaking of the Southwest, says that "it has ever been marked by lawlessness, frequency of crime, and the impunity with which vice is committed." While bowing our heads in shame before the truth of this charge, I think it can be clearly shown that it depends not, as has been asserted, upon causes necessarily inherent in the constitution of our society. Indeed the charge contains, in its specifications, one of the reasons, why they all exist. "The impunity with which vice is committed" is the cause of "lawlessness" and "frequency of crime." The fault, then is either in the character of our laws, or in their administration. Indeed it is in both: although the evils of the latter result principally from the former. The best guarantee for the execution of the laws is that those laws should themselves be good. If they are of that kind which cannot command the respect of the people, or are such as cause the moral sense to revolt at their execution, they had better be blotted from the statute-book. You cannot expect the officer to enforce the laws, unless the feelings of the community are with him in the discharge of his duty. The history of judicial administration in the Southwest, sustains this assertion. Our laws have been impotent, in many cases, because they have been disproportioned to the offences; and the guilty have consequently gone unpunished. One such omission affects the whole character of justice. Seeing the laws disobeyed or neglected in one instance, the people see no reason why they should not be in others. In many cases, too, we have had no laws where they were much needed. This enables gross and shocking offences to be committed against the community, for which there is no ample or appropriate penalty. Is it to be wondered at that, under such circumstances, the people should take, as it is termed, the law into their own hands? This produces that odious, disgraceful and dangerous practice called "Lynch Law"—which has so frequently, of late years, cast a blackening stain upon the fair character of our region, and which, like the blood of the murdered, upon the hands of the Scottish usurper, will not out, at our bidding.

These evils have all resulted from the fact that we have not had a proper criminal code, in the two States —Alabama and Misissippi—to which the charges are chiefly applicable: and this has, no doubt, arisen from the youth of these States. It takes some time to create a system of penal laws suited to the character of a people. It can only be done by a philosophical examination of that character. The early legislators of our State, and of her western neighbor, erred in thinking that a severe code was best calculated for the times. It is a maxim of law, that severity is not so sure a preventive of crime, as certainty, of punishment; and that there should be a gradation in the penalties, as there is in the turpitude, of offences. It is a gratifying fact that the law-makers of these States have, at length, discovered the truth of these maxims, and have set about reforming their criminal codes. It is to be hoped that the Penitentiary system, which was adopted by our Legislature at its last session, will be so arranged in its details, as to furnish us a system of penal laws, which will fully answer the purposes of justice, and save us, in all future time, from the bitter reproach of being a lawless and semi-barbarous people.

If this subject is properly attended to throughout the Southwest, the dark shadows which rest upon our name will be removed : the ennobling causes of moral and intellectual prosperity, to which I have referred, will have a full and free operation ; our character will become such as we may well be proud of ; and our section of the Union will ascend in every respect to that lofty excellence, of which it has such ennobling prospects. A few remarks upon these Prospects will conclude, Gentlemen, what I have to say to you, to-day.

I have sometimes, in hours of contemplation, attempted to imagine what is to be the destiny of this vast region which we inhabit. In my fancies I have never, for a moment, seperated her from the rest of the Union. The chain, which binds us together, seems, to my mind, to be composed of moral and political motives, and of physical causes, which must always keep us one. And yet that unity can only be best preserved by the citizens of each section, emulating in the progress of improvement. If we stand still here in the Southwest, our section—in military phrase—cannot keep step with the rest of the confederacy ; we must hang like a dead limb upon the body national. No improper motives, therefore, enter into the seperate contemplation of the prospects of our own peculiar region. In my mind such a contemplation gives birth to the purest species of patriotic pride. I look around over our extended territories, and I find them in the possession of a race of men, upon which, for near a thousand years, the choicest benedictions of heaven seem to have been bestowed: the Anglo-Saxon race. They are living beneath the ennobling influence of Republican institutions, and under the blessed light of the Protestant religion. With that spirit which has ever marked their path in history, they are applying to the vast natural resources of this region, all the inventions and improvements which science has given to art. By their efforts, gigantic and savage forests have been changed into scenes of fruitfulness and beauty. Towns and villages have sprung up with the suddenness of a magician's transformations. Rivers, which but a few years ago rolled in unfettered majesty through wide solitudes—"hearing no sound save their own dashing,"—have been converted into channels of commerce, and are now to be seen, lined with floating palaces, conveying to the sea the rich productions of the soil. Across the high hill, and through the deep valley, the long Railroad is visible, passing like a thing of life, uniting distant communities together, cheapening and facilitating transportation and travel, scattering riches around its path with the prodigality of sunshine, and giving to the immense advantages of the country, their full operation upon the rest of the world.

And the tide of this improvement is onward! There is no pause—no exhaustion! Our population itself is rapidly increasing. Where forty years ago there were scarcely five thousand civilized inhabitants, there are now nearly two millions. Well might Mr. Everett say that, when in Germany he spoke of these things, his auditors regarded him with the same surprise and disbelief, with which the Emperor of China viewed the English merchant, who told him that, in the cold climate of Great Britain, water frequently became as hard as stone. And yet this great increase of population is going on with the same rapidity. If it should continue, in a few years how very vast will be the number of our inhabitants! No States in the Union will surpass those of the Southwest.

From these manifestations, and from the mental and moral influences to which I have referred, what is it reasonable to expect will be the destiny of our section of the Union? Is it enthusiasm, to believe that at no very distant day, we shall, in all the constituents of true greatness, in all that can render a people prosperous, happy and respected, in no manner, be inferior to any part of the world! Will you look to Agriculture? Already, but with scarce a tithe of our resources developed, we are furnishing to the world, the great staple commodities of trade and manufactures. Even now, the failure of one of our crops would affect the financial and mercantile interests of Europe to their core. South of us, in our own continent, nations are springing into existence, which are demanding our productions, and will increase the demand for the future. This will force us into Commerce. It is true that, in past years, our trade has been carried on by others, and that through unnatural, and to us expensive, channels : and that there are pseudo-philosophers, even in our own borders, who tell us that this course of things is inevitable, and must always continue. "You want the means—you want the capital!" Such talk is unlettered nonsense. We have the means—we have the capital! We have them in our invaluable natural products, which the world must have. Nothing but an unjust system of national legislation—nothing but the consequent indebtedness of our merchants in the Northern cities—has ever wrenched our trade from direct communion with Europe, and kept it in a route at once inconvenient and circuitous, and which operates to enforce a tax upon us of several millions of dollars annually. If the people of this section will reflect properly upon this subject—if we are left unfettered by restrictive, and oppressive, though indirect, legislation—if the leading minds of our region will devote their time and energies to this object—as that master spirit, who recently fell in a neighboring State,* like Muly Moluck, with his harness on, in the very onset of the battle—the efforts of interested individuals to control our commerce will be as impotent as the struggles of the Persian to fetter the heavings of the sea of Greece ; and the South and her younger sister the Southwest, will flourish to a degree which they have hitherto never known. This exalted consummation, I confidently expect, as not very remote.

But the most ennobling and gratifying prospect,

* Robert Y. Hayne, of South Carolina.

which opens to the citizen of the Southwest, is the excellence which this section of the Union is to attain in Literature. I have looked very erroneously upon the natural advantages of our region; upon the kind and character of its inhabitants; upon the form and nature of its political and social institutions; upon the moral causes which are at operation among us; and at our prospects in every other respect, if we are not destined to an exalted position in the Republic of Letters. A contemporary poet, not more imaginative than philosophical, has told us that "coming events cast their shadows before;" and, if we may deem the appearances about us at all indicative of the future, they surely warrant the anticipation that here the Arts and Sciences—the whole circle of Belles-lettres—are to flourish with the freshness and beauty of their Grecian morning.

This anticipation, Gentlemen of the Erosophic Society, is particularly appropriate to the present occasion. It blends with, and terminates, the character and design of your association. Your object is, by improving yourselves, to improve the Literature of your country. By Literature, I understand not that trivial, puerile and evanescent species of composition, which is produced by love-sick school boys, and bread and butter misses—not that ginger-bread work of the fancy, whose highest ambition is to embalm, in immortal nonsense, the miraculous feats and failings of monks and nuns, of counts and robbers—the very spawn of distorted intellect—nor yet that phosphoric effulgence, which gleams luridly, as in the infidel and infamouswri tings of Voltaire and Rousseau, from the putrid corruptions of the times—but by Literature I understand those exalted manifestations of mind which show that the people of a country think for themselves, think much, think correctly; that their morals, as well as their intellect, are improved; that they are not busied with the frivolous and fantastic incidents of a day, but that they look to that knowledge which developes and enlarges all the capacities of man; which dwindles the distance between the denizens of earth and the higher intelligences of heaven; and which not only receives its own form and fashion from the character of the people and the times, but, as the sea answers to the sun, serves as a mirror in which those people and times are properly reflected for their own gratification and improvement, and which flings back upon them a reforming and beutifying lustre not primitively their own Such is the Literature of which a nation may be proud. Such was the view the Abbe Rollin took, when he included in his course of lectures, at the University of Paris, upon Belles-lettres, the whole circle of ancient and modern learning, and such too is the order of Literature, which I am sure I shall have your warmest sympathies, in predicting, from her natural, political and social characteristics, for the Southwest. That the period is distant when we shall have such a Literature, is perhaps true; but that it will come is as certain as that we shall arrive at great agricultural, commercial and political power. You, Gentlemen, may not live to see it; but by using your exertions, throughout life, to develope and improve the intellectual resources of our region, to disseminate a just appreciation and taste for the higher branches of learning, and to teach our people that there is something more valuable and exalting in life—something better suited to the destiny of beings whose immortality, has already begun—than the mere arts of traffic and amassing money—you may accelerate the dawn of this ennobling period—may produce a " circle in the waters," which unlike the emblem of ambition, will not break by its own extension!

When this period shall arrive, our section of the Union will be in its full power and glory ; our history, our character, our capacities, will be properly understood and appreciated. We may then expect to see our orators occupying the most conspicuous stations in the chambers of National Eloquence: our authors illuminating the age by the philosophy and beauty of their productions. Then, perhaps, the Genius of Immortality shall—as in the beautiful emblematic device of your own Society—place the wreath of Fame upon the brow of many a native Franklin: and then the voice of Poetry—not in her character as a prophet, but as a historian—shall fitly exclaim, in the slightly altered language of an accomplished female writer of our own state:

> 'That, not for northern latitudes alone,
> The stars of virtue and of Genius shone;
> These, moving onward from our country's birth
> To bless, successive, all its spots of earth,
> Shed their full beams' their brightest, and their best,
> Upon the regions of the sweet Southwest."

CLAIMS AND CHARACTERISTICS

OF

ALABAMA HISTORY:

AN ORATION

BEFORE THE HISTORICAL SOCIETY OF ALABAMA,

AT ITS

Anniversary at Tuscaloosa, July 9, 1855.

ORATION.

Gentlemen:

The most elegant of Roman historians, in the introduction to one of his memorable works, complains of the want, in his time, of associated effort for the collection and preservation of the elements of history. He tells us that to individual enterprise it was almost ex-exclusively left to gather and perpetuate the memorials of the past, the records of distingushed achievements, and "the images of those illustrious men, whose examples powerfully animate to virtue, and enkindle an inextinguishable flame of emulation in the breasts of their descendants." Thus, the cultivated era of Sallust had not the advantages of Historical Societies. These, the most powerful auxiliaries of the recording pen, are the product of a period of more extended intellectual refinement. It is in comparatively modern times, that the lovers of historical composition,—the generous minds who would chronicle the deeds and virtues of their ancestors; the growth, progress and renown of their country; the advancement of the arts and sciences; the diffusion of light, liberty, and literature; the amelioration of humanity, and all the other chequered events and influences, which form the life of a people —leaving lessons of instruction for the future,—have availed themselves of the obviously vast advantages derivable from communion in the prosecution of their laudable efforts. Historical Societies are the most efficient agencies ever established for the accurate and comprehensive preparation of history. They not only seize upon the fleeting memorials *temporis acti,*—so as to present the very form and body of the time, more faithfully and fully, than individual ministry could perform,—but they rectify, in the light of common perceptions, the errors of conflicting accounts, the obliquities of personal vision, and the crudities and inconsistencies of partialities, prejudices and passions, and serve, at the same time, the lofty offices of critical judgment and historic philosophy. Such at least would be the character and functions of such associations if they were properly conducted.

To every country its own history is of prime importance. Upon this, its national character and its national sentiments depend. Patriotism, the first of civic virtues, can have no intelligent basis, beyond a blind instinct, save in a just appreciation of the excellences which have marked the career of a country;—of the services, sufferings, and devotion of its sons; of the justice, beauty and utility of its institutions; of its adaptation to the wants of civilized society, and of the lessons of heroism, philanthropy, and intellectual and moral grandeur which its annals present. How essential then, to every State or nation which aspires to be more than a mere Zahara in history, that its records should be compiled and embodied, and its chronicles,—vivified and embellished by the touches of genius,—be rendered imperishable monuments for future ages.

To aid in this great object is, I repeat, the chief office and excellence of Historical Associations. The Society, whose anniversary we commemorate, though but yet in its infancy; is one of these. The American States, in their confederated nationality, present the proudest manifestation of man's moral grandeur, in a political organism, ever yet given to the world. Each of these States, though they blend in historical as in political analogies, has a history of its own, peculiar in its parts, and demanding separate illustration. This has led to separate histories of our several republics, and in most of them to the establishment of Historical Societies. Massachusetts, New York, Pennsylvania and Virginia, have had such institutions for near half a century, and their scholars, statesmen and worthies of every class, have taken especial pride in contributing to their advancement and prosperity. How many memorials of the fickle fortunes of the times, of the transitory but yet interesting incidents of the day, of the services, sacrifices, trials and triumphs of heroes, statesmen, orators, philosophers and divines, have thus been rescued from the remorseless jaws of time, which, like another Saturn, loves to devour his own progeny.

Other and younger States have also their flourishing Historical Societies. I will but mention those of

Georgia and Louisiana, our neighboring sisters, whose institutions, though recently established, have contributed largely to the fund of historic knowledge, particularly as relates to their own territories. They have garnered from the waste and perishing harvests of the past, much useful and interesting information, and the light from these sources, shed over the incidents of their colonial period, invests them with an interest that fascinates the student, and makes him linger with delight over the career of Oglethorpe, or the still more wonderful adventures of Marquette and La Salle.

To appreciate how much Historical Societies may do, for the furtherance of History in its most elevated sense, let us glance at the materials which properly enter into and compose their collections. Their libraries embrace all the rare and curious books, charts and manuscripts, which illustrate or bear upon the discovery, exploration, first settlement and future fortunes of the State. All the materials, however minute or ephemeral, from which the great narrative of events is subsequently to be framed, are thus collected together. Biographies of individuals of all classes, local histories and sketches, transactions and journals of public assemblages, proceedings of legislative bodies, laws, ordinances, discussions, and debates, judicial trials and decisions, statistics, essays and addresses, periodical publications, magazines, reviews and newspapers,—those "brief abstracts and chronicles of the time,"—all these,—the elements of History—are gathered and preserved by such associations as this. They are the *disjecta membra*, which some future Prometheus is to combine and harmonize, and inform with that fire from heaven—the Godlike flame of Genius.

For no portion of our country is such an association so important as for our own State of Alabama. This Society has before it as inviting a field and as potent inducements as are presented in any other member of the Union. Though ours is but one of the younger States; though she has no Revolutionary heraldry; though the dynasty of the wilderness, with its red and roving tenants, has but recently passed by; though two-score years have not elapsed since the establishment of our Constitution; and though but a small part of our adult population are natives of the soil,—yet Alabama has a history as extended and remarkable, as diversified and romantic, as abounding in strange particulars and incidents, as full of the most wonderful phases and contrasts of human life in savage and civilized conditions, and as marked by the bloody struggles of contending forces, as any other part of our country; and over this wide field, so picturesque and attractive, hangs a misty veil,—a morning fog, wreathed around its hills and vallies,—which the first dawn of the sun of historical research has not entirely lifted from its repose, so as to render luminous with golden rays, the attractive regions beyond.

The mission of the Alabama Historical Society is to penetrate this *terra incognita*, and to bring its hidden places to light. Your scope includes the whole extent of our history from its earliest discoverable period to the present day. You stand, in some sort as De Soto did, three hundred and fifteen years ago, with his steel-clad chivalry—his centaur-like warriors, and his white stoled priests, upon the borders of our unexplored territory. Far as his eagle-eyes can pierce, from the last elevated spur of the Look-out Mountains, he beholds a virgin wilderness of all forests, intersected, like lines of silver, by giant rivers, along whose banks rove, in savage and defiant magnificence, the most powerful of all the primeval races that tenanted this continent. His purpose is to explore, to conquer, and to reduce to the uses of civilized man, those boundless regions, in which he fondly thought to find the golden treasures of Mexico and Peru, or the still more precious waters of the Fountain of Youth, which was to restore his decaying faculties and give him an immortality upon earth. The fabulous narratives of Ponce de Leon, and Pamphilo Narvaez, had thus brought the lingering remnants of the Age of Chivalry—of the Flower of Spanish Knighthood—to expend their last waves upon the Indian-guarded forests of Alabama.

With far different objects, but in certain similitudes of research, you stand upon the borders of Alabama history. It is yours to bring to light all that concerns the primeval condition of our territory—to trace, with the first explorers, their blood-stained paths, along our winding rivers and through the heart of the mighty wilderness; to fight over with them again their sanguinary battles; to view the wild and romantic aboriginal races contest with the invader every inch of the soil; to hear that first of patriot warriors, the unconquerable TUSCALOOSA, peal forth his kingly battle-cry; and to see him die with more than the grandeur of Sardanapalus, amidst the flames of his sacked and suffering city—the *first* city of Mobile. What a field of historic research thus opens up, even in this imperfect view! The veil is now lifted from the condition of the first possessors of our territory, and their long and curious career, pregnant with enigmas, and often as silent as the Sphinx of the Sands, presents itself for philosophic investigation. Coming on down through the successive eras of French, British, Spanish, and Anglo-American colonization and possession, what shifting and motley hues are exhibited in the kaleidoscope of our past. These are the domains of the Alabama Historical Society. To collect the confused and scattered accounts of these times long gone; to draw, from the slumbering Herculaneums of French, Spanish, and British archives, the original narratives and reports of the first European explorers and occupants, and render them accessible in our vernacular; to garner the fast fading memorials of our Indian progenitors; and from a later day, to draw forth, embody, and compile, appropriate narratives of the adventures of the pioneers of the present population, as they gradually, through wars and perils, and trials of every kind, passed into the bosom of our State, hewed down the wilderness, opened the broad and fertile fields, laid the foundation of social comfort, and civic prosperity, and eventually organized a State Constitution, distinguished above all others for its guarantees to freedom of conscience, freedom of thought, freedom of speech, and freedom of individual action—to gather and perpetuate the evidences and mementoes of all this, are the functions, the opportunities and the duties of this associatson.

Will any one say that the field of Alabama History is devoid of interest and attractiveness, and unworthy of cultivation? A superficial glance at its leading phases would refute the assertion. I think that, even in the limited space allowed me now, I can show you that, in all the elements which render history valuable; in contributions to a knowledge of human nature under most novel and remarkable circumstances; in the presentation of the finest materials for literary performance, alike in prose romance, and all the departments of poetry; and in the possession of the noblest subjects for the graceful offices of painting and sculpture, our past is truly classic ground, and that there the genius of Prescott and Irving, of Scott and Cooper, Allston and Weir, of Powers and Crawford, might have found the richest opportunities for its exercise. I will glance along at a few passages which will illustrate my argument, and may, at the same time, bring to light, times, events and personages which the recording pencil has not yet delineated or developed.

Some of the most remarkable and romantic chapters in our history have already been frequently portrayed. The story of De Soto, at which I have glanced, is familiar to all. I shall not dwell upon it, but only remark, that in my estimate, it, above all others, affords the best opportunity for a great American Epic. The fierce and fiery chivalry of Spain, with gleaming helmets, and ringnig armor, with champing steeds, and waving banners,—accompanied by a pious priesthood ever bearing aloft the symbol of Christianity,—pushing its way, like the path of some great fiery dragon, through the immemorial homes of the ever hostile and untamable savage, whose superstitions were all as grotesque, as his traditions, his manners and customs were marvellous,—all this, through the noblest region that the sun ever illuminated, still in its fresh and unshorn verdure,—presents a theme from which the genius of a Homer would have framed more than an Odyssey, and the warrior-harp of Tasso would have kindled into as glowing verses as celebrated the Delivery of Jerusalem. Some youthful American Homer, not blind like old Mæonides, but eagle-eyed and fiery-hearted, may yet "fling a poem, like a comet forth," worthy of this great Pilgrimage, and of the genius of our country. Meanwhile, Powell, a native painter, has given us, in a great Historical picture, the "Discovery of the Mississippi, by De Soto," which deserves its conspicuous place in our national Pantheon at Washington.

The period of the possession of Alabama by the French, is replete with remarkable occurrences and romantic details. They came with the closing months of the seventeenth century, and held for sixty-five years. Besides their principal settlement at Mobile, they had military and trading posts, at Fort Toulouse, near the junction of the Coosa and Tallapoosa, on the recent site of Fort Jackson; at the mouth of the Cahawba; at Jones' Bluff, on the Tombeckbee; at the present site of Saint Stephens; at Nashville, on the Cumberland; and at the Muscle Shoals, on the Tennessee, then called the Cherokee river. The erection and intercourse of these several stations, and their dealings with the Indians were constantly attended by difficulties, perils, massacres and conflicts, of the most exciting character. The French traders and missionaries were ever bold, adventurous and enterprising, and it is not extravagant to say that every inch of our territory was trod by their feet, if not watered by their blood, more than a hundred years ago. Numerous wars were also kept up with the Indian tribes, exhibiting instances of heroism upon both parts. But I cannot notice them at present. Time will only allow me to dwell upon some of the general characteristics of the French inhabitants, who varied in number, during this protracted period, from three hundred to three thousand persons, dwelling principally at Mobile. They were a gay, light-hearted, adventurous population. From the first, their national flexibility and vivacity of temper enabled them, with conspicuous facility, to ingratiate themselves with the Indian tribes. Their young men readily adopted the manners, tastes and pursuits of the wilderness, and soon became as expert woodmen, hunters, and trappers, as the natives themselves. Many a "Hawk-Eye" or "Leather-Stocking" was to be found among the *courieurs de bois* from Mobile. Marriages, temporary, or permanent, with the lithe-limbed maidens of the Choctaws or Alabamas, formed links of amity and influence, and gave rise to mixed races, long after clinging to their paternal names. The adventures of the forest, along interminable rivers, over lofty mountains, or across flower-enameled prairies, whether in pursuit of furs and game, or in the hazardous enterprises of war and traffic, or with the mild-minded missionary in the dissemination of the doctrines of the Cross, among the benighted savages, furnished fascinating topics of narration, with which the curiosity of the women and children, around the domestic hearth-stone, was regaled upon the return of the adventurers. The body of the population, at Mobile, were however, engaged in small mercantile avocations, and the constant caravans of Indian ponies, laden with packs and kegs and tin-cups, afiorded picturesque evidences of their inland traffic. Their persons, their houses, their tables and couches were decorated or supplied from the spoils of the chase, in contrast with the embellishments of French finery. The construction of the town facilitated the nimble conversations, across the narrow huddled street, from door to door of the low wide-eaved houses. The days were generally spent in industry; the evenings in dancing and merriment. Many of the colonists had been gentlemen in France; some of them of noble origin; and most of them had pursued military careers. Spirited and adventurous, they had their packs of dogs, their guns, their boats, their Indian beauties, with the influence of a voluptuous climate, and the boundless opportunities and invitations of a new world, fresh and blooming, to provoke and minister to their desires and imaginations. These were the Arcadian days of the French *regime*, and such in part, were the characteristics of the population of Mobile, an hundred years ago! *Tempora mutantur, et nos mutamur in illis!*

What mind is there, but must be destitute of imagination, that does not find in times and scenes and conditions like these,—in the picturesque contrasts between the colonists and their savage neighbors; in their wars, skirmishes, captivities, and perilous adventures; in the fearless Jesuit or the bare-footed Carmelite threading the wilderness to propagate the tenets of his creed; and in the countless diversities of individual character, the finest materials for fictitious composition. What a series of romances, equalling in interest the Waverley Novels, might be founded upon the single career of the gallant and chivalrous Bienville, during the many vicissitudes of his administration as Governor, for more than forty years. He was the heroic founder of Alabama—the Father of our State. The incidents of its early history cluster around him, like the leaves of the oak around their parent stem, and the historian or the novelist can scarcely have a finer theme than to depict his character and career.

The autumn of 1763 saw the dominion of Mobile and its appendages in the interior pass from France to Great Britain. They were a part of the acquisitions of the Seven Years' War, which lost to France all her possessions in North America. The newly acquired territory was made a part of West Florida, with George Johnston, a captain in the Navy, as Governor. Mobile was taken possession of, on the 20th of October, by Major Robert Farmer, as the agent of the King. A regiment of Scotch Highlanders, under Col. Robertson, was sent to garrison Fort Condé. They arrived from Pensacola, by way of the Bay. The act of transfer was signalized by appropriate ceremonies. The Scottish bag-pipes sounded the national anthem of England, as the lillies of St. Denys were lowered from the flag-staff of Fort Conde, and the lion of St. George elevated in their stead : and a *feu de joie* announced that the name of the fortress, in compliment to the Queen of Great Britain, was changed to Fort Charlotte. Soon after, for the purposes of civil jurisdiction, that portion of the province west of the Perdido, as far as Pearl river, was erected into a county, called after the same princess, Charlotte County ; and appropriate judicial and ministerial officers were appointed. Some of the papers executed at this period, and evincing these facts, are now among the records of the Probate Court of Mobile County.

The period of British possession embraces twenty years, and includes the era of the American Revolution. As from this fact it has a peculiar interest, and has never been described by any writer,* I may add something to the fund of historic knowledge, by dwelling more protractedly upon a few of its leading incidents than would otherwise be appropriate. It may, however, be remarked that we have but little accessible information as to the condition and progress of affairs at Mobile and in the interior, during the dynasty of the British, for when they evacuated the province, some years after, they carried with them all the documents referring to this period, and deposited them in Somerset House, London, "where according to positive information," says the Spanish Surveyor General, Vincent Pintado, they were to be found in 1817, and undoubtedly still remain. Would it not be an object worthy of your association, Gentlemen, to endeavor to obtain copies of these papers? Meanwhile, we must grope our way through obscure chronicles and incidental allusions, for any information as to this period.

The first British governor of Alabama, Major Robert Farmer, appears to have been a personage of marked peculiarities of character, and, if we may credit the portraiture of a French cotemporary at New Orleans, would form a not unfit companion-piece for the Knickerbocker functionaries of Irving,—Walter Von Twiller, and Peter Stuyvesant. Aubry, writing to the French government, (May 16, 1765,) says: "The correspondence which I am obliged to have with the English, who write to me from all parts, and particularly with the governor of Mobile, gives me serious occupation. This governor is an extraordinary man. As he knows that I speak English, he occasionally writes to me in verse. He speaks to me of Francis I. and Charles V. He compares Pontiak, an Indian chief, with Mithridates; he says that he goes to bed with Montesquieu. When there occur some petty dfficulties between the inhaitants of New Orleans and Mobile, he quotes to me from the Great Charter (Magna Charta) and the laws of Great Britain. It is said that the English Ministry sent him to Mobile, to get rid of him, because he was one of the hottest in the opposition. He pays me handsome compliments, which I duly return him, and, upon the whole, he is a man of parts, but a dangerous neighbor, against whom it is well to be on one's guard."

This is certainly a graphic sketch of the poetical and classical predecessor of the later Chief Magistrates of our State.

The first step of the new authorities was to take possession of the military and trading establishments in the interior, which had been partially dismantled by the retiring French. Tombeckbee, now Jones' Bluff, was delivered to Captain Thomas Ford on the 20th of November; and a garrison was soon after placed in Fort Toulouse. These stations respectively commanded the intercourse with the Choctaw and Creek Indians.

The spring of the next year saw at Mobile, one of the largest assemblages of aboriginal chiefs and warriors, ever collected in our country. It was a congress of the head-men of all the tribes south of the Ohio, convened to meet Capt. John Stewart, the British Superintendent of Indian Affairs in the South. The career of this functionary is a romance of thrilling interest. He was one of the few survivors of the terrible massacre at Fort Loudon, on the Tennessee, having been spared by reason of his popularity with the savages. The chiefs now flocked to meet him to the number of more than two thousand, and, with their fantastic equipments, presented a most imposing spectacle of savage grandeur. They were encamped for many days within sight of the frowning battlements of Fort Charlotte. The Superintendent was a man of eloquence and shrewdness, as well as of great experience and knowledge of Indian character, and he delivered an able speech, still extant, in Hewitt's History of

Carolina, which had a powerful influence on all the tribes, and induced them to enter into the desired treaty with the British. Only the Six Lower Towns of the Choctaws, and some of the contiguous Creeks dissented, and preferred following the banner of the French to the west of the Mississippi. Thus the many scattered and nomadic villages of Alabama and Mississippi Indians—the Tensaws, Biloxis, Pascagoulas, and Alabamas,—which have bewildered some speculative historians,—made their homes in Louisiana.

Liberal grants of public land were speedily made, by the British authorities, to induce settlements in the interior. These I cannot stop to note. But among the earliest beneficiaries of the govermental bounty, was a colony of French Protestants, whose amiable characters and melancholy fortunes give them a peculiar interest. Their story is but little less romantic than that of the French Emigrants in Marengo, with which you are familiar.

Anxious to secure that dearest of earthly privileges, —"freedom to worship God,"—they solicited, under the patronage of the provincial governor, and received from the King of Great Britain, a large grant of land upon the Escambia river. This they undertook to cultivate with the olive, vine and mulberry, and with rice, indigo, and tobacco,—staples whose culture the government was solicitous to promote. To the number of sixteen leading families, embracing sixty-nine persons, male and female, many of them educated, intelligent and refined, accompanied by carpenters, coopers, blacksmiths, tanners, and other artisans, to the number of two hundred and nine, they were transported in the spring of 1767, at the royal expense, to their concession. At once they entered industriously upon the purposes of their emigration. Their white cottages rose amid the live-oak groves of the region, and the spire of the little neighborhood church pointed its finger of Protestant faith to the sky. But unfortunately the next summer and autumn proved one of those fatal seasons of visitation from "the yellow tyrant of the tropics," and well-nigh all of this interesting colony fell victims to that terrible disease. The Arcadian scheme of Agricultural life was totally destroyed, and the few survivors made their way to Pensacola or Mobile, to lament their friends and seek for more salubrious scenes of employment. What materials for description and pathetic delineation would the genial pens of a Mitford, a Crabbe, or a Wilson have found in this simple narrative from the Lights and Shadows of Alabama Life!

The period of the American Revolution was now at hand; and it will be interesting to learn what relation our colonists held to that great movement. The inhabitants of Mobile and Pensacola, as well as of East Florida, were united in interest, and had but little intercourse or sympathy with the other British colonies. They were too weak, too isolated, and felt too sensibly the gurdian care of the parent government, to desire independence. Accounts of the earlier struggles of the Revolution reached them, but only produced a smile of derision at the "Bostonian Liberty Boys," as the patriots were termed. A few ardent spirits got up a remonstrance against local grievances and the proceedings of Peter Chester, the Governor, and transmitted it to the British ministry; but it was utterly disregarded. Still the people could not be induced to unite in the rebellion of the other colonies. Various efforts were made by Captain James Willing, of Philadelphia, and Oliver Pollock, the agents of the Continental Congress, to seduce them from their allegiance. These gentlemen came by way of New Orleans to Mobile, and circulated clandestinely, many copies of the Declaration of Independence. But the effort was abortive. After many narrow escapes, Captain Willing was at length apprehended through the vigilance of the British officers, and was kept closely confined, a part of the time in irons, in the stone Keep of Fort Charlotte. He came near expiating his temerity upon a gallows in the *plaza* in front of that fortress, but was eventually exchanged at the close of the year 1779, for Colonel Hamilton of Detroit, a British officer, upon whom our government had retaliated for the rigorous treatment of the imprisoned agent.

But the inhabitants of Mobile, though they would not participate in the struggle for Independence, were not to be exempt from the ravages of war attending that event. Spain took part with France in the hostilities against Great Britain, and ordered her American subjects to join in the conflict. Galvez, a gallant and gifted officer, was Governor of Louisiana, and speedily seized the English establishments at Baton Rouge and Fort Bute, on Bayou Manchac. He then proceeded to invest Mobile, with an army of two thousand men.

This force, finely equipped, and provided with artillery, was brought in vessels, by sea, from New Orleans. Landing below Choctaw Point, Galvez advanced to the assault upon Fort Charlotte. This fortress was garrisoned by only eighty regular troops, but they were considerably reinforced by the inhabitants who took shelter within its staunch and solid stone walls, which, defended by British troops, were not to be yielded without a struggle. The Red Cross at the top of the flag-staff returned a stern defiance to the summons to surrender.

The future Viceroy of Mexico, whose name is so honored in Spanish annals, erected his batteries, six in number, with heavy artillery, to the north and west of the Fort. The intervening houses were burned, and a spirited cannonade was carried on for several days. At length, on the 14th of March, 1780, a breach in the walls had been effected, and the commander was compelled to capitulate. Honorable terms were allowed for the gallantry of the defence; but the town had suffered severely from the siege. Among the dwellings destroyed, was the handsome residence of Major Robert Farmer, the former "Governor," who had become a rich landholder, but had died a short time before.

A visitor at the present time to our State emporium would scarcely imagine that occurrences like these had ever happened upon its wide and peaceful site, overbuilt with graceful edifices and adorned with flowering gardens; though it is but only the other day that, in cutting the foundations for the new City Market, the spade of the laborer encountered the still solid relics of old Fort Conde, which, after having stood for a hundred and ten years, was destroyed by the orders of the American Government, that the ground upon which it stood might be used for more civic and utilitarian purposes.

The close of the American Revolution left Mobile and its dependencies in the hands of Spain, and hers it remained for thirty years. This era is one of great interest, and full of events that increase in attractiveness, as they approach our own times. But I must pass them, noticing only a commercial house of large capital and extensive transactions, which had sprung up during the British possession, but now became still more powerful, indeed a ruling influence in the whole Southwest. It was known under the firm-title first, of "Panton, Leslie & Co.," and subsequently of "John Forbes & Co." The partners were intelligent and enterprising merchants of Scottish origin, and had branches of their house at Matanzas and Pensacola. They owned and employed many vessels, and their principal object was to supply the Indians with every species of merchandize. For many years they had carried on a large and prosperous business; but when Spain took possession of Florida, it became a part of her policy to obtain the exclusive trade of the Indians, by drawing it off from the English of Georgia and South Carolina. For this end, they made treaties with the Alabamas, Choctaws, and Chickasaws, to deal only with some one Spanish house, to be chosen by their chiefs. Panton, Leslie & Co. secured this rich privilege, by admitting, as a secret member of their firm, Alexander McGillivray, the celebrated chief and emperor of the Creek Confederacy. This was the secret of the influence which the Spaniards ever retained over that powerful chieftain, and which the authorities of Georgia and the General Government, with Washington at its head, could neither understand nor destroy, and it led to the many bloody hostilities in which they were involved upon the frontiers.

This grasping and powerful house thus established business connections with all the Southern Indians. In every tribe and quarter they had their agents and pedlars; drew constant crowds of Indians to their stores and ware-houses at Mobile and Pensacola; granted extensive credits to chieftains and tribes; despatched their vessels to the West Indies and Europe, laden with peltries, furs, and other products of the country; received returned cargoes of every variety of merchandize; amassed immense profits; and wielded a commercial power and influence not before or since equaled by any one house in either of the emporiums of the South. Some of the partners resided at Mobile, throughout the Spanish period, in fine residences, elegantly supplied with the luxuries of taste and comfort; and they lived in a style of princely magnificence. By taking the oath of allegiance to the Spanish crown, they secured the right of citizenship, and became grantees of large tracts of land, which have been subjects of frequent legal investigation under our government. The firm was at first composed of John Forbes, William Panton, and John Leslie. The last two retiring,

John and James Innerarity, brothers, became members under its second designation. The several associates, excepting McGillivray, were all related by either consanguinity or marriage, and were connected with wealthy Spanish families in Cuba.

Towards the termination of its existence, this opulent house found all the Indian tribes largely in its debt, and was compelled to take from them in payment extensive tracts of land, which were ceded by treaty. The Choctaws, thus made compensation for a debt of more than forty thousand dollars; and the Lower Creeks and Seminoles (McGillivray being dead) granted, in liquidation of a much larger debt, a million and a half of acres, on the Apalachicola. How forcibly do the fortunes of this house verify, even in the primitive days of Alabama, the assertion of Carlyle, that "Commerce is King!"

The lingering dynasty of the Spaniard fades into the morning dawn of Anglo-Saxon settlements in our State. The hour and the man had now come to subdue and possess the wilderness. As early as the Revolution, large bodies of the unfortunate adherents of the British cause had fled from South Carolina and Georgia, through the dense and pathless forests between, to the shores of the Tombeckbee and Mobile Bay. They laid the first foundations of American inhabitancy in the counties of Clarke, Washington, and Baldwin. Some of the stragglers lingered on the way, and intermarried with the Creek Indians, giving rise to the half-breed chieftains, such as the Mackintoshes, the Manacs, the McQueens, the McGirks, and others subsequently winning sanguinary celebrities. What an atmosphere of romance hangs over even this portion of our story; but how it is deepened and brightened with sunnier hues, as the streams of population now pour in, from the eastward, through savage perils, across giant rivers, and through unopened woods, to the Southwestern quarter of our State. The various treaties of the French, British and Spanish, with the Indians, made this region the resort of the first emigrants. The experiences of this backwoods life, for more than twenty years, were quite as singular and wonderful as those of Boone and Kenton in Kentucky, or Sevier and Robertson in Tennessee. They had their quarrels and conflicts with the Spaniards on their Southern border, and more than one *fillibuster* enterprise was projected for the seizure of Mobile.

But time as it passed on and filled these solitudes with settlers, at last brought the most sanguinary era in Alabama history. The leading incidents of the war that begun at Burnt Corn and Fort Mims, and ended at the Horse Shoe—the bloody Illiad, in which the form of Jackson stands conspicuously forth, a greater than Achilles—is better known than other chapter in our annals. The subordinate events of the time, forming the no less interesting, though more private history of our people, have generally been overlooked, living only in perishing traditions. The first pioneers and settlers of our State encountered dangers, privations and sufferings, and performed heroic actions well worthy of being registered by the Muse of History. They were a hardy, gallant, adventurous race. Take one, a central figure, as an example. I see before me, in imagination, as I saw him more than twenty years ago, the stalwart form, the Herculean proportions, of Gen. Samuel Dale. He was the Daniel Boone of Alabama. Inured from his boyhood to Indian conflicts on the frontiers of Georgia, and early trained to all the wiles and stratagems of savage warfare; winning the highest character for dauntless courage, vigilance and strength; then a trader among the Creeks and Cherokees, exchanging manufactured goods for cattle and ponies; then a guide for emigrants along the blind or blazed paths that led from Georgia to the Tombeckbee; and eventually a settler, with his wife and his axe in Clarke county,—this man, when the war with the Indians broke out, was the very man for the time. The Red Men of Alabama knew him well, and dreaded his prowess. In their descriptive language, they called him Sam *Thlucco*, or Big Sam. And well did he justify, by his performances, the fear of his enemies. The Canoe Fight, where with only two assistants, he vanquished nine of the most gallant Creek warriors, is but one incident in the chronicle of his deeds. On another day, solitary and alone, he had slain with his own hands, five warriors, and rescued a female prisoner, who speedily evinced her gratitude by saving him from the knife of a sixth foeman, who would otherwise have succeeded in taking his life.

This is the Representative Man of the era of our War with the Creeks. And well might his statue tower in marble in our halls of State. He was a Richard Cœur de Leon,—a Godfrey of Bouillon—moulded and fashioned to the circumstances of his forest home. After the war he served in our Legislature, honored a new country with his name, and then went to Mississippi, to die in the fulness of years, in May, 1841, honored and beloved.

Cotemporary with the advent of Dale to South Alabama, was the arrival of another pioneer, of somewhat kindred though milder taste, in the Valley of the Tennessee,—a hunter rather than a warrior. Stories of the fertility of that region were circulated early after the American Revolution. Hunters and adventurers, who had explored the wilderness, brought back glowing accounts of its unexampled loveliness; its wide sweeps of luxuriant soil, clothed with the noblest of all forest trees; its bold and gushing limestone springs, and swift streams abounding in fish or suited to ply the water-wheel; its game of every variety,—the bear, the deer, the beaver; and its pure and genial climate, locked in by the overtopping mountains of the south and east, which furnished picturesque views of the inviting panorama. This was the favorite border hunting ground of the Cherokees and the Chickasaws, which their rivalry had kept sacred from the possession of either. An ineffectual attempt had been made as early as 1784, to settle it, by Colonels Robertson and Sevier, and Georgia had actually erected it into a county, denominated Houstòn, after one of her earlier Governors; but it was not until July, 1805, that its title was ceded to the whites by the Indians. About that time an adventurous pioneer from Tennessee, named Hunt, penetrated the region, and, charmed by the beauty and advantages of the spot, erected his cabin on a bold and elevated bluff overhanging an immense limestone spring, which poured forth a large stream of clear crystal water, and around which the wild deer were wont to collect in great numbers, while he, concealed in the tops of the surrounding trees, could easily, with his faithful rifle, pick off as many as he wished of his favorite game. Soon other adventurers sought the spot, and a village sprang into existence, forming the nucleus of the population which flowed rapidly from Tennessee, North Carolina and Kentucky, into the adjacent fertile lands. Madison county was established in December, 1808, and the next year the village was incorporated under the name of Twickenham, after the villa of the illustrious author of the "Essay on Man," some of whose collateral connections were among its first settlers. But the democratic inhabitants did not fancy the poetical designation, and at the next session of the Territorial legislature, the original name of Huntsville, in honor of its first founder, was restored to the picturesque and thriving village. It is no idle or uninteresting reverie to stand upon the summit of *Montesana*, and, while gazing down upon the broad and cultured panorama of the Tennessee Valley, with its now flourishing capital, lying in a white and green mosaic of loveliness at your feet, thus to recall the incidents of the first settlement of North Alabama.

But scarcely had the adventurous pioneers opened the woods and erected their cabins in the pine forests of what is now Clarke, Washington and Monroe counties, and in the distant and secluded recesses of Madison, when the period arrived, of the most terrific and destructive Indian wars that have ever occurred in the United States, baptising our soil with blood. It was my intention, while anticipating this address, to have dwelt upon the history and characteristics of our Aborigines, as most forcibly illustrating my theme. But *non nobis nunc hoc perficere.* Time, and the evident though unavoidable tediousness of a narrative discourse, admonish me to forbear. I may however remark, that the Red Men of Alabama, if properly reviewed, would be found to present more interesting facts and features, upon a more extended scale, than any other American tribes. The peculiarities which had ever invested the character of the Indian with so much romantic interest, making him the chosen child of fable and of song, were here exhibited in bolder relief than elsewhere. In numbers ; in the extent of their territories, all converging to the heart of our State ; in their wide and terrific wars ; in intercourse and traffic with the whites ; in the mystery of their origin and migration ; in the arts, rude though they were, which gradually refine and socialize man ; in their political and religious forms, arrangements, and ceremonies ; in manifestations of intellectual power—sagacity and eloquence ; and in all those strange moral phenomena, which marked "the stoïc of the woods, the man without a tear,"—the native inhabitants of our soil surpassed all the other primitive nations, north of Mexico. The study of their history is peculiarly our province,—for they are indissolubly connected not only with the past, but the present and future of the State.

Yes! "though they all have passed away,—
That noble race and brave,
Though their light canoes have vanished
From off the crested wave;
Though, 'mid the forests where they roved,
There rings no hunter's-shout,—
Yet their names are on our waters,
And we may not wash them out!
Their memory liveth on our hills,
Their baptism on our shore,—
Our everlasting rivers speak
Their dialect of yore!"
'Tis heard where CHATTAHOOCHEE pours
His yellow tide along;
It sounds on TALLAPOOSA'S shores,
And COOSA swells the song;
Where lordly ALABAMA sweeps,
The symphony remains;
And young CAHAWBA proudly keeps,
The echo of its strains;
Where TUSCALOOSA'S waters glide,
From stream and town 'tis heard,
And dark TOMBECKBEE'S winding tide
Repeats the olden word;
Afar where nature brightly wreathed
Fit Edens for the Free,
Along TUSCUMBIA'S bank 'tis breathed
By stately TENNESSEE;
And south, where, from CONECUH'S springs,
ESCAMBIA'S waters steal,
The ancient melody still rings,—
From TENSAW and MOBILE!

The Thirty Battles, fought by Weatherford and his dusky followers, with Claiborne, Flournoy, and Jackson, and terminated by the treaty on the site of Fort

Toulouse, in August, 1814, lost to the Creeks all their dominions west of the Coosa. The astonishing celerity with which the conquerors prosecuted the war is one of its most notable characteristics. The battle of Tallashatchee was faught the third of November; Talladega, the tenth; Hillabee, the eighteenth; Autossee, the twenty-ninth; Emuckfaw, the twenty-second of January, 1814; Echanachaca, or the Holy Ground, the twenty-third; Enotichopco, the twenty-fourth; and To-hope-ka, or the Horse Shoe, the twenty-seventh of March. These, with numerous smaller engagements, almost exterminated the nation. Not less than four thousand warriors are believed to have fallen victims to their wild fanaticism and martyr-like courage.

Alabama emerged, like Miriam, from the Red Sea of her struggles, and now a new era of growth and prosperity began. The streams of population flowed rapidly into all parts of the interior of our State. I can follow only one,—for its present interest.

The spot upon which we are assembled, with an indefinite strip of territory on both banks of the Black Warrior (originally called the *Choctaw*,) to its junction with the Tombeckbee, had been, from time immemorial, a neutral ground between the Creeks and Choctaws. Both tribes abstained from its occupancy. About the year 1809, however, a Creek Chief named *Oseeche-emathla*, obtained permission from the Choctaws to establish a settlement near the falls of the Black Warrior, for the purpose of facilitating trade with the American Factory at St. Stephens, then under the charge of Col. George S. Gaines. This settlement, which speedily grew into a village, was just below what is now known as New Town. Its Chieftain was in the habit of purchasing on credit, annually from the Factory, about one hundred and fifty dollars' worth of goods, which he retailed to the Indians. In the spring of 1812, he went to St. Stephens, and boasting of a great increase in his business, was extremely solicitous to obtain credit to the amount of $1,000. The suspicions of the Factor were aroused, and he refused to enlarge the bill beyond its ordinary size. That night, Tandy Walker, an old and astute Indian trader, gleaned from some of the incautious and maudlin companions of the merchant-chief, that the Creeks were preparing for war. The Indians departed with their goods, which were never paid for, as hostilities were commenced in a few weeks by the Battle of Burnt Corn, and the Massacre at Fort Mims. The Indian village of Tuscaloosa, so called from an immemorial family name among the Choctaws, soon witnessed some of the effects of the war. A party of hostile warriors had made an incursion into Tennessee, and after many murders, made prisoner Mrs. Crawley, an interesting and intelligent woman, whom they brought to Tuscaloosa and detained in captivity. News of her situation reaching Col. Gaines, he induced the fearless and adventurous Tandy Walker, to undertake her liberation. This he accomplished with a skill worthy of any of Cooper's heroes; and the fair prisoner was safely conducted to St. Stephens, whence she was sent by that noble pioneer of our State, whose name is worthy of all praise for his services at this period,—Col. Gaines,—to her friends in Tennessee. The insolent savages at Tuscaloosa, not long after, met a deserved retribution. The friendly Choctaws under Pushmataha, with a band of Chickasaws led by Col. John McKee, subsequently for many years Representative in Congress from this District—in October, 1813, attacked the village and reduced it to ashes,—most of the inhabitants having fled. The spot remained abandoned until after the war, when in 1816, the first settlers, Emanuel York and John Barton, from Tennessee, pitched their tents and raised their crops of corn on the beautiful upland plain where now stands the city of Tuscaloosa. The harvests of the next year were reaped by a considerable population ; the outlines of the future town were laid out ; and in January, 1818, the Alabama Territorial Legislature, then in its first session at St. Stephens, established the county of Tuscaloosa. The ensuing spring, Thomas M. Davenport, an enterprising printer, commenced the publication of the "Tuscaloosa Republican," a weekly newspaper, which in twelve months, took the name of the "American Mirror," which was continued to a period within the memory of many of my audience.

The flight of the honey-bee is said to mark the progress of the Anglo-American race; but the presence of the printing press is a surer index of its growth in intelligence and refinement ; and, in this connection, I may state that the first newspaper ever published in Alabama, was the "Madison Gazette," at Huntsville, in 1812. "The Halcyon" was established at St. Stephens, 1814, by Thomas Eastin, who became the first Territorial printer, executing the Laws and Journals of the first Legislative Assembly. A man named Cotton commenced the earliest newspaper at Mobile, in November, 1816. It was called the "Mobile Gazette and General Advertiser." In 1820, "The Clarion" was published at Claiborne; "The Free Press," and the "Alabama Watchman" at Cahawba; and the "Republican," at Montgomery, by J. Battelle. These were the exponents and *avant couriers* of the rapidly increasing intelligence of their respective communities. It may also be added, that "Green Academy," at Huntsville, still in existence, was the first organized institution of learning in Alabama, having been incorporated by the Mississippi Territorial Legislature, in November, 1812. "Washington Academy," in Washington county, had been chartered a year previously, but did not go into operation until some time after. From these simple primitive sources—these small Castalian fountains,—originated the streams of knowledge, which now, with more than the fertilizing influence of the Nile, and with richer deposits than the golden sands of the Pactolus, irrigate our soil, and flow with a converging wealth and beauty, into that noblest of Southern educational institutions, the University of Alabama, thence to diffuse throughout the State, as has already been done, despite the cavils of the insolent and the ignorant, in the persons of her Alumni, the noblest of influences for the promotion of the intellectual, moral and social welfare of our people. Standing here, with the bridge of time behind me, which I have crossed for this presence,—after an absence of more than twenty years,—with its memories and its merits crowding upon my mind, and the exemplars of its excellence all about me, and chief of them, its distinguished President, (the Rev. Dr. Manly,) who is about retiring, amid the regrets of the whole State, from the station he has so honored and adorned, I can but exclaim,

> "*Salve magna parens, Saturnia tellus,*
> *Magna virum!*"

This local termination brings me to the conclusion of my address. Have I not, Gentlemen, sufficiently vindicated the claims of our history to the study and research of our scholars? Have I not shown that, though obscured through hither neglect, by the fast gathering twilight of time, and buried amid crumbling ruins and accumulated dust, it has treasures, the richest, to repay for exploration and development? There is a chamber in the Mammoth Cave of Kentucky, whose stalactites are said to be luminous. It is thus with the almost subterranean halls in which the memorials of our past lie concealed. We push our way through the dimness, and across the barriers, to our French, Spanish, British, Aboriginal, and Anglo-American eras, and by patient effort and studious toil advance until their long hidden beauties hang brilliantly before us. The lovers of literature, in all its departments, find there the precious metals, which might be moulded into all the most graceful and elegant forms of thought. The stimulants to an intelligent and appreciative love of country are there. Shall these treasures continue to lie unused and unregarded? This Society becomingly answers the question. It has undertaken to supply for our State what Sallust lamented as wanting at Rome. Its members are performing an important public service, and will receive the thanks of posterity. To their own minds also, their exertions will be productive of benefit; for, as the great English moralist has happily said, "whatever withdraws us from the power of our senses; whatever makes the past, the distant, or the future predominate over the present,—advances us in the dignity of thinking beings." Go on, then, Gentlemen, energetically in your noble undertaking, consoled by the assurance that you are collecting the materials that shall illustrate and embellish the annals of your State, in the far distant, when they shall receive the plastic touch and vivifying breath of some future Xenophon or Polybius, some Tacitus or Livy, who, like the Hebrew prophet, shall bid the dry bones—live!

AMERICANISM IN LITERATURE:

AN ORATION

BEFORE THE

Phi Kappa and Demosthenian Societies of the University of Georgia,

AT

ATHENS, AUGUST 8, 1844.

ORATION.

Gentlemen of the Literary Societies:

The return to scenes, with which we have been familiar in early life, constitutes much of the pathos and poetry of manhood. The changes time has made in each once familiar object, the developement into new life and beauty of some, the decay, the significant absence, of others, impress us with mingled emotions of pride and tenderness. We look with a calm gratification upon the improvements that have been made; we mourn, with a patient sorrow, for those things, which, too obviously, have passed away from the earth forever. Such are my emotions to-day. You have called me back, from a distant home, over a wide interval of years, to the scene of my earliest collegiate life. I have come, gratefully, at your bidding, and find well-nigh all things changed about me. The unadorned edifice, in which prayer was wont to be said, and where the feeble voice first attempted to pitch its tones to the music of eloquence, has passed from the view, and this beautiful temple, with its architectural elegance, now occupies the site. The fair village, that then lay in almost pastoral quiet amid its embowering trees, has become a populous town, the home of cultivated wealth, and the mart of an active and far-reaching commerce. But the greatest changes have occurred with those who then gave life and social pleasure to the scene. Where are the young forms that bounded in the elasticity and luxuriance of untamed feeling, upon yonder grassy slope when last I looked upon it? All gone and changed; scattered through all parts of this busy, diversified land of ours. Some of them are holding high trusts in Legislatures and Congresses, winning proud reputations for statesmanship and eloquence; others fill noble places in the pulpit, and professor's chair; and I have met not a few amid the pine forests and wide prairies of Alabama, engaged in the hot-handed struggle, at the hustings or the barbecue, for this or that presidential aspirant. But alas! when I again have asked for others, I have been answered, in melancholy tones, that their names have been carved, for many a season, upon the marble of the grave-yard!

One other remembrance comes before me at this hour. I see the form of the venerable individual who presided over this institution, at the period of my first entrance into its halls. Through a long life, he has devoted himself, with the love of a christian, and the capacities of a scholar, to the intellectual and moral elevations of the young men of the South. His exertions have been most nobly rewarded. Hundreds, under his guidance, have passed up the paths of usefulness, and reflected light upon the institutions of the country. He has been the foster-parent and vivifying spirit of this University. Now,—at the period to which I revert,—in the fullness of his fame, and while the sun of his life is sinking amidst the mellowed clouds of three score years and ten, he is about to sever his connection with this institution. I remember the morning when we marched in procession to his residence, to take our leave of him. I see him standing bare-headed beneath the grove, affectionately grasping the hand of each student as we passed, and fervently ejaculating, in a voice tremulous with emotion, while the tears streamed from his eyes, "God bless you, my sons!" A few years,—and the venerable patriarch was borne from the scene of his earthly usefulness to the beatitudes of the Just; but, while the walls of this institution remain, they will stand a fitting monument to the memory of MOSES WADDELL.

At the same period, to which my memory now goes back, another distinguished individual shed the light of his intellect and the influence of his example, upon this community. Though his life was not spent in the quiet bowers of literature, but in the turbulent field of politics, yet he united much of the gracefulness of the scholar with the solidity of the statesman, and was ever active in the promotion of those enterprises, which have for their object the diffusion of intelligence and virtue among the people. Neither the blandishments of office, nor the voluptuousness of foreign courts could corrupt his republican simplicity, and he was, in all the leading features of his character, the model of an American statesman. This Georgia of yours owes him a debt of gratitude for his services in the federal councils, and not till talents and integrity, patriotism and stateman-ship are unappreciated in the land of Oglethorpe, will she neglect the fame of her CRAWFORD.

Not inappropriate to the subject, upon which I propose to address you to-day, are these reminiscences of two of the most eminent men in the history of this State. They both struggled for the same end,—the elevation of the best interests of our country. The one sought to accomplish this by giving a proper impulse and direction to our political institutions; the other placed his chief hope of regeneration, in the establishment and diffusion of an elevated intellectual system. The one was a statesman—the other a scholar. Herein then we recognize, to some extent, our subject, which is to include a discussion of the influence, upon mental developement, of the physical, social and political characteristics of our country, and which I therefore call AMERICANISM IN LITERATURE. An enquiry into the modifications, which our forms of government, as well as our other peculiarities, are destined to work in that chiefest of a nation's interests, its inellectual efflorescence, can never be devoid of interest on an occasion like this, if at all philosophically conducted. There are lessons kerneled in such an enquiry, for the instruction of the statesman as well as the scholar.

But, at the outset, let us look a little into the legitimate purposes of both governments, and literatures. Mankind too frequently mistake these for ends, when they are only means for the achievement of an end.

They are but instruments whereby to accomplish the great design for which man was created. And what is that? Is it to hold Congresses, crown kings, write poems, fight battles, invent steam engines, or build magnetic telegraphs? Oh no! These are but episodes in the great epic of immortality. There is a higher design, an ulterior purpose. What then is that? I repeat. For what did God make man, and place him on this revolving globe? Is there any key to this mystery of life and motion? Why do the constant generations come and go athwart this earth like the waves of the sea upon a coast of breakers? Why this ceaseless production and reproduction? For what was this great complex machinery of worlds, and centuries, and seasons, and souls,—thought, sunshine and vegetation,—life, death, resurrection,—fashioned into shape and motion, and hung out in the heaven of time? What good does it do? What end can it accomplish? Ah! these are the old enigmas, which no Œdipus has solved. Reason, revelation, only let us know that man is an immortal, ethical being, and that the great law of his nature is incessant progress,—progress to the infinite, the eternal, the omniscient, the perfect. Ever onward, never attaining! All things, when aright, move upward, unceasingly, (by a great spiral revolution,) to the unattainable throne of God!

This moral law obtains in this world as well as in the next. Bards and prophets from the old centuries, have foretold and prayed for a state of intellectual and moral perfection; not the wild dream of a Condorcet, but a social millenium, when between the smiling hemispheres of beauty and refinement, the world should roll round in the warm flush, the *purpureum lumen*, of Divine intelligence and love. For this we implore when we say, "Thy kingdom come!" Not only do we invoke a moral dynasty, but also, an intellectual. The two must go together. God is all intellect, as well as all love! Literature, in its purity, no less than religion, is a scion of his beneficence, and one of his provisions for the redemption of man. All human institutions, whether intellectual or political, should contribute to this great law of progress. Unless they are founded upon and vivified by its spirit, they have no right to be. They are tyrannies and falsehoods, and should be extinguished. In every enquiry then, as to the value or validity of a government or literature, we should measure them by this standard, judge of them by this rule.

Bad governments and bad literatures tend ever to the demoralization of the human family. They not only retard, but roll back the wheels of progress. The old tyrannies, and their intellectual systems, were manifestations and promoters, not of civilization, but of barbarism. Radically wrong in their whole philosophies of man and life, they led upward to no glorious zenith, but lay, like stagnant oceans, weltering in rottenness and error, breathing pestilence, woe, and degradation. This, in main part, is why man, in the sixty centuries, has risen so little above his primeval condition.

But in modern times, a better philosophy of both Government and literature has begun to prevail.

Mankind have learned that governments are somewhat more than games or machines kept in curious motion for the amusement and edification of rulers; and literatures are beginning to be regarded, not as the phantasmagoria of poets and dreamers, the sunset scaffoldings of fancy, but as something very far beyond that. The old secret has come out, that man's immortality has already begun, and, by these things, you are moulding and fashioning him in his destinies forever.

Surely now, no enquiry can be more appropriate or profitable than whether this American Government, this American Literature of ours, in what they are now, and are destined to be, correspond with the principles and designs of Providence, in the creation of man: that is, are they in faith with the great law of intellectual and social progression? The question is double, but it may still be answered affirmatively. In my judgment, there has never been a social organism in which the two greatest motive powers of elevation, government and literature—for under literature I now include religion—were more happily accommodated, or gave "fairer promise of a goodly morrow," from their reciprocal operations, than in this young twenty-six headed giant of the West. Let Sydney Smith sneer as he may, but verily this Americanism of ours, with all its physical, historical and political aspects, is destined to be, as it already has been, a powerful influence on man, and will necessarily modify and fashion the literature of the world. Literature, in its essence, is a spiritual immortality; no more than religion a creation of man; but, like the human soul, while enduring the mystery of its incarnation, is subject to the action of the elements, is the slave of circumstance. In the sense in which I would now view it, it is the expression of the spiritual part of our nature, in its .intellectual action, whether taking form in philosophy, history, poetry, eloquence, or some other branch of thought. The sum of all this, in any nation, is what constitutes her literature, and it is always modified and colored by the peculiarities about it. As the river, sliding under the sunset, imbibes, for the time, the hues of the heavens, so the stream of literature receives, from the people through which it passes, not only the images and shadows of their condition, but the very force and direction of its current. Every literature, Greek or Roman, Arabic or English, French, Persian or German, acquired its qualities and impression from the circumstances of the time and people. The philosophic eye can readily detect the key, cause and secret of each, and expose the seminal principle from which they grew into their particular shape and fashion. The same scrutinizing analysis will enable us to determine the influences among ourselves, which are to operate in the formation of our literature; as well as to decide whether it will comport with those high spiritual requisitions which, I have already avowed, should be demanded from it. Let us then attempt to see how Americanism will develope itself in Literature. We shall discuss some of its preliminary conditions first.

1. The physical attributes of our country are all partial to the loftiest manifestations of mind. Nature here presents her loveliest, sublimest aspects. For

vastness of extent, grandeur of scenery, genial diversities of climate, and all that can minister to the comforts and tastes of man, this heritage of ours is without a parallel. In its mountains of stone and iron, its gigantic and far-reaching rivers, its inland seas, its forests of all woods, its picturesque and undulating prairies, in all its properties and proportions, it might well be considered, in comparison with the Eastern Hemisphere, the work of a more perfect and beneficent artist. To the eyes of the Genoese mariner, the wildest dreams of Diodorus and Plato were more than realized. Seneca sang:

> "——————Venient annis
> Sæcula seris, quibus oceanus
> Vincula rerum laxet, et ingens
> Pateat tellus, Typhisque novos
> Detegat orbes:"

Yet not even in the mirror of his prophetic fancy were these more than Elysian fields glassed with all their beauty and sublimity. Even the bilious British satirist, who could see no good in all our institutions, was compelled to confess that here

> "——————Nature showed
> The last ascending footsteps of the God!"

Well-nigh all this vast expanse of fruitfulness and beauty, too, has been subjected to the control of civilized man. Our country has extended her jurisdiction over the fairest and most fertile regions. The rich bounty is poured into her lap, and breathes its influence upon her population. Their capacities are not pent and thwarted by the narrow limits which restrict the citizens of other countries. No speculating theorist, a Malthus, Stultz, or Liceto, has cause, here, to apprehend the dangers of over-population. Room, bountiful room, is all about us, for humanity to breathe freely in, and to go on expanding in a long future.—Do these things afford no promise of intellectual improvement? Are they no incitements to a lofty and expanded literature? Do they furnish no *materiel* for active, generous, elevated thought? Is there no voice coming out from all this fragrance and beauty and sublimity, appealing to the heart and fancy of man, for sympathy, utterance, embodiment? Why, it was once said, that the sky of Attica would make a Bœotian a poet; and we have seen even "the red old hills of Georgia" draw inspiring melody from the heart of patriotic genius.—Physical causes have always operated in the formation and fashioning of literature. In all the higher productions of mind, ancient and modern, we can easily recognize the influence of the climate and natural objects among which they were developed. The sunsets of Italy colored the songs of Tasso and Petrarch; the vine-embowered fields of beautiful France are visible in all the pictures of Rousseau and La Martine; you may hear the solemn rustling of the Hartz forest, and the shrill horn of the wild huntsman, throughout the creations of Schiller and Göethe; the sweet streamlets and sunny lakes of England smile upon you from the graceful verses of Spenser and Wordsworth; and the mist-robed hills of Scotland loom out in magnificence through the pages of Ossian, and the loftier visions of Marmion and Waverly.

Our country, then, must receive much of the character of her literature from her physical properties. If our minds are only original; if they be not base copyists, and servile echoes of foreign masters; if we assert an intellectual as well as political independence; if we dare to think for ourselves, and faithfully picture forth, in our own styles of utterance, the impressions our minds shall receive from this great, fresh continent of beauty and sublimity;—we can render to the world the most vigorous and picturesque literature it has ever beheld. Never had imagination nobler stimulants; never did nature look more encouragingly upon her genuine children. In poetry, romance, history and eloquence, what glorious objects,—sights and sounds, for illustration and ornament!—I have stood, down in Florida, beneath the over-arching groves of magnolia, orange and myrtle, blending their fair flowers and voluptuous fragrance, and opening long vistas between their slender shafts, to where the green waters of the Mexican Gulf lapsed upon the silver-sanded beach, flinging up their light spray into the crimson beams of the declining sun; and I have thought that, for poetic beauty, for delicate inspiration, the scene was as sweet as ever wooed the eyes of a Grecian minstrel on the slopes of Parnassus, or around the fountains of Castaly.

Again: I have stood upon a lofty summit of the Alleghanies, among the splintered crags and vast gorges, where the eagle and the thunder make their home; and looked down upon an empire spread out in the long distance below. Far as the eye could reach, the broad forests swept away over territories of unexampled productiveness and beauty. At intervals through the wide champaign, the domes and steeples of some fair town, which had sprung up with magical suddenness among the trees, would come out to the eye, giving evidence of the presence of a busy, thriving population. Winding away through the centre too, like a great artery of life to the scene, I could behold a noble branch of the Ohio, bearing upon its bosom the already active commerce of the region, and linking that spot with a thousand others, similar in their condition and character. As I thus stood, and thought of all that was being enacted in this glorious land of ours, and saw in imagination, the stately centuries as they passed across the scene, diffusing wealth, prosperity and refinement, I could not but believe that it presented a nobler theatre, with sublimer accompaniments and inspirations, than ever rose upon the eye of a gazer from the summits of the Alps or the Apennines.

Such are some of the physical aspects of our country, and such the influence they are destined to have upon our national mind. Very evidently they constitute noble sources of inspiration, illustration and description. For all that part of literature which is drawn from the phases of nature, from the varying moods and phenomena of the outward world, the elements and the seasons, they will be more valuable than all the beauties of the Troad or Campania Felix. Rightly used, they would bring a freshness and spirit into the domain of high thought, which would revive it like a spring-time return, and we might take up, in a better hope, the exultation of Virgil,—

> "Jam ultima ætas Cumali carminis venit,
> Magnus ordo sœclorum nascitur ab integro,
> Et jam virgo redit, Saturnia regna redeunt !"

2. These pleasant anticipations are also justfied in part, by the excellent and diversified character of the population of our country. Herein will reside one of the strong modifying influences of Americanism upon literature. Though our population is composed principally of the several varieties of the Anglo-Saxon stock, yet every other race of Europe, and some from the other continents, have contributed to swell the motley and singular combination. Coming from every quarter of the globe, they have brought with them their diverse manners, feelings, sentiments, and modes of thought, and fused them in the great American alembic. The stern, clear-headed, faith-abiding Puritan, the frank, chivalrous, imaginative Huguenot, the patient, deep-thoughted, contemplative German,—pligrims from every clime, creed, and literature,—are to be found in contact and intercourse here. They interact upon each other to fashion all the manifestations of society, in thought or deed. The contrasts and coincidences, they present under our institutions, afford new and graceful themes for the poet, the novelist and the philosopher ; and the historian will have to give us pictures of life and humanity here, such as are found not elsewhere. I need but allude, in this connection, to the existence of three distinct races of men

upon our continent, with their strongly marked peculiarities of conditon, color and history. The immense rapidity with which our numbers are increasing—well nigh doubling in every fifteen years !—will produce an unexampled demand for knowledge, and act as a powerful impetus to its elevation. Already has the great and fluctuating intermixture of our population had an influence upon the English language. In no part of the world is our mother tongue spoken with such general purity of pronunciation, as in our country. The constant tide of internal emigration tends to rectify the provincialisms into which stationary communities so frequently fall. Otherwise is it even in England. The whole kingdom is broken up into dialects as numerous as her counties; and the respective inhabitants are almost as unintelligible to each other, as if they spoke languages radically distinct. Is it Utopian to expect the proudest results, when one common language shall be employed by the many millions who are to occupy this almost illimitable republic ?—But, it is upon the strong, industrious and wholesome character of our population, that the best hope of our national mind depends. Their habits of life will generate a *muscularity* of intellect, becoming their position and destiny. No effeminacy of thought or feeling will be tolerated among a people, composed of the choicest varieties of every race, stimulating each other to mental exertion, and accumulating wealth and power with almost miraculous rapidity and extent. Such a people, if they should have no powerful impediments, are better fitted than any other to render the world an intellectual illumination, and to bring round in reality the poetic vision of the golden age.

3. Pass we now to the consideration of the most potent influence of Americanism in Literature : the form and spirit of our political institutions.—If there is a truth strongly exemplified in history, it is, that free governments are the best calculated of any, to promote the intellectual and moral progress of man. Of all the vast tyrannies of antiquity, how few contributed to the advancement of letters ! There is not in existence a line of verse or philosophy by Chaldean, Babylonian, Assyrian or Phœnician author. Populous, powerful and magnificent as those kingdoms were, they yet stand in history like the huge pyramid of human skulls which Tamerlane erected before the gates of Damascus, great, dumb monuments of human misery and oppression. In beautiful contrast are all the free states of the past. Under their genial institutions, the arts, the sciences and the refinements of life rose into prosperity and beauty, and, like the swinging flower-gardens of oriental sumptuousness, diffused a fragrance which still floats upon the breezes of history. This is particularly true of Athenian, Roman and Italian literatures. Just in proportion to the liberty existing among them at their respective eras, was the extent, the luxuriance of their mental developement. It is so in the nature of things. Tyrannies are restrictions upon thought and its utterance. Their every influence must be directed to the suppression of those great truths of philosophy, religion, poetry and life, which are the soul and efflu-

ence of every genuine literature, and which great men, the prophets, and apostles, and martyrs of thought, are sent into the world to preach. It is true that, under monarchies, there have sometimes been glorious revelations of genius, learning and intellectual luxury, as in the eras of Augustus, Louis XIV., and Elizabeth; yet they were either outbursts of coming or going freedom, or contained, in themselves, but little that could add to the elevation or happiness of the mass of men. How few truths, tributary to the perfect law of life, were brought to light by any, the most gorgeous, of these intellectual dispensations!

But this government of ours is established upon principles more genial to the literature of humanity, than any other that has ever existed. The noble, broad, philosophic truths at the basis of our constitution, the rocks upon which our house is built, are all conducive to intellectual development. The fundamental maxim, that all men are politically equal, which has done so much to elevate humanity, infuses into literature a new spirit, as well as into government. The man of genius now, however obscure his parentage, or humble his condition, can proudly hold up his head, in the light of the common sun, unrestricted, unabashed, by any of the miserable fictions of prerogative, and utter forth, in the emphasis of thunder, the solemn truths he has learned in the Patmos of his imagination, and which shall make all mankind feel that the propitious bend of the heaven comes equally close to every descendant of Adam. In its whole organism, our government provides for the unrestrained exercise of mind. This is the permeating spirit of our political fabric. The sages and statesmen who received their lessons of wisdom between the clouds and thunder, covering the Sinai of the Revolution, knew that literature had always been the truest friend of the rights of man, and they consequently provided, in all our fundamental charters, for the encouragement of the faithful instructress. Freedom of conscience, freedom of thought, freedom of speech, and freedom of the press, the essentials of literature, are the pillars of our national edifice. No other government has ever held out, in itself, so many incitements to intellectual action. There is a pervading necessity for the application of high thought to its management, in every department. About its movements there is nothing of brute force ; all proceeds under the guidance of constant, indispensable mental power. That old dumb, central principle of monarchies, about which Blackstone, De Lolme and Montesquieu were so much troubled, the absolute sovereignty, is here an active, thinking, vital essence, like the atmosphere we breathe, embracing all, yet in every man's bosom, and calling on each for the exercise of his intellectual faculties. The countless offices of our system, open equally to all, are so many spurs to enterprize. How wide and minutely diffused is the influence,—how constant, how potent ! All of us are daily invoked to the discussion and decision of questions, in law, philosophy and economy, which demand for their proper adjustment, all the learning of experience, and the profoundest operations of the mind.

Universal suffrage is, in its end, universal knowledge. Democracy is the parent of literature. Verily, under these aspects, we may apply, in an intellectual, as well as political sense, to every American citizen, the bold parallel which Wordsworth draws to the Highland freebooter:

> " The Eagle, he was king above,
> And Rob Roy, he was king below!"

But, it has been said, that though our institutions thus hold out excellent opportunities and stimulants to intellectual exercise, they are yet prejudicial to literature proper, because of their almost exclusively political tendency. This is to some extent too true. Very evidently the greater part of our talent has hitherto been monopolized by politics. But that has been owing chiefly to the infancy of our country. In the outset of a government so peculiar as ours, so complicated and popular, in which so many arrangements without precedent had to be made, and so many apparently conflicting principles adjusted, it was natural that the talent of the country should be principally directed to the affairs of State. The shining names in our history, who had won distinction in our first political councils, became beacon-lights to guide the emulous spirits of our youths into similar careers. Both these influences have now begun to subside. Besides, nations in their infancy, like individuals, are apt to mistake the obvious and fascinating, for the useful and the true. As both advance in life, they acquire deeper and wiser lessons. So far, we have rushed headlong into politics, as much from the novelty of the attraction, as from any other cause ; and the intellectual stature of men has been measured more by the number of offices they have held, than by their solid contributions to the permanent thought of the country. This is a sad error, and must die out. As we grow older, we will learn that literature is a far nobler pursuit than "the vain, low strife, that makes men mad ;" and that the philosophers, historians, poets and scholars, the preachers and teachers, are the great men of the time. Politics itself can never be a science, never more than a barbarian scramble for office, unless it is purified and rounded into form by the spirit of literature. Already have other nations learned the necessity of making their statesmen out of their scholars. At this moment the illustrious Humboldt is prime-minister of Prussia, and in France, we see Thiers, Guizot, La Martine and Arago, all distinguished as authors, occupying the most prominent political positions.

This spirit, at no distant day, must obtain in our country. It is not our form of government or its tendencies, that are inimical to literature. It is the public taste that is depraved, the public mind that is in error. Let these be rectified, as they are fast being, under the progress of intelligence—before the outpourings from institutions such as this all over our country—and literature may have a Lazarus-like resurrection in these occidental forests. Even now, if common justice were done to the authors of our country, in protecting them from the piratical and nefarious system of plunder from foreign authors ; if, guided by the plainest principles of justice, Congress would allow the foreign writer, a copy-right to secure to him the labors of his own intellect, to which he is as honestly entitled as the people of Alabama are to their cattle which may stray across the line into your Georgia ; if we would protect ourselves from this "blue and yellow literature," the scum of the French and British press, which is contaminating our morals, and depraving our minds ; if, in short we would be actuated by elevated sentiments of patriotism, justice, morality and love of letters, to the adoption of an international copy-right law,—we should have the heralding of as pure and noble a literature as ever dawned upon the eyes of Pericles or Tacitus, Ariosto or Addison. But ah ! the present Serbonian system is worse, far worse, in its morals and moral effects, than Mississippi repudiation !

4. Let us glance now at another aspect of Americanism from which we may hope something for literature. Our general government is constructed upon the principle of having as little to do as possible with the internal, domestic affairs of society. By its enumerated powers, its rightful province and jurisdiction are mainly external. Consequently, after the general, and, as they may be called, incidental influences, I have enumerated, and the fact that it guaranties to each state a republican form of government, it has but one specified provision by which it can encourage literature ; that is the power "to promote the progress of science and the useful arts, by securing, for limited times, to authors and inventors, the exclusive right to their respective writings and discoveries." Beyond this, the entire control and jurisdiction of all the vast

territories of intellect,—the flowering Palestines of mind,—are left exclusively to the separate populations of the several republics composing the confederacy. Each State is the legitimate and only guardian of all the great interests of knowledge within her borders. Unlike the general government, she can do everything for the promotion of letters not prohibited by her constitution; while the former can do nothing, for which it has not an express grant of power. This leaves the destinies of education, of literature, science, and the arts, in safer and more potential hands, than if they were confided exclusively to national control. In my estimation, our system of confederated sovereignties, one of the most marked features of Americanism, is peculiarly favorable to the production of a pure, earnest, life-bestowing, beauty-breathing literature. Let us elaborate a little the reasons for this belief.

It was the benevolent desire of Henry the IV., to which he was prompted by the philosophic mind of his minister, Sully, to see all the kingdoms of the earth united in peace under one harmonious government. This generous vision, if feasible at all, could only be realized under some system similar to ours. Our confederacy is susceptible of indefinite extension. The addition of new States tends but more firmly to confine the Union to its legitimate functions, and to diffuse wider, and wider, the blessings of democracy, peace, and security. Under no other organism, could these fundamental requisites of literature, be so extensively attained. A vast consolidated government could but ill provide for the comfort and welfare of its remote parts. It could not meet the domestic wants and intellectual demands of its diversified sections, nor proportion its encouragements to the peculiar characteristics of the people and the place. What general system even of common-school education, would extend equally to all parts of this vast and motley Union? The sun himself shines with a varying splendor upon the sands of Nantucket and the corn-fields of Alabama. In no vast, unbroken empire, has literature ever flourished. The gigantic despotisms of Asia are great Zaharas in the intellectual world. But one star illuminates the darkness of that long, wide, Chinese night,—the star of Confucius. Russia, with her teeming millions, has never struck the harp of Apollo, nor caught the glintings of the silver shield of Minerva. There they stand, in blank, grey stupendousness, like the sphinx upon the sands of Egypt, giving no answer to the questionings of intellect! So evermore with these giant consolidations. Government must come down, and shape itself to the varying conditions of men. As with us, it must have its wheels within its wheels, each one, as in the vision of the prophet, vital with a distinct interest, yet moving out sympathetically to the whole. This then becomes disembarrassed of those minute details, and innumerrble complex duties, which exist in every social system, and which have to be observed and nourished before a literature can be created.

But this federated system prevents another detrimental influence of consolidated governments. Wherever there is a great central capital, the whole intellectual wealth of the country, whether invested in literature or politics, becomes accumulated in it. It forms a conspicious reservoir, to which all the fountains have to flow, before they can be distributed through the land. Imperious laws are there given to the world of letters, and all other competition is frowned down and destroyed before the fashions of the metropolis. We see this illustrated in France and England. Before genius can find an audible utterance, it has to travel up to London or Paris: even such men as Johnson and Voltaire were not exempt from the necessity. They had to prune and warp their intellects to the whims of the book-pedlars and play-mongers in Grub-street, or the *Rue de la Paix.* So evermore: Every thing provincial is denounced and rejected. The best book, issued in Leeds or Manchester, in Bourdeaux or Marseilles, is consigned at once to oblivion, before the literary dictatorship of the metropolis. No good thing can come out of Nazareth; there is no divinity among Gallilean peasants. The result of all this is most pernicious. Poor genius is compelled to languish in obscurity in the provinces; the God dies in the manger; and the entire literature of the country, instead of being the large, fresh, oak-like growth of the heart of the whole people, becomes the dwarfed and noxious vegetation of a hot-bed of vice and effeminacy.

These evil influences can never exist with us. Our institutions disseminate their influence through every portion of the Union. Each State has its own capital, whence proceeds the legislation which is to develope and form the mind of its inhabitants. True, as yet, these several centres are weak and uninfluential; but, as the States swell in power, wealth, importance; as they begin to feel, each for itself, as every community sooner or later must feel, the necessity for a home literature; then the advantages of our distributive system will be happily discovered. At the least, we shall always have a number of large cities in this Union, at remote points, with equal centrifugal forces; thus preserving our literature from being concentred in one metropolis, while the rest of the country is left in comparative darkness, and the bright servitress becomes, as she too frequently has been forced to be, a vile pander to the bad passions of the enemies of free institutions.

The rivalry and emulation which must always exist among the several States of the confederacy, will be highly favorable to literature. Each State will be unwilling to be surpassed by a sister in the promotion of letters. This feeling has already given rise to the many institutions for high learning which exist in our country. Even now we have well-nigh a hundred universities or colleges, a larger number than any other country upon the globe. These are the nurseries of that genius and talent, which must blossom into beauty,—into literature. The young men of each section will not consent to fall behind those of any other in those elevated achievements, which, while they shed a morning-light of gracefulness over the institutions of their country, will make their own names as musical upon the lips of history as those of Cicero or Milton, of Thucydides or Shelley. Every one will strive to be faithful to the highest interest, the honor and dignity, the faith and lineaments, of his nourishing parent. The intellectual manifestations of each section will thus partake of the peculiarities of the State in which they may arise, its moral and physical phases, and thus our national literature, while, in its parts, it is stimulated by a generous rivalry, will imbibe an originality and freshness thereby, that will make it not unlike our national government, receiving its vigor and permanence from the individual prosperity of its component sovereignties.

The lessons of history, that experimental philosopher, might be quoted in behalf of the position that belles-lettres have ever flourished, to the greatest advantage, under an associated system of small, independent States. But the illustrations are familiar, and I shall pass on, content with only pointing you to the contrast between the intellectual conditions of Greece and Italy, during the existence of their republics, and when these were extinguished in the broad expanse of consolidated dominion; as also to the history of the Swiss Cantons, the Hanseatic Towns, the Baltic Circle, and the present condition of the States of Germany. Though none of them can be compared, in excellence of political arrangement, with our country, yet it is certainly a significant fact that, in proportion as they have approximated to the system of confederated sovereignties, literature, science and art have flourished in their borders. Well, then, might Sismondi, in his glowing picture of the Italian republics, a book every American should read, regret, with a deep pathos, the extinguishment of their separate existence, as the stoppage-up of so many well-heads of moral and social refinement.

We have now taken a general view of some of the principal features of Americanism, as I call it,—its governmental, social and physical aspects,—in reference to their influence upon the developement of literature. These, it must be admitted, are highly auspicious for the future, even if, as is too true, they have accomplished but little as yet. They must work out our intellectual redemption in the long *to-come*, and give us a republic of letters, as vigorous, symmetrical, lovely and expansive, as its kindred political system,—as the broad theatre upon which our many millions are to move. This new literature is to be something unlike any thing of the past. It is not to be a re-production of the worn-out articles of faith, philosophy, poetry, or fable, of antiquity. No, God forbid! I would not reproduce here, if I could, that golden age of Augustus, nor those diamond days of Elizabeth, of which we have before spoken. No! Americanism has a destiny of its own to accomplish in literature. It has to work out a system of thought, unlike any that has gone before, mirroring truly the new phases of humanity, of society, of government, that are here coming forth. The literatures of all other nations are entirely inadequate, unfit for Americanism. We must have a literature congenial to our institutions, to our position, to our great democratic faith. This we want exceedingly now. We want a literature not unlike that which Milton, and Marvell, and Sidney, and

Harrington, and Fletcher of Saltoun, foreshadowed in the times of the Protectorate: a literature, sailing like a ship across the ocean of time, freighted with the noblest interests, the Manilla ransom of humanity, and bearing onward ever, all sails set, before the steady breezes of that old Millenial progress. Yes! Americanism is to achieve important modifications in the spirit and faith of literature. What some of these will be, it is not difficult to determine.

Is it not singular that, in the six thousand years we have been upon the earth, so little has been established in political philosophy? Few truths touching the rights or relations of man, the authority of rulers, or the best forms and essential principles of government, are of general reception even among the most intelligent and cultivated minds. The details of policy and practice are still more diverse and unsettled. Well-nigh every government has proceeded upon some radically erroneous tenet. This has dislocated and disordered the whole machinery. Ours is the first that has squared its foundations according to the immutable laws of human nature. Taking for its polar-star, its watchword—"equality and justice to all," it has been enabled, in its spirit and practice, to comport with the requisitions of sound reason. Thus our government will be able to present to the world, not only the model of a system approaching perfection, but more correct and elevated postulates and maxims in political science, than have ever before been propounded. This we must do, in justice to ourselves and our institutions. The very text-books used in our schools and colleges, and by our law students, are filled with iniquitous sophisms and falsehoods. All other governments are bending their genius and learning against the faith and polity upon which we practice. It is ours to justify these in the eyes of the world, from the insidious as well as open attacks of our enemies, and to sow broad-cast the exalted principles of democracy, until every people, within the blue girdle of the sun, shall lift up their hands in joy upon their hills, and shout aloud, in the ecstacy of regenerating freedom. Political philosophy is, as yet, scarcely a recognized science; but I firmly believe that it is to be the destiny, as it certainly is the duty, of our country, to give to the world, lessons of wisdom, in both its branches, of ethics and economy, which will do more for the diffusion of truth, and the elevation of man, than any other influence since the writings of Luther and Melancthon. The Declaration of Independence was the first star of the morning, but it will be followed, in the figurative language of Shelley, by its "flocks of golden bees," until the whole sky shall be luminous with truth and beauty.

Another great achievement for American genius, is to rectify the erroneous spirit of history. From the times of Herodotus to Hallam, all history has been written wrong. It has been, throughout, a specious and cunning defence of the assumptions of the few, against the rights of the many. Kings and courtiers, knights and warriors, Ghengis Khans and Cœur de Leons,—the tyrants and murderers of mankind,—have been made to walk in stately procession, through its dramatic scenery, while the mighty people, each one more truly preserving the image of his maker, have been treated as so many dumb beasts of burden. Instead of being, as it was first called by Dionysius of Halicarnassus, "philosophy teaching by example," it has been, example distorting philosophy. Well might Sir Robert Walpole, in his dying hours, exclaim, "Read me not history ; I will believe any thing but that." Verily, the world has always been imposed upon by these lying Books of Chronicles ! Look for instance, at the histories of the French Revolution. What writer has ever faithfully portrayed the spirit and incidents of that great struggle for the rights of man ! All have attempted to excite our sympathies for the stolid Bourbons, and the supercilious *noblesse* of the *old regime*, and to stir our indignation against the tumultous upheavings of long depressed hnmanity. Even Scott prostituted his fine genius to the miserable task of framing a distorted argument in defence of the aristocratic principle ; and Archibald Alison has recently strutted forth, in pompous tomes, to hurl his anathemas upon every manifestation of democracy, whether in France or America !

All this, I say, has to be rectified. The whole volume of history must be re-written in a different spirit, with kindlier principles and a better faith. Our sympathies should be stirred in behalf of the suffering citizen, not the bloated despot : for the father toiling in the long afternoon of those days, gone a hundred years ago, to earn a scanty subsistence for his children, and not for the pampered patrician, revelling in wealth acquired only by governmental fraud and extortion. This is the spirit of our institutions, and should be the spirit of our literature. Written in this faith, what a change would take place in the philosophy of all history, and chiefly of that French Revolution! No longer should we have it depicted only as a savage outbreak of the worst passions of depraved humanity, but, what it was, in some sort, an honest, faithful, yet terrible, bloody, and dreadfully perverted struggle of an injured people to free themselves from the grinding oppressions of a long-continued loathsome tyranny. The heart-sickening excesses and horrors of the time would be charged, in the main, to those who attempted to resist and crush the popular spirit. Through the whole fell, demon tragedy, we should see one benevolent purpose at work, like the memories of his youth in a bad man's heart, which would justify many acts now regarded with odium and reproach. What a different estimate, too, would be placed upon some of the most conspicuous actors in that bloody drama. Robespierre is commonly represented as a fiend incarnate. This sentence, it has recently been contended, is, to a great degree, unjust. Those who knew him well, say that in the private and domestic virtues, in amiability of character, and in strong religious feeling, he was not the inferior of any of the cotemporary leaders of the Revolution. While it is admitted that he was driven, by the exigencies of the time, into many desperate expedients, over which humanity must ever shudder; yet it is contended that he was by no means the author of the long catalogue of crimes which were laid at his door. How the truth may be I shall not now pretend to determine; but certainly we should receive the popular versions with some critical hesitation, when we reflect that the commentators upon Robespierre and the Revolution have, with scarcely an exception, been monarchists or aristocrats. They have delighted to heap all obloquy upon him and his party, because they were the ultra-republicans of France, and would hold no middle-ground short of unqualified freedom. It is success that turns the rebel into the hero; and if those Jacobin clubs had succeeded in their effort to establish the broadest democracy, the name of Robespierre, instead of being cast out among men, as a synonyme for all that is brutal and bloody, might even, perhaps, have been recorded in history, by these sycophantic dispensers of fame, as one of the benefactors of the human family.

To do justice to this great Revolution, as well as in all the other chapters of history, is a part of the mission of Americanism. It is a noble enterprise, and, to my mind, presents a powerful inducement to the cultivation, by us, of letters. Already has a native author, of ample capacities, given us a glowing history of our own country, and of connected events in Europe, conceived and executed in the right spirit, with a genuine philosophy. Two others, inspired by the same high faith, have thrown the sunlight of American genius, over kindred provinces of history, and become honored apostles of the creed which I would inculcate to-day. Already the names of Bancroft, Prescott, and Irving, are uttered by the genuine lovers of the literature of humanity, with deeper regard than those of Tacitus, Livy, Hume, or Gibbon. When American genius shall, in a similar spirit, have encircled the whole field of the past; drawn out from eras, governments and occurrences, their proper lessons of instruction; weighed, in an equal balance, emperors and peasants, conquerors and captives; and tried all by that great test of merit,—what have they done for human progress?—then, and not till then, can history assert any claim to the attributes of philosophy. Oh! ever be the past brought to us in its truth, that it may guide us aright in our wanderings through the future!

Other fields stand invitingly open, with similar persuasives for culture by American minds. Poetry, metaphysics, ethics, each and all, need accommodation to the faith and polity adopted here. In their spirit, their essence, not in their form and embellishment only, they are philosophic powers for the promotion of the highest happiness. Hitherto they have achieved little of their proper evangelism in the world. They have stood, with the materialists of the last century, upon the external accidents of man, and reasoned inward to the soul; rather should they stand, like angels in the door of that temple, and look out through its portals, upon the blue sky and the green earth, the revolving wheels and the inclined planes, the ethical positions and relations, that are framed and energized by the out-running laws propounded in there. This spiritualism is the increasing faith of the age; and it alone is reconcilable with enlightened democracy. How it must manifest itself in the more ideal part of our literature, I would gladly linger to examine ; but we have tarried too long with these imperfect speculations, and must pass to a conclusion.

Though I have insisted that Americanism, in all its various phenomena,—in the magnificent and imperial spread of our country, its diversified climates, scenery, and productions—in the excellent character of our population, their rapid increase and extension, their hardy habits, and unity of language, faith and feeling—in the noble principles of our national constitution, and in the excellent arrangement and operation of our confederated system :—though in all this, I have insisted that Americanism is highly auspicious to literature, and that in every department of thought, there is imperious demand for the rectifying spirit ;—yet I would not be misunderstood. I have little faith in American literature, in its tendencies and achievements, thus far. We have shamefully neglected alike our mission and its opportunities. A multitude of pernicious influences, chiefly coming from our social condition, have checked and thwarted intellectual development. Some of these I have incidentally mentioned ; the others need not now be enumerated. Suffice it to say, one of the strongest impediments has been the timid and time-serving spirit of the great body of the scholars of our country. Entrusted with the care and keeping of the ark of the intellectual covenant, they have yet suffered it to be polluted by the hands of the ignorant and vulgar, and have yielded themselves to the blind infidelity, the anti-literary prejudice, of the day. Shame, shame, to the faithless disciples of this great religion of the mind! They have sold themselves and their salvation for thirty pieces of silver!—It is to her scholars,—those whom her institutions have nourished into intellectual manhood, that a country has the best right to look for the preservation of her highest interests, and they should be willing, with Gallileo, to endure solitude, poverty, derision, even martyrdom, in behalf of the "good old cause."

Yes: the speculations we have indulged in to-day, look chiefly to the future. Come however slowly it may, a literature must come beneath these occidental sunsets. The influences enumerated, will work out an intellectual reformation, as certain as the laws of vegetation, or the going round of the day-time. When the low philosophy and material purposes, now dominant, shall have perished, as they must, before the steady progress of education; when the hundreds of scholars, who are annually poured out from our colleges and universities, shall have swelled to thousands, all faithful to the high interests committed to their guardianship; when our literary men shall appreciate properly the true dignity and nobleness of their vocation; and when our country shall feel the old necessity of employing in her councils, her philosophers and scholars, instead of the brawling demagogue and vapid dunce;—we shall have the fulfilment of the vision whose prophetic rays have touched our eyes to-day. The period may be remote, but its advent is certain. The cause of literature cannot be stopped. It is the cause of civilization, refinement, virtue, religion, human progress! Let us then abide in the faith that this country of ours, as she is destined to present to the world, the proudest spectacle of political greatness ever beheld, will not be neglectful of the other, the highest interest of humanity, its intellectual ascension; but that both shall flourish here, in unexampled splendor, with reciprocal benefit, beneath the ample folds of that banner, which shall then float out, in its blue beauty, like a tropical night, brilliant with the stars of a whole hemisphere!

JACK-CADEISM AND THE FINE ARTS:

AN ORATION

BEFORE THE

LITERARY SOCIETIES OF LA-GRANGE COLLEGE,

ALABAMA,

JUNE 16, 1841.

ORATION.

GENTLEMEN:

In this age and country of ours, it requires a bold spirit to assert, amid the din and bustle of ordinary life,—the stir of the market place, and the excitement of the exchange,—the pure and elevated claims of literature. The world, at least that portion of it which lies about our doors, is essentially mechanical The grinding of the mill and the rattle of the railroad constitute the music which is most complacent to the ears of men. Every other spirit is absorbed in a feverish struggle for gain. "Put money in the pocket,"—is the ruling precept of the day. Nothing, the value of which you cannot calculate in dollars and cents, is tolerated by society. The blotting-book and the ledger, the shipping list and the broker's bulletin, make up the popular literature of the mass.

This spirit rules in every department of life. Even the precincts once sacred to a better divinity have been violated by its approch, and "the camp, the court, the grove," so sweetly devoted, by the Wizard of the North, to the gentlest faith of man, have yielded to its sullen dominion. It may truly be said to be the dominant Spirit of the Age.

Every era has been denominated in history from the ruling characteristics of the people. Thus, we have the Golden Age of Augustus, and the Reign of Terror of Robespierre. Our time has received many appellations. By some, it has been called the Age of Mechanical Science; by others, the Age of Utility.—By none, even of its self-gratulators, or pseudo-perfectionists, has it been denominated the Age of Moral Refinement. Whatever appellation, the History Builders of after time may give us, unless a deep regard is paid to the spirit I have mentioned, will be a gross misnomer.

The manifestations, from which our era is to be distinguished, unlike those of antiquity, are confined to no one country. The world is not now, as it was some six centuries ago, spotted all over, like a tesselated pavement, by a thousand contrarieties of color; by every diversity of purpose and ambition. Everywhere, from the land of Hong Foy and Houqua, the Tea Merchants, to the home of Sir Mulberry Hawk or My Lord Verisopht, from the quays of Liverpool to the cabins on the Oregon, the passion for pelf, for money-making, is the arch monopolist,—the insatiable Neptune that eats up all other Gods.

But it is in our own country, that this creeping autocrat has its firmest home.—We talk of the greatness of these American States; of their power and glory; their commerce cresting every sea; their agricultural and mechanical wealth; their iron muscles on the land, and their great pulsating arteries; their emigrants pitching their tents by the brackish waters of the far prairies, or felling forests through which the buffalo and moose had roamed unscared since the cradling of Time. All this is true, and more. But what is it all? It cannot be denied that we have done much for the conveniences of civilized man; that we have extended the arm of dominion over the elements; made them draw on the turnpike and spin in the manufactory. We have truly given man a right to the title of the Queller and Controller of physical nature. Yet, what does all this, in its best phase, imply? Does it not all look one way, down one vista, to one end,—the accumulation of property? Have not all our efforts been directed to the developement of the physical energies of the country; to the improvement of the national sinews, and not the national mind, to say nothing of the national heart? And has not the result,—boast of it as we may,—declaim in heroics about it, as all may do, from the unbearded sophomore to the Elisha-like senator,—been but commensurate with the cause? Loving my country with all the fervor and enthusiasm of a heart by no means cold; loving her more for what she might and ought to be, than for what she is; I must yet confess, with a lowering of pride, that I see, in her vaunted stupendousness, more of physical, than of moral or intellectual greatness!

If, from our country at large, we direct our minds,

under the same train of thought, to the section in which we live; this proud Southwest, the land of the cotton plant and the magnolia, the palmetto and the sugar cane; how sad is the contemplation! With all her acknowledged superiority in climate, in soil, in natural productions, in her mighty fretwork of navigable rivers, in the intrinsic character of her population; do we not find that she is thoroughly engrossed in the paltry passion for pounds and pence, and that her greatest proficiency is, to speak symbolically, in the limited philosophy of the ploughshare and the jack-plane, or the degraded cunning of the yard-stick and the packing screw? You must pardon me if this language is too plain; for I have a duty to do, and in sincerity it shall be done.

Any one, who will cast an observant eye upon the pursuits of our people, will find how deeply this spirit of utilitarianism, as by courtesy of speech it is called, is ingrained in the very constitution of our society. All our occupations—professions and trades alike,—have in view only one end. The great study of the farmer, the lawyer, the physician, the merchant, the mechanic, is how to double his profits. Even those in high places,—the legislators of the land,—would not "patriotically serve the public" a day, if you withdrew their per diem allowance. This inordinate passion is like the lean kine of the dreaming monarch; swallowing up every better purpose. It gives its hue and impress to every phase and feature of life. The parent, in the education of his child, must have him taught only those things, which will be of practical value! Education itself is curbed and fashioned by the influence. After delving in a miserable way, for a few years, over the primary branches of instruction, the hopeful youth, now that he is bearded and built like his father, assumes the full stature of an educated man ; with just knowledge enough, neglected as it is ever after, to addle his brain, and engender a spirit of ignorant vanity,—self-chuckling and deaf,—which besets and debases his whole moral nature. The limits, which the law sets up between the man and the minor, being passed, or the Baccalaureal Letters Patent obtained, whoever heard of the student continuing his studies in our country ? He at once launches out into all the petty plans and speculations of "the good old way, in which his fathers went." He loses all remembrance of the Pierian fountain, if ever he had knelt at its moss-covered curb-stone ; and remembers the beautiful days of his youth, only as so much time squandered in idle pursuits, under tyrannical taskmasters. This is the character of the greater portion of our youth ; and verily, it may be said, few of them are likely to die of that disease which Festus thought had affected Paul. The noble race of the olden scholars has never existed in our land. We know nothing of that generous order of intellectual Palestræ, who, from youth to manhood, from manhood to age, with an enthusiasm as deep as woman's love, drank of the golden waters of philosophy in the sacred grove of Academe, or, in a later age, bent, with a fever at the heart, and a hectic flush upon the pallid cheek, over dingy scrolls, in the midnight quiet of a German University.

All the sentiments and habits of our people are at war with such a life. They regard purely intellectual pursuits in a man, as mere idle revery. They only

> "Bend the pregnant hinges of the knee
> Where thrift may follow fawning"—

and, not comprehending, they despise the habits of that man, who gives his days and nights to Letters. Indeed, the opposition goes so far, that the man who is at all literary is deemed unfit for any practical part in life. No matter how great may be his intellect; no matter though he could thread and untangle, almost with the ease of intuition, the thousand little intricacies, over which they blunder and fumble with painful perseverance; he is yet elbowed aside in the press of life, to make room for men as far his inferiors, as the shrivelled shrub of a summer's garden is to the tempest-stemming pine. It is the fate of genius to be suspected if not despised; and nothing is more common in all our village streets than to hear the sneering prophecies of the dunce and dotard—those human moles who ridge the footpath,—that such a one will never be of any account in life; for he is a literary man! This is not the case in our country alone. "Beggary and genius have become proverbial synonymes with the vulgar of almost every nation; and nothing is so distressing to the green-grocer or the butter-merchant, as the dreadful apprehension that his favorite son Jacky may yet turn out to be a Genius."*

---

* W. G. Simms,—in the Magnolia.

Such being the spirit of the community in which we live, it may be well said that it requires a bold spirit to advocate, within our borders, the cause of literature. Degrading to the land as the imputation is, it is nevertheless true. The man, who comes out, upon any occasion, from the engrossing avocations of the day, to lift a voice in behalf of the better impulses of humanity; who ventures, amid the frog-like croaking of the great marsh of society, above the buzz of the cotton-gin, the rattle of the bacon-waggon, and all the sounds of the workshop, the hammer and the yard-stick,—those Merlin sceptres of modern life,—to raise the low, sweet music of philosophy, is encountering a species of voluntary martyrdom; is exposing himself to an *experimentum crucis*, as stern as ever brutalized the streets of Avignon or Seville.

And yet this spirit must be encountered. Every man, who loves his country, who loves his common nature, should do something to eradicate this curse; worse than the curse of Adam, if not the full developement of that curse itself: should use all his powers to remove this foul incubus which sits upon society, like the old man upon the shoulders of Sinbad, stifling every generous impulse, every noble effort, and forcing poor man, proud man still, to plod through the ruts and ravines of life, as little conscious of the God within him, as the rude hut of the patriarch was of the angel it sheltered.

As the potency of this spirit of utilitarianism is perhaps greater in our portion of the Union than any other; as it here darkens and destroys many of the better, if not the best, capabilities of humanity ; it here needs the most powerful resistance,—it is here that the strongest effort for a nobler philosophy should be made. What subject is worthier of our thinking men ; of our patriots ; of our philanthropists ? There can be none ; for it includes in its purview, man's whole social, moral and intellectual destiny.

To you, Gentlemen,—a Brotherhood of Scholars,—the sunny waters of whose youthful affections are yet undarkened by the shadows of a colder creed,—this contemplation is particularly appropriate. You are shortly, from these ambrosial arcades, to step into the world, to participate in its practices and purposes, to move in its dusty whirl; and I speak but the voice of many a man's experience, when I tell you that, if you yield implicitly to its requirements, if you do not, like a strong swimmer, stem a torrent's progress, it will be in vain that you have outworn long years of scholastic toil; that you have bowed with a deep reverence over the curious diagram ; that you have garnered instruction from "Tully's voice, and Virgil's lay, and Livy's pictured page !" Worse, worse than wasted, will have been your time. You will individually become one of a poor, pitiful, plodding race,—I speak in no unkind spirit, for I love every creature that partakes of the inheritance of our first Father,—who go through life in such a way as seemingly to sanction the bitter sneer of the caustic satirist, that the whole purpose of man is

> "To draw nutrition, propagate and rot!"

Oh, let me, my friends, beseech you to resist this

Circéan influence ! Let me, upon this occasion which you have so generously furnished me, file a plea in behalf of a better faith. Let me, in short, point out the evils of this gross system of materialism, of JACK-CADEISM,* as it should be called; its blightiug operation upon the noblest interests of our country; as well as attempt to exhibit the best means of modifying, if not eradicating, its influence. Those means, I shall endeavor to show, reside in a proper culture of the Imaginative Faculty, and in a generous encouragement of its visible manifestations,—the FINE ARTS: to whose moralizing influence, I hold, we are to look for all our better hopes of intellectual or social excellence. This is one of the great truths of history. And when men forget the existence of any important truth, or suffer it to die out among them, they are forced, by a thousand resulting ills, to weep heavily over its tomb

The pernicious influence of the utiltarian doctrines may be more forcibly illustrated by a reference to the moral condition of our section of the confederacy. There has been little variance among writers in describing the characteristics of our population. The whole corporation of European tourists,—from De Tocqueville, down, down, down to Captain Marryatt,

---

* "*Cade.*—Let me alone:—Dost thou use to write thy name? or hast thou a mark to thyself, like an honest plain-dealing man?

Clerk.—Sir, I thank God, I have been so well brought up, that I can write my name.

All.—He hath confessed—away with him—he's a villian and a traitor.

Cade.—Away with him, I say; hang him with his pen and ink-horn about his neck."—*Second Part of King Henry VI.*—*Act* 4, *Scene* 2.

—that Peter Simple on shore,—disagreeing in many things, have all concurred in their portraitures of us. We are every where represented to be lawless, violent, irritable, haughty, vain, unsocial, quick of entrance in a quarrel, reckless of life, heedless of the obligations of religion. A few of the ruder virtues are allowed us; but they are such only as appertain to a semi-barbarous state. The picture is undoubtedly over-colored; but many of its features may be found. Where did you ever hear of a country in which there were fewer of the incentives to the higher virtues? A man must be honest, brave, industrious; for these qualities are necessary in his trade or profession. He can't be trusted unless he is. But where are the motives to generosity, to benevolence, to charity, to courtesy,—"the old unbought grace of life,"—to a refined and filial patriotism? These certainly form no integral part of our social economy. They are all engulfed in the tide and temper of traffic. That spirit, whose approaches Edmund Burke so loftily lamented, is upon us. All our philosophers teach us to regard only those things which shall increase our store. This is our great motive principle. Under its influence the gentler virtues die. Religion herself—the beautiful embodiment of all the better rules of morals, with an infusion of never-paling divinity; the sweet monitress that teaches us how much of heaven a good man may incarnate in himself,—is set aside or adopted as convenience dictates, and her elevating precepts fall upon the hearts of men, only like cold and scattered stars through the gloom of a northern heaven!

The *savans* of our land have attempted to correct these evils by legislation. That is beginning at the wrong stage of the disease. They train up a child in the way he should not go ; and then they punish him for following the bent of his education. You may pile law upon law ; adopt penal codes, as systematic as the Pandects of Justinian, or as tyrannical as the tablets of Draco ; and yet you will produce little moral reformation. You must mind the seeds of the evil. The parable of the Tares is no unmoralized fable. A people, to become refined, must have some motive else than to grow rich. They must have some other catechism than Poor Richard's Almanac.

We are usually told by flippant sciolists, that the way to correct these evils is by education. I shall not refute the assertion ; I shall not so sin against science. But if we are to understand by "education," that species of teaching commonly given to the mass of our youth, honesty must own that it is entirely inadequate to such an end. At best, it is but a brief cultivation of the grosser faculties of the mind. To moral culture it has no relations. The feelings of the heart, the finer fancies of the intellect, are all left dormant, to perish in their sockets. There might be a nation of men highly educated upon the utilitarian plan, who would all be villains. Frankenstein's hero was composed of parts, each one perfect in itself, and yet their combination produced a demon. There was wanting a pervading spirit, a genial sympathy, blending the discordant members into one harmonious whole. So with a nation. Unless its constituent portions are united by something more than a mere insulated excellence; unless there is a refined fitness for each other; a going-out of each in love and generosity through the whole; in short, unless its virtues as well as its intellect be cultivated; it will be but a chaotic mass of incoherent materials:

"Like sweet bells jangled, harsh and out of tune!"

This is the great secret of civilization: and it is against this principle that Jeremy Bentham and his implicit disciples have most deeply sinned. Their doctrine not only blights the social virtues, by failing to cultivate their sources, but it would quench every exalted Literature. Adopt the maxim, that we are to pursue only those things which are of immediate practical value; whose utility can be computed by arithmetic; and you would extinguish the main glories of the world. Where would go the storied splendors of antiquity? They who carved, and they who dug; the cyclops in his smithy, and the tanner at his vat; the utilitarians of Rome; have perished entirely, leaving no epitaph to after times; and yet the names of Cicero, and Virgil, and Juvenal, and Terence—of the unproductive classes—still travel with the stars; moulding opinion through all the Subsequent. These, the sage of Queen-Square Place would, with one of his solemn sneers, extinguish forever.

The evil does not stop here. Its barbarous extent would obliterate every nation's proudest inheritance; the fame of her scholars and literary men. Erase from the tablets of England's history, the names of Bacon,

Milton, Shakespeare, Spenser, and Byron only, and how much of her glory would you extinguish forever! What would be the barren heath and winding lochs beyond the Tweed, without the moonlight halo that emanates from the pages of Burns and Scott?—Eclipse the fame of Dante, Petrarch, Tasso, Alfieri, and Boccacce, and how the sky of Italy would be darkened! Deprive Portugal of her Camoens; Spain of her Lope de Vega, her Calderon, and Cervantes; and what a pall of gloom would cover the Peninsula! What would France be without Corneille, Racine, Rabelais, Montaigne, Voltaire and De Stael; or Germany without Goethe, Schiller, Martin Luther, Herder, Lessing and Erasmus?

These illustrations show the absurdity of the doctrine, as well as its pernicious influence upon Letters. In our own country, it has had a repressing influence; has kept down everything like literary elevation. There have been occasional efforts to develope our native genius. "Prithee Poins!" did you not speak of such a thing as Southern Literature? Like the sounding of a bell in a vast wilderness, we have heard the faint chimes of a scattered few, who would awaken us to an elevated devotion. They have been the neglected prophets and apostles of an impracticable creed. The Jack-Cadeism of the day has quenched their vestal fires. "Hang him with his pen and ink-horn about his neck," has been the constant verdict of our backwoods' juries. Southern Literature indeed! *Lucus a non lucendo!* Throughout this broad, green, beautiful land of ours, as it is sometime rapturously called;

from Mason and Dixon's, to Hunt and Carroll's line; there is not one native author; exclusively an author! Yes, there is one: one of whom we may be justly proud. Solitary and alone, in this barren Patmos, he has been struggling for years, to develope and illustrate an indigenous literature. And well, though perhaps unrewarded,—certainly unrewarded by those for whom be has done the most,—has he accomplished his exalted mission. His numerous productions have arisen like a line of beautiful hills around the literary horison of his country. Could my voice reach him in his far home, amid the palmetto groves of Carolina, I would bid him—God speed! in his proud vocation. I would tell him that he is a worthy herald of the noblest faith save one,—a sister spirit—that has ever brightened our common nature. Though his immediate countrymen may not appreciate his efforts; though, like Dante, he may struggle in darkness; I would tell him to remember Dante's prophecy; remember its fulfillment! The time will come when the brow of the author of "Atalantis" and the "Yemassee," of "Mellichampe" and the "History of South Carolina" shall be crowned with the green garlands of unforgetting love!

It is in the history of our Periodical Literature that the influence of this iconoclastic spirit is most manifest. Many efforts have been made to establish among us the higher class of periodicals. They have all been ineffectual. The truth has been fully proven that our people do not want,—that they are positively unfit for, such intellectual establishments. How sad is the history of the SOUTHERN REVIEW! For profound learning, elegant scholarship, lofty and generous criticism modelled upon the purest standards of taste and philosophy; it was but little, if at all, inferior to the great Coryphæus, the Edinburgh itself. Its pages were regularly adorned by the most finished productions of such minds as Legare, Cooper, Grimke, Elliott, Harper, Drayton, Hayne, Nott, and England. Fearlessly, eloquently, it defended our peculiar social economy, and better constitutional creed; wreathing at the same time, the graces of literature, like the myrtle of Harmodius, around the ruder implements of attack and defence. And yet,—though many of its articles were regularly translated into other languages, and read with rapture by the illuminati of the Continent,—it was permitted, by our all-patriotic population, to die by that most painful of all the processes of decomposition—starvation. Ah! how far below zero, our intellectual thermometer sank, the day those funeral obsequies were performed!

That such has been the result of all our attempts at literature is not strange. Our scholars, like our legislators, have begun in the wrong way. The minds, the feelings of the people must first be accommodated by a proper culture, before they will yield to the dynasty of either. That culture, we repeat, does not consist in the development of the grosser faculties of the mind alone. There are other and higher attributes of the intellect. Man is not a mere Babbage's Calculating Machine. He has sentiments, feelings, emotions; a love of the beautiful, the true, the sublime; a yearning for immortality, an impulse to the perfect. These,—the divine part of his nature; the attributes of the unperishing essence, his soul,—the German metaphysicians have denominated The Ideal. Our writers, pursuing a less exact phraseology, have classed them as constituents or objects of a more familiar term, the Imagination. Either phrase, if rightly understood, will answer our purpose; and it is in the cultivation of this faculty, in its most extended sense, that we shall insist, reside the only remedy for the evils of which we have spoken; the only antagonist principle to the horrors of utilitarianism; the only hope of social regeneration. For,—to use the thought of Frederick Von Schlegel, in his admirable "Philosophy of History,"*—"there can be no comprehensive culture of the human mind,—no high and harmonious development of its powers, and the various faculties of the soul; unless all those deep feelings of life,—that mighty productive energy of human nature, the marvelous imagination, be awakened and excited, and by that excitement and exertion, attain an expansive, noble and beautiful form. Were the mental culture of any people founded solely on a dead, cold, abstract science, to the exclusion of all poetry, *in action or thought;* such a mere mathematical people, with minds thus sharpened and pointed by mathematical discipline, would never possess a rich and various intellectual existence; nor even probably attain to a living science, or a true science of life."

Under the influence of the popular philosophy, men

* Vol. 1, p. 305.

have come to greatly mis-appreciate, if not wholly to misunderstand, the character and functions of the imagination. It is regarded, at its best, but as a generous weakness of the mind; an intoxicating mental champagne, generating vapors and phantasms in the brain, fit only for the amusement of children, or the idle gratulation of some love-sick girl. How false is the notion! What injustice is done to the great motive principle of all moral or intellectual excellence!

The human mind may be briefly divided into two grand departments: the Actual and the Ideal. The first regards things,—the plainer things of life,—only as they have been or are. Its speculations extend thus far, and no farther. The last prompts to every new and high enterprize; to every improvement or discovery in art, science or feeling; to every reformation or regeneration; to every thing "not of the earth, earthy;" to every revelation of the hidden or future; to every effort or aspiration for the true, the beautiful, the immortal! This is the imagination, and these are its offices. It urged "the world's grey fathers" to all their efforts for civilization and refinement. It led them up to the summits of their rugged mountains, and pointed them to the far-smiling Palestines, beckoning to perfection. It prompted the bare-footed Egyptian to the invention of symbols for thought, and taught the Asiatic sheep-tender "to unwind the eternal dances of the sky." Socrates, when he mused at the Bonquet of Plato; Gallileo, before and after he recanted at the Inquisition; Columbus, as he floated in his polacre, in the bay of Genoa, dreaming of a means of realising the fiery Macedonian's last ambition; all felt its divine impulse. Leibnitz tells us that all his philosophy resulted from his Ideality; and the apple-watching Newton caught the secret of his greatness from his imagination. It is, in short, an attribute without which perception is dull, memory weak, and judgment inactive.

But we do not propose a dissertation upon all the offices of this faculty. Addison, in his finished prose, and his imitator Akenside, in his finely modulated verse, have adequately painted its pleasures. Our purpose is to show that its development, and culture should be more attended to in every system of education; that this is peculiarly essential under our frame of government,—this "fierce democracie;"—and that no people ever reached a refined social position without a cultivation of the faculty itself, and particularly of its external manifestations: the Fine Arts.

It is in these manifestations, that this imperial faculty, which dwells in the recesses of the bosom, like a hermit in a cave, has accomplished its triumphs. The Fine Arts have, in all ages, been the main civilizers and refiners of man. Before letters were invented, Poetry trembled from the lips of the wandering bard, sanctifying the rude heart of the attracted barbarian: Music, as in the metaphoric story of Orpheus, calmed the bestial passions and roused the timid virtues into play: Painting caught the fleeting vision, and hung her miracles upon the walls which Architecture and Sculpture had adorned. These,—the arts, which that beautiful poetry of religion, the early Greek mythology, embodied in the forms of the Muses, as a part of its faith,—the unphilosophical have usually regarded as the effect, and no part of the cause, of civilized refinement. I have looked at the chronicles of the past, with an erring eye, if this be so. True, we usually find the Arts in their most palmy prosperity in periods of the greatest social splendor. But they had originated long before. They were but glowing in the sunshine of that day whose meridian, —whose long unstooping, Joshua-like meridian,—they had accelerated.

Every era of great excellence will be found to have been preceded by the enlarged development of one or more of the Fine Arts. Homer, whoever he was,— "whether," as Dr. Parr says, "he was Homer or somebody else,"—flourished long before the sabbath of Grecian glory. He sang his martial stanzas in a rude and unlettered country. They, who heard his metrical chant, at first paused from curiosity to listen to the ravings of the blind old Sciote. The boys hoot: the maidens titter: the utilitarians of that day, the bullock-driver and the pulse-gatherer,— where are they now?—sneer. But he strikes up a bolder and a wilder strain. He tells of Hector's bravery, of Helen's beauty, of Priam's woes.—Their hearts become entangled in the song. Now a strain of fervid patriotism; now a gush of genial sympathy, of generous pity, of expanded benevolence; now a burst of fiery indignation at unholy wrong, at sacrilege, at fraud, at cowardice, at tyranny,—roll upon the mild air of that Ægean evening. Like Roderick Dhu before the highland harper, their hearts have sympathized in every note of the blind, old poet. Think you that they did not lie down that night in their wretched hovels, better and braver and more generous and patriotic than they had been? Models of excellence,—ideal it is true but not unattainable,—were swimming in their hearts, were pictured before their imaginations, which in long days after, when old Melesigines had passed away, had a moulding and glorious influence, had their full revelation in the age of Pericles!

This is undoubtedly, when taken in connection with the sister arts,—the paintings of Zeuxis, the sculptures of Phidias, and the friezes of Apollodorus,—the philosophy of Grecian history.

Other eras exemplify the same truth. It is somewhat singular that the greatest poet of modern times arose in the darkest hour of the world. And what an upward impulse did he give to man! In that long night of ages,—the ten centuries of degradation,—when humanity "had lost all her original brightness," what hope was there for the world? The gorgeous crests of Roman and Grecian glory had, like the hosts of Pharaoh, been whelmed completely from the sight: and no Miriam struck her harp of triumph and promise above the cold, Lethean waters. From the holder of the keys of St. Peter to the beggar in the lazaretto, all was squalid ignorance, sensuality and crime. At this dejected moment, a faint sound, like a ringing cymbal, is heard in the West. Nearer it comes, until it swells into a hymn of indignation and triumph! It speaks of hope and redemption to man. It lashes vice in her high places. Tyranny and bigotry tremble at the omen. The clouds break away; and a faint dawn for humanity is seen in the east. Need it be said that that song was the Divina Commedia; that that poet was Dante?

This is the origin of the Revival of Letters. The poet gave an impulse to the painter, to the statutary, to the architect. The Fine Arts began to revive; and, from the course they took, the Reformation—so essential to clear away the last shadows of the ages of delusion,—was brought about. There can be little doubt,—though it has seldom been awarded him,—that Dante did as much to reform the abuses of the Romish church, as Martin Luther. He depicted, in a language never equalled for music and persuasion, all the long-accumulated evils of the Papal hierarchy. With a boldness unsurpassed even by his own heroes, he rent the veil of the unhallowed temple. Neither the cap of the pontiff, nor the horned bonnet of the bishop, was free from the sarcasm of his verse. With a well-becoming joy, he dared to consign several of the boasted Vice-regents of Jesus themselves, for their unnatural crimes, their open infidelity, to the tortures of his *Inferno!* Nor was it upon Religion alone, but upon Liberty and Literature, that he had an awakening influence. "He was the congregator of those great spirits that presided over the resurrection of learning; the Lucifer of that starry flock which, in the thirteenth century, shone forth from republican Italy, as from a heaven, into the darkness of the benighted world!"*

* Shelley's "Defence of Poetry," p. 51.

Nor are these triumphs confined to Poetry. The other Arts have, in many instances, had as manifest an influence for good. Who can doubt that much of the mystic literature of Egypt; much of the peculiar, refined character of her people; much of her social and political economy, was derived from the influence of her strange and gigantic architecture, her wild but polished sculpture, and her finished painting; so early established and patronized by her kings? The fabled harp of Memnon was but an emblem of the exquisite music, which the constellated arts daily infused, like a gift of sunshine, into the hearts of the people.

The most notable instance, history furnishes, of social, political and intellectual superiority, is in the Democracy of Athens. There never was an instance of such thorough and diffused refinement. Destitute of the beneficence of nature, she had made art supply the deficiency. That statesman, who could make a modern state equal to hers in every excellence, would possess a cunning superior to Macchiavel or Metternich. And yet, what seems to have been the secret of her excellence? Will it not, upon a philosophic view, —not such a *coup d'œil* as that intense sensualist, Bulwer, has taken,—appear to have resulted from the encouragement given to the Imaginative Arts? Modern commonwealths far transcend her in all the exact sciences, in a control over the energies of nature. They have, in the cant phrase of Brougham, the schoolmaster abroad in the land: but is it not to be feared that his teachings are more like those of Teddy O'Rourke, the Irish tutor,—wild lessons of blundering and folly—than the training and perfection of the moral man? Say what we will, the barren little peninsula, between mount Cithæron and cape Sunium,—with her violet crowned city,—far excelled any modern state in her whole social and educational polity. Let us, for the sake of illustration, transport ourselves in fancy, like the Abbe Barthelemi, to her territory, in the time of her power and glory.

We are entering the gates of Athens. Down the broad street, that opens before us, a crowd is collected around the portico of a temple. Let us approach.—They are gazing with delight upon an architect who is erecting the statue of a divinity. As the beautiful form displays itself against the sky, they shout the name of Praxitiles. We wander on by graceful temples and elegant dwellings, beneath whose colonnades, priest, and poet, and philosopher, and artist, and orator, and rhapsodist are mingled in indiscriminate conversation. In a little while we enter a spacious grove. How tastefully adorned! Gay crowds are wandering through its shady walks. Now they collect in the centre; and Plato arises to speak of the immortality of the soul. Among the audience you see many who are distinguished. That small, old man, with the long beard, dressed much in the style of a Carmelite friar of the present day, is Diogenes. Yonder meagre, lank young man, with the red eyes, is Aristotle, the Stagyrite. That pale, delicate, scholarly-looking youth, who so continually shrugs his shoulders, like a Frenchman, is Demosthenes. Others of no less reputation are around. From the Academy, we proceed to the

Lyceum. What a profusion of matchless paintings and sculptures deck its walls. Pericles is illustrating the powers of eloquence, and propounding the laws. Thence we seek the Theatre. First a tragedy of Æschylus, and then a comedy of Aristophanes: each, unlike our modern dramas, illustrating some important moral truth. Now for the house of Aspasia. She gives to-night, one of her ambrosial feasts. The collection of philosophy and wit would make Madame Recamier, or the Countess of Blessington, die of envy.

Such is a day in Athens!* Such were all her days! Can any modern university boast so excellent a system of education? What wonder that her citizens were the most refined population on earth!

But we need not resort to these pictures of the past to illustrate the esthetic influence of the arts. What Athens was, Rome, from the same cause, in a later day became. The rude passions of her populace were humanized and refined by the presence of the Muses. The habitual contemplation of the beautiful tends to soften the asperities of the heart; and make its stony places gush with the waters of charity and love. This is the Philosophy of the Imagination. Its beautiful revelations, whether in verse or stone, upon parchment or canvas, have ever been the most eloquent preachers of morality. They are so from their nature. Directing all their radiance to the heart, they awaken its holiest sympathies. They rouse the passion for

---

* Macaulay, in one of his essays, has a similar scene.

the pure, for perfection. No man, with such gentle ministrants of good, such graceful persuasives to refinement, could be content to live and die as though he had no soul.

In a survey of the Fine Arts, it would not do, to pass unnoticed the epoch of their greatest modern perfection. As has been said, Dante was the prime reviver of the Imaginative Arts. He was soon followed by many worthy disciples. Petrarch and Boccacce, in the flowery wilderness of song; Michael Angelo, and Raphael, and a host of others,—whose footsteps are yet beautiful upon the mountain tops of history,—in painting, and sculpture, and architecture,—enriched Italy with the proudest wonders of art; and elevated her to a lofty position in the university of nations. This made her capitols "the cities of the soul," and drew the pilgrims of every literature, of every art, from Shelley to Thorwalsden, to drink at her immortal fountains. We cannot linger over her teeming history. It is one of the most brilliantly illuminated pages in the chronicles of man. There the plastic arts exemplified their influence in the conversion of a barbarous people into a refined, intellectual community; and left a lesson for all the succeeding. But to nations, as that solemn plagiarist, Coleridge, has said of individuals, "experience is like the stern lights of a ship, illuminating only the track over which they have passed." Few modern statesmen have treasured the instruction. Napoleon, who, if he had not been Europe's mightiest conqueror, would perhaps have been her first philosopher, did not overlook the lesson.

When he had erected the architrave of his stupendous power, he saw that one thing was wanting to adorn, to endear, the edifice. Under the guidance of Canova, he struck upon the right secret. He attempted to fill the Louvre with the treasures of Italy.—But alas ! the pedestals of his power were too slippery with blood ; and he only left the collections of his genius to brighten and beautify the reigns of the stolid Bourbons. And what an influence must they have had upon the mind, and, that most social of all its manifestations, the manners, of the French people ! The most imaginative of English-essay writers, William Hazlitt, has finely described the effect that the reccollections of the Louvre had upon him. "Wherever I was," says he, "they were with me, above me, and about me, and hung upon the beatings of my heart, a vision and a joy unutterable. There was one chamber of the brain, at least, which I had only to unlock and be master of boundless wealth,—a treasure-house of pure thoughts and cherished recollections. Tyranny could not master, barbarism slunk from it ; vice could not pollute ; folly could not gainsay it. I had but to touch a certain spring, and lo ! on the walls, the divine grace of Guido appeared free from blemish,—there were the golden hues of Titian, and Raphael's speaking faces, the splendor of Rubens, the gorgeous gloom of Rembrandt, the airy elegance of Van Dyke, and Claude's classic scenes lapped the senses in Elysium, and Poussin breathed the spirit of antiquity over them. There, in that fine old lumber-room of the imagination, were the Transfiguration, and the St. Peter Martyr, with its majestic figures, and its unrivalled landscape back-ground. There were also the two St. Jeromes,—Domenichino's and Correggio's,—there stood "the statue that enchants the world,"—there were the Apollo, and the Antinous, the Laocoon, the Dying Gladiator, Diana and her Fawn, and all the glories of the antique world."*

What finer school for moral refinement or classical instruction could exist, than the opened doors of the Louvre?

Among the Moderns, there is one nation at least that has been philosophical in her social structure. We usually regard the Germans as a dull and phlegmatic race; yet, in the true science of life, they are far our superiors. In domestic polity they have few equals. Although, through a disregard of the maxims of Malthus, they have an over-teeming population, yet, unlike the Irish, they are not in a constant state of fermentation; the lowest dregs of society welling up, and muddying the whole social system. Their youth are early fashioned into virtue by the influence of imaginative culture. Music and poetry are made a part of their common school education. You cannot travel through a town in Hesse Darmstadt or the Circle of Meissen, without hearing the pleased tinkling of the laborer's guitar, as he pauses from his toil at the evening twilight; or the sweet song of the maiden, as she blends the mild religious melodies of Klopstock or Burger with the busy humming of her wheel. What

---

* "Tour through France and Italy." Chap. 4.

a transcendant social fabric! What wonder that they have the richest, most varied and humanizing literature now known! What wonder that the heart of the German emigrant, amid our western wilderness, oft sighs, with child-like tenderness, for the joys of Faderland!

The instance of our great maternal progenitor is frequently pointed to, by the advocates of the ultilitarian philosophy, in illustration of their creed. Great Britain is proudly called the mightiest demonstration of political and commercial power that the world has ever seen. This is perhaps true; and this, to a great extent, may be traced to the culture of the mechanical sciences. But is this all? Have no other ingredients entered into the composition of her social and moral condition? Are the peasants of Cumberland, or the merchants of Threadneedle street, better citizens, better men, more patriotic, more liberal, more devoted to the domestic virtues, because, as Croly has proudly boasted, "the sun never sets upon the British dominions," or that the Cross of St. George has floated in triumph in the bay of Canton, or the steamships made a great turnpike of the Atlantic? No! For the secrets of England's happiness, you must look to other sources. The myriad-minded Shakspeare, the gentle Spenser, the mighty Milton, the benevolent Wordsworth, Lawrence, Reynolds, Hogarth, Chantrey, and West, have done more for human happiness and virtue, for fireside comfort and purity, for patriotism and philanthropy, than all the inventions of Arkwright, or Bolton, or Watt, or Bentley. The sources of moral purification are most usually silent and imperceptible in their operation. Like the sunshine, they give fragrance, beauty to the flower; sparkle, freshness to the fountain; music, blandness to the breeze; health, bloom to the cheek; and yet the whole process goes on with the calmness and silence of the old, mysterious bounty. There is no creaking of the axle; no stirring of the dust! Thus, for ages, have the benefactions of the arts been poured, like a river, upon the descendants of the old Saxon stock,—the inheritors of Rollo's Scandinavian blood. Who can tell the influence that the architecture of their old Gothic cathedrals, standing all over the island, living proofs of the antiquity, if not the authenticity, of their faith, has exerted, for ages, upon the religious character of the English people, from peer to peasant? Has not Westminster Abbey, —that magnificent repository of the illustrious dead, and of glorious historic recollections, from the banners of the Armada to the Round Table of Alfred,—with its high and sculptured arches, its almost speaking statuary,—fashioned much of the manners and literature of the white-cliffed isle? What impulses to patriotism and patriotic valor! He, who can overlook these things in an estimate of the seminal principles of national character, must be blinder than the blind old king of Corinth.

These glimpses at other nations will verify the position that no people have ever attained an exalted character in literature or ethics, who have neglected the Fine Arts. Then,—to apply the lesson to our own country,—should not greater devotion be paid to their encouragement among ourselves? Are we not sadly deficient in every thing like objects of taste or imagination? It has been said by a subtle sophist that these arts cannot flourish in a democratic government: that they are ungenial to its very nature. This, if true, would be, as it was intended to be, one of the strongest arguments against Republicanism. It would prove that there could be no refinement in a republic. But all history contradicts Montesquieu. It is precisely in such a government as ours that the influence of the Muses is wanted to complete the system of social balances. A people to rule themselves must be virtuous and refined. They must have a taste for the graces and beatitudes of being. Their selfish propensities,—the primitive barbarism,—must be checked and removed. "The decent drapery of life" must be thrown over the deformities of nature. Loveliness must be made an attribute of their country, before they can love her like a mother. This is the moral which we, as a nation, have to learn.

But,—to confine our speculations to the section of the republic, in which we live,—how vast would be the benefit of the Fine Arts to the Southwest! We have seen that there is much in our situation to be deplored. The vices that mark us, are precisely such as would be removed by imaginative culture. An infusion of the atmosphere of Attica into our Southern breezes would regenerate the clime. Our people would no more degrade themselves by organized violations of law, or be lashed into tempest by the miserable passions of the hustings. The cunning aphorism of Fletcher of

Saltoun,—"let me make the songs of a people, and you may make their laws," has recently been tested in our land.—Let those songs be the pure breathings of the vestal muse, and the great heart of the country would pulsate with virtue. If our public buildings were decorated with tasteful creations of art; with noble pictures, breathing grand historic recollections; with lofty statues, placing the images of our gallant ancestry continually before the eye, and sending, to the degenerate heart, by the mute appeal of a steadfast look, the noble precepts of their sacred legacy; if, instead of that meagre, pinched style of architecture,—the double cabin, with the passage through the centre,—so common in all our towns, the graceful shafts of the Ionic, or the ornate entablatures of the Corinthian, the massive Doric, or the aspiring Gothic, won the admiring eye, an elegant taste would manifest itself in all the relations of life. The old fabric of humanity has to be disintegrated, or this must be so!

The beneficial influence of such imaginative culture would demonstrate itself in another respect. The wealthier portion of our youth, instead of wasting their patrimonies in idle follies or flagrant dissipation, would have higher and better objects. So much superfluous wealth, indeed, would not be expended on the favorites of the Turf,—some Leviathan colt or Pacolet filley, or,—to descend in the scale of being,—upon the *pas de seul* or the pirouettes of a foreign danseuse. All that classical chit-chat about the pedigree and performances of a Bascombe or a Black Maria, or the swimming grace and abandoned voluptuousness of an Elssler or a Celeste, would be terminated ; but other and nobler purposes and phraseology would engage the mind ; purposes and thoughts more worthy of beings who have already commenced the grand march of immortality.

When a taste for the Fine Arts is excited among us ; when that mighty slumbering attribute of the mind,—its only immortal part,—the Ideal, is stirred ; and not till then ; may we hope for a native Literature ; a Literature that shall redeem and illustrate this mighty sugar-cane and cotton-growing region. All previous efforts will be a wasteful dissemination of pearls. You might as well scatter, with the vain hope of vegetation, the delicate seed of the chrysanthemum or the dahlia, upon the sandy slopes of the Chandeleur isles. A few periodical works,—such as that noble Monthly, the Southern Literary Messenger, at Richmond, or its worthy collaborator, The Magnolia, at Savannah,—may be maintained by the untiring efforts of an exalted purpose upon the parts of the publishers ; honoring and beautifying the region in which they are issued ; but they will meet with no adequate and spirited patronage.

The cultivation of the Fine Arts in our country being so desirable, it is the part of patriotism to inquire as to the means by which it can be promoted.

We are apt to look too much to our National Government for an interference in the affairs of life. Such an interference would be inconsistent with the purposes for which it was established. And yet, belonging as I do to the straitest sect of our political Pharisees, I can see no impediment to its extending a liberal hand of encouragement to objects of literature and art. The wild project of Joel Barlow, for a vast National University, is perhaps too heretical for any political sect of the present day. But the General Government, in the exercise of its undenied powers, might do much, it has done something, for the Fine Arts. The capitol at Washington is a noble specimen of Architecture. Measures have been taken to decorate its halls and galleries with splendid specimens of the sculptor's and painter's genius. Much more might be done. The various buildings through the country,—the custom-houses, arsenals, public offices, and the like,—might be made chaste models of taste and elegance; and a generous love of the picturesque and beautiful be thus engendered. Surely, if the Federal Government had the authority to fit out the South Sea Exploring Expedition,—so creditable to American character,—*a fortiori*, it has the authority to promote, by similar means, the moral and social improvement of the people.

There is one undoubted means by which Congress might readily promote the culture of the Moral Arts. It will be remembered that a wealthy foreigner, a younger son of the noble house of Percy, a few years since, made our government the trustee of a bequest of a half a million of dollars, for "the increase and diffusion of knowledge among men." Over the disposition of this trust, Congress has been squabbling for several sessions. What nobler disposition could be made of it; better in accordance with the wishes of the testator; than the establishment of a National Academy of the Fine Arts! Such an institution would give life and energy to the Arts. It would serve as a solar center from which taste and refinement might be radiated through the land. Our artists would have a Louvre of their own, to which they might journey for instruction; a shrine upon which they could fondly lay their offerings to Genius. The better stars of our country's destiny, grant that such may be the character of the Smithsonian Institute!

But it is by our State Governments that the most liberal patronage might be extended to the Arts. If that niggardly spirit of parsimony, which has ever marked our legislation, could be exorcised, we might look for generous results. Our public buildings would not linger in a half-finished condition; as our State Capitol has, its bare walls nearly as blank as the minds of many of its occupants. What an influence, upon the deliberations of our Collected Wisdom, would several such noble paintings as Trumbull's "Signers of the Declaration," or White's "Marion," exercise. The legislature of North Carolina sat a laudable example in the purchase of Canova's Statue of Wasington. Its destruction by fire, a few years since, is more to be regretted than the conflagration of the capitol itself. The last has been restored; but of the other and nobler possession, we may well ask, "where's the Promethean spark that can that light relume?"

After all, it is not to our governments, state or national, that we are to look for the principal culture of the Fine Arts. Our social organization is mainly in the hands of the people. They must weave and fashion their own destiny. If then, we would acquire the excellences of every civilized community, let us go about the work with the proper spirit and in the right way. Let the minds of our youth be properly instructed; let more of the Ideal be infused into their education. They should be taught to love the beautiful and spiritual, as well as the practical. "What shall we eat, and what shall we drink, and wherewithall shall we be clothed?" should not be the whole burthen of their song; their tuition but the degraded pander to such a litany. If parents and teachers shall have a proper regard to the welfare of the young immortals under their guardianship, we shall, in the next generation, have no deficiency in the noblest graces of a nation.

It is, however, from our educated young men, that our country has the most to hope; that she has the right to hope the most. Under the bend of a smiling heaven, she has bestowed upon them all the blessings of matchless political institutions. At the wells of olden wisdom, they have been led to drink. The lessons of philosophy,

> "Not harsh and crabbed as dull fools suppose,
> But musical as is Apollo's lute,"—

have been instilled into their minds. Our country,—by no distorted figure of speech,—may be said to be looking to her sons, with an anxious, agonizing look for a requital of her favors. She has a right to insist that they shall not bend to the parricidal doctrines of the day. Many, many, many have yielded to the blandishments of the importunate sibyl. Forgetful of all the admonitions of history, they have caught the epidemic of the age ; have been content to float with the tide, and pass away, after their little bickerings are over, to swell but the drift-wood of the grave. This is an unhallowed perversion of all the purposes for which they were educated. This is doing violence the best interests of their great Alma Mater. If our young men ; the thousands who are annually poured out from our universities and colleges ; were to pursue a different course, how much good might be accomplished for the country ! What centres of refinement and instruction might they be ! One true, generous, unflinching, uncompromising, right-onward, scholar can make himself be felt in a whole community. Alone and unaided, he can do much to refine the taste, elevate the views, and beautify the structure of the society in which he lives. How much more might the co-operation of many such do ! By the establishment of lyceums and societies, they could easily disseminate better views among the people. The unreading would listen from curiosity, and be unwittingly improved. To such institutions, we may look, as an easy means for the diffusion of the Imaginative Arts. Valuable collections of painting and sculpture, libraries of wholesome books, might be made at little individual expense. Let our educated men attend to these things, and we may have, at no distant day, the dawn of an elegant literature,—of a refined social state. The Southwest will no longer be mapped in the moral geography, as the land of barbarism and Bowie-knives !

But, as a part of the Omar-like philosophy of the day, a sentiment prevails in our community that the culture of the Imaginative Faculties is incompatible with the purposes of practical life ; that the man who cultivates literature or the fine arts, even to the slightest extent, is unqualified for any thing else. This sentiment,—the dread of it,—has kept many a man of genius, from pursuing the bent of his inclination. How gross is the fallacy ! It is true that there are many instances of men of purely imaginative minds, such as Chatterton, Savage, and Rousseau, who have, in the gratification of the *amabilis insania*, neglected to provide for the necessaries of life. It has been said of poets that poverty is "the badge of all their tribe." This results, not from any incapacity, upon their part, to meet the sterner labors of life, but from an exclusive devotion to the Muse. Disregarding the advice of Walter Scott, they make literature their sole dependance ; their crutch and not their staff. On the contrary, in all the principal professions, there are numberless instances of men of genius, who have not only discharged, with exactitude, all the requisitions of business, but have found ample opportunity for literary exercises. These are the examples which we would place before the minds of our young countrymen, and incite them to imitation.

Let us look to the dry and laborious department of the Law : the "jealous mistress" as she is called by Coke ; into whose limits many of you will perhaps one day enter. Do we find that those, who have risen to the highest eminence of this profession, were mere technical proficients ? The incumbents of the Woolsack, have, with scarcely an exception, been men of letters. "The greatest, wisest of mankind" was no less the Chancellor of nature and art, than of English equity. Though his mind was stored with all the "learned lumber of the law,"—from estates in remainder, to actions of assumpsit,—he still found time to develope the richest and most accurate philosophy, that the world has seen; and his profoundest investigations are covered all over with the hues of poetry. Run along the biographical annals of the English lawyers, from Sir Thomas More to Sergeant Talfourd, and you will find that all the most eminent cultivated the imagination, as well as the reasoning powers and the memory. Blackstone acquired that polished elegance, that chastity of expression, which invest the beautiful system into which he brought the chaotic confusion of the Common Law, from a long experiment of the flexibilities of our language in poetic diction. His immortal Commentaries are rich with the colorings of fancy. There is not a happier specimen of ideality in English poetry, than his extended comparison of the Common Law to an antique Gothic castle. Numerous other examples of literary excellence in lawyers; of those who have loved to tread in the prim-rose paths of poesy; might be drawn from the chronicles of legal life. They are not needed. Indeed, there is scarcely an instance of a lawyer, whose name has survived him; who, in short, rose above the dead-level of green-bag mediocrity; who did not court the Muses. Erskine, the Demosthenes of the modern bar; Grattan, the eloquent defender of Irish liberty,—who "stood by her cradle and followed her hearse;" Curran, who said that when he could'nt talk law, he talked metaphor ; and Jeffrey, who raised English composition far above the range of Addison, and illuminated the pages of the Edinburgh Review for a quarter of a century ; are a few eloquent instances. There is one lawyer of the present day who should not be overlooked. Though the *viginti annorum lucubrationes* have, with him, been more than doubled, still in the midst of all,—a crowded practice while young, heavy official duties in age,—he has found opportunity to do more than any living man, for literature and science. The coming age will receive much of its intellectual form and direction from the extra-judicial exertions of Henry Brougham.

These instances, without reference to the similar lives of great American lawyers ;—to Wirt, Story, Webster, Butler, Gilpin, and the like ; ought to silence all cavillers, and convince our young men that, so far from being injured in professional attainments, they would be greatly benefitted, by an assidous cultivation of Letters. Let me not, however, be misunderstood by those who are going to this profession. The black letter should not be neglected for the illuminated text. Literature should be the embellishment, and not the substance of a lawyer's life. There will, however, to any habitually industrious man, be time and opportunity enough for both. To none of my friends may the witty sneer of the English judge, upon the maiden effort of a young attorney, be ever applicable ; "Poor young man, he has read the wrong Phillips !"

If the cultivation of the Ideal of life is thus proved to be not incompatible with the "Perfection of Reason;"

on still stronger grounds may it be shown to be not inconsistent with the other learned professions. Accordingly we find that the most distinguished lights of Medical Science, and of the Sacred Desk, have possessed refined imaginations and cultivated taste. Astley Cooper, Abernethey, Darwin, Abercrombie, Haller, Zimmerman, Ramsey, Mitchell, and a host of others, entitled themselves as well to the laurels of their tutelary deity, as to his secret healing spells. The Pulpit has ever been the friend of Letters. Its triumphs, in philosophy, in poetry, in eloquence, are so numerous that, when named in this connection, they come over the thought like thronging stars. Would that more of our Apostles would imitate the noble examples of Jeremy Taylor and Warburton, of the Wesleys and Clarke, of Irving and Hall, of Croly and Milman, of Channing and England, of Bascombe and Maffitt. Their divine mission could not be better promoted than by the cultivation of those branches of learning, which, like religion, refine and adorn society, improve the heart, elevate the intellect, and, in short, benefit and beautify all the relations of life. The dawn of the Millenial Sabbath can never come until the material purposes and barbarous philosophy of the present age are exchanged for a more exalted and spiritual faith.

In the view we have taken of the manifestations of the Imagination, we have said nothing directly of one of the principal; the art of the Orator. Those only have been considered which are popularly included under the appellation of the Fine Arts. Eloquence, however, is as much an art as painting or architecture.

It is one of the forms in which the Ideal of the soul elucidates itself. In every age and country it has checked and guided the passions. From the thrilling cry of Demosthenes, "let us march against the man of Macedon," to the enthusiastic shout of Peter the Hermit, ringing all through the dark headlands of Europe, "Rescue the Holy Sepulchre;" from the senatorial grace and energy of Mirabeau and Chatham, to the wood-notes wild of the Orator of Virginia; from the calmness and dignity of Paul before Agrippa, to the fervor of the Blind Preacher,—"Socrates died like a philosopher, but Jesus Christ like a God!"—it has asserted its triumphs. Well might Chancellor Kent, in such a relation, say "peace has its victories as well as war!" For of all the victories which humanity has accomplished, there are none to compare, in moral sublimity, with those of the mighty orator, standing single-handed and alone, with no ally but his own internal energies; standing calmly and boldly, with his brow unruffled and his form erect, in a tempest of opposition, upon some mighty moral Waterloo; checking the advance of Wrong, and directing the marshalled masses about him, with the same ease and exactness of sway with which the sun whirls worlds around him, as if every ray of his glory were an arm of Titan power.

We cannot stay to paint those victories. The field is illimitable. Eloquence has ever been the greatest of moral agents. From the pulpit, and the bar, and the forum, and the hustings, it has fallen like a wizard spell upon mankind. Alas! how low is its state in our country! To what a degradation has it been reduced, when the Congregated Wisdom of the nation, —occupying the places once held by the Fathers and Prophets of constitutional freedom,—can stoop for days to the vile vandalism of an Ogle, or the disgraceful diatribes of Doctor Duncan!

It would be ungenerous in a survey of the condition of the Fine Arts in our country, to neglect the mention of some of our own artists who have shed honor upon the South. In the Cimmerian gloom which covers us, the name of Washington Allston shines like a star. The boy of Carolina, by the staunch liftings of an eagle spirit,—unaided and unencouraged,—has risen to the highest pinnacles of his profession. The stern voice of criticism, and the gentle lips of consenting beauty, even in the old world, have hailed him as the Apelles of the age. When American genius is spoken of, abroad, the name of Allston is linked with Irving, and Bancroft, and Bryant. Of less reputation, but of no mean attainments in their profession, are Cogdell, Fraser, Crawford, Mills, and White, natives of the South: while, from our kindred West, kindred in character and origin, Power, and Brackett, and William West have stepped to exalted niches in the temple of art. These have proven that, if our people would but encourage genius, we have material, native with us, from which a lofty intellectual Vatican might be erected.

But we must hasten to a conclusion. You have been detained too long, Gentlemen, by this weak effort to depict the evils of the mechanical exclusiveness of the day ; its blasting effects, particularly in our section, upon morals, literature, and all the refined purposes of social life ; and by the attempt to show that those evils can only be eradicated, as they have been from all nations distinguished for a lofty intellectual and moral existence, by a generous culture of the Plastic Arts. Yet the subject is one of vast importance. There is a Philosophy of the Imagination,—though never chaptered in Political Economy,—as profound and as productive of extended practical benefit, as ever Ricardo, or Adam Smith, established for the grosser objects of sense. It is precisely such a philosophy we want most. We need no renewed incentives to traffic or accumulation. They are as strong with us as the all-compelling principle of gravitation. We want motives to loftier and less material creeds. I could not, therefore, upon this occasion,—when called to speak before those who are hereafter to stand, perhaps at the helm of State, certainly at the helm of mind, in our land,—decline an effort to do something, however little, for principles so essential to our weal as a people ; so interlinked with all our better hopes and duties ; so pernicious if overlooked ; so fraught with happiness and excellence if rightly cultured. Their neglect is not merely a temporary evil. Every age bears, in some manner, within itself, the age that is to follow. If we would have our posterity intellectual and refined, we must begin the improvement. Oh, if we would but rightly act, what a glorious reversion might be theirs ! I am apt, in spite of all discouragements, to be enthusiastic upon the destinies of my country. When I look upon all her giant physical resources; her matchless political institutions; and, more than all, when I cling, with a prophet's fondness, to the belief that her people will yet waken up to the nobler purposes of social being; I feel a pride in our plain democratic patrimony, which I would not exchange for all the tawdy furniture and gilded trappings of aristocratic institutions. At such an hour, the young American patriot can, like the old Welsh bard upon the rock of Snowden, take his stand, as we now do, upon the summit of one of our overlooking mountains, and see, far off, through the lifting haze of futurity, the domes and turrets of a mighty people, flashing in the eyes of the gladdened sun; the mingled harmonies of intellectual and religious excellence going up from every vale and hill-top; social and domestic beauty covering the land like a smiling atmosphere; each successive billow of time rolling up an accumulation of improvement; and the whole mighty heart palpitating with virtuous emotions of pride and joy at the rapid strides which these young republics have made, and are still making, to perfection. Heaven grant that such visions may prove something better than the wild dreams of Plato, or the Utopian fancies of More!

NATIONAL WELCOME

TO THE SOLDIERS RETURNING FROM MEXICO:

AN ORATION

Delivered by Appointment, at Mobile, Alabama,

JULY 4, 1848.

ORATION.

WHEN a Roman army had achieved some important victory, and returned to the city, accompanied by spoils and captives, the gratified inhabitants, with exulting shouts, welcomed them at the gates, conducted them through the long and glittering streets, beneath flower-wreathed and sculptured arches, and, from the lofty porticos of the capitol, proclaimed that the occasion should be commemorated as a national holiday. In a kindred spirit, we have met, upon this our country's anniversary, to welcome the return of a portion of a gallant army, who, battling in their country's cause in a foreign land, have won laurels as glorious and brilliant as ever decked the brow of Roman conqueror or consul. The time is fortunately adapted to the occasion; and we can but regard it as a happy coincidence, that we should now be able to greet the return of the gallant soldier, the war-worn patriot, the choicest spirits of the fame-covered army of Mexico, amid the light and exultation of another Sabbath of our political independence. Their deeds have served to elucidate afresh the primal splendors of this morning of liberty; and it is fit that we, while meeting around the old altars upon which were kindled the fires of seventy-six, should mingle, with the gratitude and reverence we pay the sainted fathers of our land, our admiration and our love for their worthy descendants who have lit the fires of freedom and fame anew. The lessons of the day would indeed seem to demand such an acknowledgment; and even now, throughout all portions of this broad continental republic of ours, amidst the hymns of thanksgiving and shouts of joy with which the day has been hailed, is heard one universal sentiment of praise and panegyric for the heroic hearts who have placed the standard of the stars above those lofty palaces where once floated the golden gonfalon of Cortez, and was heard the wild music of the teocallis of Montezuma.

To the soldier himself, it must be particularly gratifying to be welcomed home amidst the national music and patriotic ceremonials which attest that the lofty sentiments of liberty, the noble lessons of ancestral wisdom, and the generous admiration for courage, patriotism and heroic self-devotion, are not yet extinct in the country of his birth and love. His own heart has recently received a new baptism and inspiration; and it exults, like a young eagle, once more to soar in the breezes of freedom, and bathe its plumage in the rich sunlight of independence now spreading like the broad smile of heaven, over the green land of Washington, from the rocky pinnacles of New England to the sunset-reddened waters of the Gulph of California!

With these emotions, we all, citizen, and soldier, hail another return of our national jubilee! It has come under circumstances of peculiar and unprecedented interest. Never before did our country, in her internal condition, as well as in her relations with the rest of the world, present herself in so imposing, so influential a position. Three score years and ten and two have passed since the establishment of her nationality, by the Declaration of Independence; and in that period she has sprung up from a state of colonial vassalage to imperial magnitude and grandeur. The infant Hercules, which could scarcely strangle the serpents around his cradle, now stands almost like the Angel of the Apocalypse, with one foot upon the mounains of the East, and the other upon the waters of the Pacific, and proclaims to the world the downfall of despotism,—the termination of tyranny.

This growth and extension of our country have no parallel in the history of the world. Man, under the influence of free institutions, seems to have been gifted with new power of increase and expansion. The thirteen meagre colonies that, in 1776, hemmed the Atlantic, with a population of scarcely three million of inhabitants, destitute of any of the higher advantages or opportunities of social, intellectual, moral, or political culture, have now become thirty flourishing States, with vast territorial dominions, more than treble their original size, bordering on all the seas of North America, and embracing a population of twenty millions of souls, existing in the highest social and political condition, blessed by all the benefactions of science, art, literature and religion.

Well may such a people rejoice on the birth-day of the nationality, which has given them all this. But it is not in this alone, nor in this chiefly, that the philosophic mind finds cause for rejoicing, upon this anniversary. The Fourth of July gave birth to something better than a nation. It gave birth to an idea, to liberty—to principles, never before recognized, without which all nationhood would be tyranny, and which are as essential to human happiness as the atmosphere to the lungs, or religion to the soul of the sinner. These principles became incarnate in our form of government—we became the Messiah of the new political creed, and we sent our doctrines into the world to preach the gospel to every creature.

The world was slow to learn the lessons of truth. Nations were like Saul of Tarsus, with scales upon their eyes, going on to the Damascus of despotism. Suddenly and of late, a light has shone out as from heaven upon the nations of Europe. The slumbering continent was heaved like a sea in a tempest. Thrones and crowns, and sceptres—the regalia of royalty, the baubles and gewgaws of aristocracy, were, like the host of Pharaoh, swallowed up in the Red Sea of Revolution. France sprung to republicanism in full beauty and symmetry ; and, from the orange groves of Sicily to the poplar avenues on the Danube, spread the great principles of our Declaration of Independence, "that governments are instituted among men only for the protection of life, liberty, and the pursuit of happiness, deriving their just powers alone from the consent of the governed."

But, while well-nigh all Europe,—France, Italy, Austria, Prussia, Holland and Belgium, at least, have been illuminated by the radiance which beamed from the burning throne of the Bourbon,—by the Promethean fire that young La Fayette snatched from the altars of American Liberty,—it is melancholy to behold the oppression, the degradation, the darkness that have covered, with a foul eclipse, the beautiful but blasted land of Emmet, Grattan, Curran and O'Connell. The cradle in which has been rocked so many of the champions of freedom in every struggling nation ; so much of the genius, eloquence and courage, which have illustrated and adorned the annals of our own country ; which gave to us a Montgomery, an Addis Emmett, and a Shields,—lies bound around by the Anaconda folds of our own ancestral tyrant ; and the world has recently beheld, in the full light of the civilization of the nineteenth century, before the eyes of all men, a gallant patriot, a man of soul and genius, for fearlessly daring to express Republican sentiments, for nobly asserting God's truth and God's freedom, snatched by the myrmidons of power from his household altars, from the bosom of his fair wife, and the arms of his young rosy children,—condemned as a felon, and hurried off in chains to the hulks of Bermuda ! Ah, sirs, this is the very sublimity of melancholy ! The incarceration of John Mitchel is a cloud that blots half the sun of the age. Great God ! shall these things continue? Shall Ireland always be the slave-yard of England and Famine?

> Oh, blood of martyrs! staining all her green,
> Soon may you wash her spotted garments clean;
> The Harp of Tara! soon may it pour forth
> The olden anthems thro' the island-north;
> And Emmett's epitaph ring o'er the sea,
> *Erin Mavoureen! thou art free, thou art free?*

But let us not sadden farther the enthusiasm of to-day, by thoughts like these. There is cause enough for exultation here in this Palestine of the West. Our country has passed through two full generations of manhood, and has signalized, both in peace and war, the stability of her institutions, and their capacity of extension at least to an entire continent. The croaking prophets of despotism told us, at the outset, that our government might work well upon a small scale; that like a summer flower it would bloom in the peaceful sunshine, but that it could not stand the storms of war; that like a circle in the waters it would dissolve by expansion; that we would be weak, distracted, and ineffective for any gigantic struggle with foreign nations. Thanks to the better wisdom of our ancestors; thanks to the sagacious pilots who have stood at the helm of the Ship of State; thanks to the stout arms and bold hearts of our patriotic yeomanry; thanks, especial thanks, to the gallant army of Mexico, the lie has been given to all such ill-omened forebodings. It has been proven that the machinery of this government, though, like the allegoric vision of Ezekiel, it has its wheels within its wheels, with nice and delicate arrangement, has yet energy and power that can resist and overcome all attacks from internal or external foes! I will not linger upon a consideration of its workings in the midst of peace; but pass at once to a review of the spectacles which have been presented in the recent war with Mexico. This will be more appropriate to the present time and occasion.

Three years ago, our country had been in a state of unexampled peace and prosperity for thirty years. She had gone on expanding in population and wealth, with magical rapidity; spreading the waves of civilization all over the valleys and mountains of the west; and making the wilderness and desert places to bloom and blossom like the rose. She was at peace with all nations. Upon her Southwestern border lay a young Republic, peopled by emigrants from her own bosom, that had won its independence and established its nationality in the eyes of the world, and had been recognised by all the leading nations of Europe as a free and separate sovereignty. For seven years it had asserted its sovereignty from the Sabine to the Rio Grande, its defined limits in its constitution, without even an effort upon the part of its original rulers to exert authority or jurisdiction over it. It was as independent then, according to the laws of nations, as the United States are to-day. This young Republic sought admission into our confederacy. By a public, peaceful act, we admitted her, with her constitutional boundaries; but at the same time avowed our readiness to make all rightful reparation for any injury done, and to treat with the neighboring nation for a proper line of boundary. This peaceful, prudent measure, Mexico, the claimant country, notwithstanding her claim had expired by every statute of limitation, besides having been lost by an original action of ejectment, chose to construe into an insult to her Castillian dignity. At once she sounded the clarion of war, and issued her national proclamation that she would not cease from hostilities till she had driven every American, east of the Sabine. Suddenly, after months of secret preparation, she poured a large army over the Rio Grande, and struck the first blow upon the soil of the United States. Congress, at once, with a unanimity that presented but two opposing voices in the Senate, and but fourteen in the House, declared "war to exist by the act of the Republic of Mexico," and preparations were at once made to conduct it to "a speedy and successful termination."

Thus, by no fault of ours, we were involved in this Mexican war; and we entered into it like Godfrey of Bouillon, with the Holy Lance, into the field of Ascalon, crying "God for the Right and the Just!" The events that followed constitute the brightest annals in our history. Upon the fields of Palo Alto and Resaca de la Palma, at Monterey and Buena Vista, the heroic Taylor and his chivalrous little army performed feats of valor and prowess which hurled back, in ignominious defeat and confusion, the multitudinous hordes of Mexico, and covered the American name with a blaze of glory. The blessings of our people every where, of every faith, are resting like a beautiful diadem upon his brow.

I cannot stop to depict the many thrilling incidents connected with these engagements. One only will I mention, as it is especially honoring to a gallant officer, now within the sound of my voice, and whom Alabama is proud to claim as an adopted son. In the terrific battle of Buena Vista, when, wave after wave, the Mexican forces, confident in their overwhelming numbers, had dashed and broken upon our apparently devoted little army, which appeared about to crumble and sink before the repeated onsets; when Santa Anna rallied his Aztec legions, his reserve corps, and brought them down to sweep all before him ;—then, when the standard of the eagle and the stars was waving to and fro, like the torn sail of a sinking ship in a storm, then, at that critical moment, when O'Brien's battery had been captured—then, says General Taylor, in his official report, "Captain Bragg, who had just arrived from the left, was ordered at once into battery. Without any infantry to support him, and at the imminent risk of losing his guns, this officer came rapidly into action, the Mexican line being but a few yards from the muzzles of his pieces. The first discharge of canister caused the enemy to hesitate; the second and third drove him back in disorder, and *saved the day!*" Proud words, proudly won!

But it is with the incidents of the war on the Southern Line, as it is called—with that brilliant series of victories, beginning at Vera Cruz, and terminating at the city of Mexico, that we have chiefly to deal to-day. We all remember when the call for volunteers was sent through our land, like the fiery cross of Clan Alpir through the hills of Scotland. We all remember, when it was announced that the gallant hero of Queenstown, Chippewa, and Niagara was to lead the expedition, with what alacrity and enthusiasm the ardent young men of our country, following the heroic example which had been set them by our gallant veteran, Desha, responded to the call of the government. They were anxious to emulate the deeds of their ancestors; and the rusted sword of the Revolution, and the tattered banner of 1812, were again given to the sunshine and the breeze. Every section of the Union sent forth its contributions of energy and valor. It is not my purpose now to designate all of these, but it is proper that I should refer specially to one regiment, whose remnant —ah, sad word!—whose remnant is before me. The citizens of Mobile had the proud pleasure to testify their admiration and regard for the Palmetto Regiment, as it passed through this city on its way to the war. It was then composed of more than a thousand men, headed by the gallant Butler, whose name was even then a synonyme for all that was valorous and noble. Long shall we remember the feast of patriotism and the flow of feeling, the gushing emotions, and the eloquent words which marked our intercourse, on the day they embarked for the scene of operations. Proud anticipations and fond hopes were cherished that they would prove themselves worthy descendants of sires who had fought and bled at Eutaw, Camden, and The Cowpens. With similar emotions, we saw the gallant sons of Georgia, and the chivalrous spirits of our own State, pass through this city, for the beleaguered confines of Mexico; and their enthusiastic patriotism, fortitude and perseverance proved that they wanted but fair fields and favorable opportunities to have accomplished as valiant performances as those that fell to the good fortune of any portion of the army.

Time would fail even to enumerate the interesting events which now followed, adding to the imperishable fame of our country. We can but glance at a few which stand out prominently above the rest.

As the yellow rays of sunset streamed along the white line of coast, and the smooth and glassy waters of the gulf, near Cape Antonio Lizardo, and west of the Island of Sacrificios, on the ninth of March, 1847, was presented the most singular and brilliant spectacle ever witnessed on this continent. A fleet of frigates, steamers, and transports, each bearing the star-spangled banner, lay stationed along the bay; and soon a long line of surf boats, bearing four thousand men, under the immediate command of General Worth, to the sound of spirited martial music, and with a shout that made the welkin ring, as a gun gave signal, bore for the shore. As the keels touched the shallow beach, the men sprang waist-deep in the water, and simultaneously ascended the sandy slope, and formed in battle array. Soon another line followed, and another, and *the American army was in Mexico*, and the city of Vera Cruz invested. With its powerful castle of San Juan d'Ulloa, it had been deemed impregnable, the Gibraltar of America; but after thirteen days' investment, it was compelled to yield to the profound scientific skill and regulated valor of the "Republic of the North."

Now began that series of brilliant victories of which I have spoken. When we compare the disparity of forces; when we reflect that one army fought upon the march, ever wearied and jaded, exposed to the inclemencies of a hostile climate, in the midst of an enemy's country; and the other from its mountain fastnesses, and well-wrought fortifications, with every advantage of a knowledge and possession of the country—we shall find nothing in all history to surpass the achievements of the American arms.

Up through the long and difficult passes of the Cordilleras; by the gigantic gorges and tremendous chasms; over the pedigrals of volcanoes; across tumbling mountain torrents, where every bridge was a fortification; beneath the eye of Popocatapetl and Orizaba,—the little army of Scott, seldom exceeding ten thousand men, pushed its way onward to the heart of the country. In vain did Santa Anna struggle to make of Cerro Gordo, a Mexican Thermopylæ. The American army bore down all resistence, and struck the mind of Mexico with a consternation from which it never recovered. Here the gallant Shields was shot through the breast by a grape-shot, Providence, however, preserving him to reap greener laurels upon subsequent fields of fame.

On the 17th of August, the army reached the turning ridge of the mountains, and here, from the spot called Buena Vista by Humboldt, was caught the first view of the valley of Mexico, containing its brilliant and populous city. A lovelier vision has never risen on the eye of man since the old prophet stood upon the summit of Pisgah, and gazed upon the flowery Palestine below. It spread out like a rich garden, teeming with every variety of tropical fruit, plant and flower. The orange tree waved its glistening foliage, but half concealing its golden apples, and the pomegranate and the cactus displayed their gorgeous blossoms, giving far other invitation than to the hostile visitations of war.

> "Oh, Christ! it was a goodly sight to see
> What heaven hatd done for that delicious land."

But man had prostituted its beauties by his evil passions and malignant deeds ; and the stern voice of duty called our gallant army on, in their effort to reduce to subjection a foe which pertinaciously refused all offers of peace. This was one great characteristic in the management of this war, which will redound to the eternal honor of our government, that we always bore the olive-branch in advance of the sword—and, before we would crush our foe, invited him to peace. But, with a fatuity almost like insanity, he continued to reject our proffers.

In the middle of the summer solstice, our army reached the fields of Contreras and Churubusco. There the enemy had rallied all his forces for a desperate and final struggle, and had entrenched himself with the most powerful fortifications. But after battles on two successive days, he was completely vanquished—the fourth army which the Mexican Republic had raised in eighteen months being destroyed, and the capitol of the "magnanimous nation" left completely at the mercy of the conqueror. These battles, called by Gen. Scott the Battles of Mexico, were the greatest ever fought on this side of the Atlantic—if we except the almost fabulous narratives given of the forces of Bolivar, Hidalgo and Morelos. The Mexicans numbered fully thirty thousand men, while Scott had not one-third of that number. Here the Palmetto Regiment won its most brilliant laurels—laurels alas! bathed in the heart's blood of its gallant commander. In the thickest of the terrible fight of Churubusco, when others had faltered, when the day seemed well nigh lost, the heroic Shields determined to make one more desperate struggle for victory. He rode up before the Palmetto Regiment, and demanded, loud above the din of battle —"Who will follow me?" "Every South Carolinian here, General," exclaimed the noble Butler, "will follow you to the death!" And through the iron hail, like the Old Guard at Lodi, the Palmettoes dashed to the charge—and the victory. But a terrible toll did they pay at those gates of death. In front of his regiment bravely cheering them on, their "father and their colonel" fell! Oh do not deem his death unfortunate. He fell as brave men love to die. Sooner or later death must come to us all;—the fresh green turf is a far sweeter couch than the feverish bed,—and there is no nobler boon than to "look proudly to Heaven from the death bed of fame." Sleep proudly, noble Butler! The children of future days will speak thy name with pride, and strive to imitate thy deeds;—and when

Carolina's sons shall be called, in their country's service, to other fields of fame, they will pray to pass like thee, in Enoch's fiery chariot to heaven.

An armistice delayed the forward movement of our troops ; and it was, with Punic faith, improved by the enemy to organise further resistance, and to collect his energies and resources in the vain hope of saving his capital from its threatened doom. The treachery being detected, hostilities were at once resumed, and the sanguinary struggles at Molino del Rey and Chapultepec ensued. These terrific contests seemed to revive all the horrors of the *triste noche* of Cortez ; and the causeways which had been baptized by Castillian blood, were bathed anew by the ensanguined torrents that flowed, as fast and freely, from the bosoms of American valor. The terrible disproportion of forces, the formidable fortifications which had to be overcome, invested the achievements of our troops with a splendor as brilliant as the richest haloes of chivalry. They are all recorded by the pencil of the historian in illuminated letters, and I need but allude to them, to fill the mind with thronging scenes of embattled contest, heroic achievements, indomitable fortitude—the waving banners, the thundering artillery, the gleaming lines, the charging squadrons—the shrieks, the roar, the carnage and the smoke of war in all its most imposing forms. Here, in cöoperation with the whole army, the Palmetto Regiment renewed its right to be called by excellency, the chivalry of the Union, and the gallant Gladden signalised his title to wear the blood-stained mantle which had fallen from the shoulders of Butler. Numberless instances of personal valor might be enumerated; but I shall content myself with mentioning one, which will illustrate the spirit, the undying resolution, that fired the bosoms of all the gallant soldiers of our country upon that memorable occasion.

In one of the storming parties, at the hill of Chapultepec, the banner of his regiment was entrusted to a regular soldier, who pledged his word that he never would surrender it. Up through the iron hurricane that decimated their ranks as they went, the chosen stormers moved, that banner borne proudly in front. Suddenly it was seen to sink; an officer leaped to the the side of the standard bearer; a grape shot had torn away half his head, and he had fallen; but still his hands were clenched to the flag staff, and it was only by a desperate struggle, and not till death had quenched all his strength, that the standard could be liberated, and borne onward to the entrenchments. That soldier passed, with the star spangled banner waving above his soul, to the battlements of heaven!

Ah! well might Mexican desperation make its deadliest stand at the hill of Chapultepec—for full in sight lay the magnificent capital, the prize of the victory—and after a few more sanguinary encounters, at the *garitas* of Belen and San Cosme, the American army passed into the plaza of Mexico—the great bell of the Cathedral tolled the death of a nation—and the commander-in-chief of the forces of the North pitched his head quarters in the vaunted palace of the Montezumas!

The war, it may be said, was now terminated—

though many subsequent and guerilla contests continued the ineffectual struggle. *A peace was conquered* —and after some months of negotiation, a treaty of amity and friendly relations was established. The American forces have been gradually retiring from the country ; and it is to greet the return of some who have participated in the noble achievnments which I have so poorly portrayed, that we have assembled here to day. In the midst of the patriotic enthusiasm engendered by another recurrence of our national aniversary, and with a full appreciation of all their heroic performances, with hearts bounding with joy and pride, we welcome them back to the shores of the Union. The glad waters of the Gulf of Mexico have borne them in triumph, and with seeming exultation in all its waves, to our arms, and our hearts, and with the thunder of artillery, the plaudits of millions, the American people cry to them welcome, welcome to the land, whose annals they have re-illuminated with a light and beauty equalled only by our Revolutionary glory.

Soldiers of Mexico, we give you here, the first greetings of the American people. Everywhere in your progress through the land, you will be met by the cheers and admiration of one sex, and the smiles and the love of the other. While we will drop with you the tears of profoundest and tenderest sorrow for the loss of those who now sleep in soldiers' graves, upon the mountain slopes and battle plains of Mexico, while we shall long keep bright their memories in the sanctuaries of the heart, we will yet extend to the survivors, our warmest gratitude, our most imperishable admiration. You have given lessons and examples which will tell upon the destinies of our country; which have elevated her in the estimation of all nations; which, while extending our dominions over territories of imperial breadth, have proven our national capacities for the trials of war as well as the amenities of peace; and which have gone far in accomplishing our great destiny of including the whole North American continent in one mighty brotherhood of free and flourishing States, that shall ever stand, a Pharos of Freedom, to illuminate and guide the world. Then, Soldiers of Mexico, in the light of this national jubilee, welcome back, thrice welcome to the blue skies, and fertile fields, the happy homes and free and peaceful institutions, of the Republic of North America!

SKETCHES AND ESSAYS.

THE PILGRIMAGE OF DE SOTO.

[This sketch was originally published in 1839, and was the first attempt made to locate definitely the route of De Soto, through the Southwest. As all subsequent writers have followed its statements, it is here retained in its original form, as the authentic basis of a most interesting and romantic chapter of our history.]

THE history of the Southwestern States commences at a period antecedent to that of any other portion of the American Union. Long before the Pilgrims had landed at Plymouth, or the bold and chivalrous Smith had led his followers into the savage wilds of Virginia, —Spanish enterprise and prowess had over-run and subjugated the greater portion of that territory, now included within the States of Georgia, Alabama, Mississippi, Louisiana, and Florida. Indeed, it was that part of North America which was first discovered and settled by European adventurers. As early as the year 1512, Juan Ponce de Leon, a hardy and adventurous cavalier, who had been a distinguished companion of Columbus, discovered the peninsula of Florida, and gave it that name from the brilliant profusion of flowers, which decorated its coast, and from the day, on which it was discovered; being the Pascua·Florida, or Feast of Flowers. The name was subsequently applied, by the Spaniards, to all the Southern portion of North America; which they claimed, by the right of discovery, for the crown of Spain. Numerous expeditions were made, within the next ten years, for the further discovery and conquest of the country, which, it was fondly dreamed, abounded in wealth and magnificence, that would cast the golden splendors of Mexico and Peru, into the shade. These expeditions all resulted unfortunately for those engaged in them. The most extensive and disastrous was that of Pamphilo de Narvaez, who, with three hundred men, undertook the conquest of Florida, in 1528. He landed near the bay, then, as now, called Apalachee, and made an expedition of eight hundred miles into the interior. His route is not known. At the end of six months he returned to the coast, with all his high hopes of wealth and conquest shattered and gone; his ranks wofully thinned by disease and death; and the remnant of his forces in a condition of most miserable penury, and without vessels to convey them from the country. Several rude barques were constructed, in which they put to sea, but they were all shipwrecked in a storm near the mouth of the Mississippi; and but four individuals escaped, who, after long wanderings and captivity, for near seven years, ultimately reached Mexico, by land, to tell the sad story. The accounts which they gave of the immense extent and magnificence of the countries, through which they had passed, though partaking of the character of the boldest fiction, were readily believed by their countrymen, whose minds already regarded Florida, as more than a Land of Promise, and as abounding, not only in unparalleled opulence, but in fountains of such miraculous virtue, as to perpetuate youth, and to restore old age to its primal vigor and bloom.

Inspired by these incitements, and thirsting for fame and conquest, HERNANDO DE SOTO, a Spanish cavalier, in the year 1538, fitted out an expedition for the conquest of Florida. He was a gentleman of high birth and connections, and had enriched and distinguished himself, by a campaign in Peru, under Pizarro. At his request, Charles V. constituted him Governor of Cuba, and invested him with absolute power over the immense territory of Florida, which he undertook to subjugate at his own expense. Fitting out a most splendid armament, in which was invested all his own wealth, and that of his companions, many of whom had amassed immense fortunes by previous enterprises in America, he set sail from the port of San Lucar of Barrimeda, on the 6th of April—" as gaily as if it had been but the holiday excursion of a bridal party." He stopped in the island of Cuba, long enough to make arrangements for its government, during his absence; and then proceeded for Florida, which he reached in the month of May, 1539, and anchored in a bay, which he called Espiritu Santo; now known as Tampa Bay. The number of his forces, on landing, was six hundred and twenty men; two hundred and twenty-three of whom were mounted on excellent horses. These,—

many of whom were cavaliers of great wealth and distinction,—all partook of the enthusiasm of their leader; and were perhaps as gallant and proud a band of soldiers, as have ever been collected together. They were provided with all the means and muniments of war; with helmets, bucklers, corslets, shields and swords; and presented as gay and glittering a spectacle as the eye could wish to look upon. In addition to arms of all kinds then in use, everything was provided, that the experience of former campaigns had proved to be servicable; chains and manacles for captives; ample stores of provisions; a large drove of hogs for stocking the country; tools of every description; bloodhounds to ferret out the inhabitants; and—in strange parallel—even the sacred emblems and implements of Christianity, for the purpose of diffusing the mild rays of the Star of Bethelem, amid the wilds of Paganism.

On the 1st of June, De Soto commenced his march into the interior. And here begins an expedition unparalleled in the annals of history. In the language of an eloquent writer on the subject—"it was poetry put into action; it was the knight errantry of the old world carried into the depths of the American wilderness. Indeed, the personal adventures,—the feats of individual prowess,—the picturesque descriptions of steel-clad cavaliers, with lance and helm and prancing steed, glittering through the wildernesses of Florida, Georgia, Alabama, and the prairies of the Far West, would seem to us mere fictions of romance, did they not come to us recorded in matter of fact narratives of cotemporaries, and corroborated by daily and minute memoranda of eye witnesses."*

It is with this bold and chivalrous expedition that the HISTORY OF ALABAMA may be said to commence. Apart from the interesting incidents of the expedition, —the chief of which occurred within her borders,—the details of the campaign, as given by cotemporary historians, tend to throw light upon circumstances and customs, which would otherwise remain mysteries; and serve to elucidate, to some extent, the situation and character of her aboriginal inhabitants. We shall therefore record, at some length, the movements and adventures of De Soto and his companions—particularly of that portion, which occurred within the present limits of the State of Alabama. Those which happened within the bounds of the other States, through which he passed, are more properly the province of their respective historians, and fall only incidentally within the object of these sketches.

Before proceeding to narrate the particulars of this expedition, let us say a word concerning the sources from which we draw our information. Of the adventures of De Soto, there are two authentic narratives.† The first is that of a Portuguese gentleman, who was one of the companions of De Soto, but whose name is

* Theodore Irving's "Conquest of Florida."

† Since this sketch was written a third narrative of this expedition, by Louis Hernandez de Biedman, a companion of De Soto, has been [illegible] and published. It was presented to the King of Spain, in 1544, and contains an original report of De Soto from Tampa Bay, dated July 9, 1539. It is very reliable.

not known. His work was first published at Evora, in 1557. It has been frequently republished and translated into different languages. The first English edition was published in 1609, by Hakluyt. To the work much faith was given at the time of its publication, and it contains internal proofs of its correctness. The other account of this expedition was published in 1603, and is denominated "The Florida of the Inca, or the History of the Adelantado, Hernando de Soto, Governor and Captain-General of the Kingdom of Florida, and of other heroic cavaliers, Spaniards and Indians: written by the Inca Garcilaso de la Vega." This work was originally published in Spanish, and has been repeatedly translated. It is not the production of an eye-witness, but of a Spanish writer of undoubted veracity, who received his account from three cavaliers of worth and respectability, who were in the expedition. These two works, though they vary in many of their details, yet sufficiently corroborate each other, as to increase their general credibility. They have been relied on by all subsequent historians, as fountains of truth, and Theodore Irving has collated a most interesting work from their respective narratives. From these sources, aided by the researches of other valuable authors,* we shall draw the statements we shall give. We intend also to trace the course of De Soto through Alabama, from the knowledge we possess, ourselves, of the country.

De Soto, as has been stated, commenced his march

* Belknap's Amer. Biog., v. 1, p. 185—189. McCullough's Researches, p. 522—531. Nuttall's Arkansas, 247—267. Bancroft's U. S., v. 1, 41—59. Williams' Florida, 152—170. Albert Gallatin's Synopsis of the Indian Tribes, 83—120.

from Tampa Bay, on the 1st of June, 1539. He proceeded in a Northeast direction. His disposition was, as much as possible, to conciliate the natives. But he soon found them true to the spirit they exhibit to this day. They impeded and harassed his march, by open and latent hostilities. Fortunately, he found, in one of the provinces near Tampa, a Spaniard, by name Juan Ortiz, who had been left upon the coast by Narvaez, eleven years previously, and who had been retained as a captive by one of the Caciques, or Chiefs. He had learned the language of the natives, and was of great service to De Soto, as an interpreter, throughout his after wanderings.

For several months, occasionally resting, the Spaniards pursued the course they had first taken. Their route must have been very nearly parallel with the present road from Tampa to Fort King, and not far from it. They found the country intersected by innumerable and extensive morasses and hammocks. Through these they fought their way, with great difficulties and losses. They passed several large and swollen streams. These were the Hillsboro', the Withlacoochee, and the Suwannee. De Soto, finding it impossible to conciliate the inhabitants, commenced a war of devastation. He destroyed their fields, and bnrned many of their towns, which were very large; some of them containing several hundred houses. The natives never asked for quarter, but fought to the last gasp. After proceeding as far North as the present Southern boundary of Georgia, De Soto was induced to direct his course to the West, to a province called

Apalachee, by the natives. Here he expected to find large quantities of provisions and *gold.* In the latter expectation he was disappointed; but he found the country abounding in food of every description, for his men and horses. It was the most populous and wealthy province he had yet entered. It was situated upon what is now known as Apalachee Bay, or the Bay of St. Marks. Here De Soto determined to pass the winter, as that season had already set in. He accordingly fortified himself, and remained until the Spring of the ensuing year. During that time numerous exploring parties were sent out; one of which discovered Ochuse, the harbor of Pensacola. A brigatine was also constructed, and sent to Cuba, with instructions to return with supplies, the ensuing year, to the harbor of Ochuse.

On the 3d of March, 1540, De Soto broke up his winter cantonment at Apalachee, and proceeded, in a Northeast direction, towards a province, at a great distance, called Cofachiqui, in which he was informed by several captives, that there was a large abundance of gold, silver, pearls and precious gems. These were the great objects of the Spaniards; and they accordingly pursued their march with much enthusiasm, continually battling with the natives, and burning their towns. They passed up the banks of the Flint River;*

* We give the modern names of these places; as they can only be learned from the descriptions of the narrators. The names as used by the Spaniards and natives, furnish but little clue to the route; that of *Achise*, or *Ochis*, a village, is to this day the Muscogee name of the Ocmulgee River

crossed it in Baker County, in Georgia; passed near the present sites of Macon and Milledgeville, crossing the Ocmulgee and Oconee rivers; and, after numerous hardships and perils, finally arrived at the province of Cofachiqui, which was situated in the fork of two large rivers. These were most probably the Broad and Savannah Rivers.*

Great was the disappointment, however, of the Spaniards, upon their arrival at Cofachiqui, in not finding the vaunted treasures, for which they had pursued their lengthy and perilous march. The "yellow metal," of which they had heard so much, proved to be only a worthless copper ore; and although they found immense quantities of very valuable pearls, yet these little repaid their disappointment. After a long sojourn in this province, for the purpose of recruiting the health and strength of his forces, De Soto, on the third of May, set out in search of other territories, which he hoped would better gratify his cupidity and ambition. The direction of his march was now to the Northwest, to a province called COSA, said to be at the distance of twelve days' journey. During the first five days, they passed over the termination of the Apalachian mountains, in Habersham county, in Georgia; and through a barren and miserable province called by the natives CHALAQUE. This is the actual name now used by the Cherokee Indians to designate their country. The na-

* Williams, in his History of Florida, locates Cofachiqui (or Catafachiqui, as he calls it,) upon the head waters of the Chattahoochee River, (p. 160.) The statement in the text is thought to be more correct.

tives were a puny, pacific race, and nearly naked. They subsisted principally on herbs, roots, and a species of wild hen, which abounded in such quantities, that the inhabitants brought De Soto, seven hundred, which they had killed with bows and arrows. After several days' march through a more fertile country, and in a western direction, the army reached a small town called CANASAUGA,* upon the banks of a river, along which the Spaniards had marched for several days. Pursuing their route for five days more through a desert country, on the 25th of June, they came in sight of a village called CHIAHA.† This is the first point the Spaniards reached within the territory that is now the State of Alabama.

The village of Chiaha is said to have been situated upon the upper end of an island, about fifteen miles in length. There is no such island now in the Coosa. It is probable that the Spaniards either mistook the peninsula formed by the junction of two rivers, (the Coosa and Chattooga,) for an island, or that those two rivers were originally united, so as to form an island near their present confluence. We have heard this latter supposition asserted by persons well acquainted with the country. There can be little doubt that Chiaha was situated but a short distance above

---

* This is now the name of a small river, which falls into the Eestanolla, at New Echota. The river referred to is no doubt the Etowah, a branch of the Coosa.

† Called by De Vega, Ichiaha. There is now a stream in Talladega County, called Chiaha, or Potato Creek. It runs into the Chocklocko, a branch of the Coosa.

the junction of the Coosa and Chattooga rivers. Here De Soto remained for several days; making diligent enquiry for the precious metals. He was informed that there were metals of a yellow color, found in a province about thirty miles to the northward. He accordingly despatched two soldiers to examine the country. They returned, in ten days, with the information, that it was a barren, mountainous region,* in which no metals, but a fine kind of copper, could be found. While in Chiaha, the Spaniards were presented by the natives with large quantities of pearls, many of which were as large as filberts. These the natives obtained from a species of oyster,† found in the river, which they opened by the aid of fire. De Soto left Chiaha, on the 2d of July, and at sunset, came in sight of a village called Acoste, situated on the Southwestern extremity of the island. He encamped his army within a bow-shot of the village, and proceeded with eight men to visit the Cacique or Chief. He was a bold warrior, and met De Soto, at the head of fifteen hundred of his braves, drawn up in battle array, painted, plumed and armed. He received De Soto with much courtesy. While they were in conversation, some of the Spaniards commenced pillaging the houses of the Indians; who, greatly exasperated, fell upon them with their clubs. De Soto perceiving the peril of his situation, with his characteristic intrepidity

* This was probably among the Lookout Mountains, in Cherokee County, Alabama.

† Probably the *muscle*, which is said sometimes to contain fine pearls.

and presence of mind, immediately seized a club, and commenced beating his own soldiers. The disturbance was soon quelled—the conduct of De Soto convincing the Indians of his amicable intentions. The Cacique was then persuaded to visit the encampment, which he had no sooner reached, than he was made prisoner. The next day, the Indians exhibiting every indication of peace, the Cacique was liberated ; and De Soto, crossing to the east bank of the Coosa river, on rafts and in canoes, proceeded on his march to the South,—his object being to reach the Bay of Ochuse, or Pensacola, where he expected réinforcements and supplies.

For twenty-four days, the army slowly pursued its course, (occasionally stopping for several days,) through a populous and fertile province, called COSA.* The inhabitants were invariably friendly and hospitable. On the approach of De Soto to the principal town, called also Cosa, he was met by the Cacique, borne in a litter upon the shoulders of four servants, and followed by a train of one thousand warriors, marshaled into companies, and gorgeously arrayed. He was a young man of fine person, and noble countenance. Upon his head he wore a diadem of brilliant feathers, and from his shoulders hung a mantle of martin skins, decorated with large pearls. The village† was situated upon the east bank of a noble river ; and con-

* This embraced the present Counties of Benton, Talladega, Coosa, and Tallapoosa.

† McCullough in his Researches, page 525, says this is the village called in the maps "Old Coosa," in latitude 33° 30 .

tained five hundred spacious houses. It was well stored with provisions; such as maize, pumpkins, beans, plums and grapes. De Soto remained at this place, until the 20th of August, and then departed, taking with him, the Cacique, and a large number of his warriors to bear his baggage. They passed through villages, called Tallimuchasse, Ulliballi, and Toasi, and arrived at a town called TALLISE* on the 18th of September. This was an important Indian post, strongly fortified by pallisades erected upon high embankments of earth. It was situated in the bend of a rapid river, which surrounded it on three sides.

At Tallise, which was the Southern boundary of Cosa, De Soto was met by an ambassador from the Cacique of the neighboring province, called TASCALUZA.† This was the name of the chieftain as well as of his kingdom. He was represented as the most powerful of all the Caciques of the country. His fame reached De Soto, long before he approached his territories; which included immense regions west and south of Cosa. The ambassador was the son of the Cacique, and came attended by a large train of war-

---

* There is no doubt that this town was situated in the elbow of the Tallapoosa river, near the present town of Tallasse, in Tallapoosa County. The same name has always been applied to the spot by the Indians; and a tribe of the Creeks was also known by the same appellation.

† This name is a pure Choctaw compound-word, from *Tasca* or *Tusca*, warrior, and *Lusa* or *Loosa*, black. It, with several other words, proves that the Indians mentioned in the text, were of the same tribe as the present Choctaws.

riors. He was of noble and imposing appearance; taller than any Spaniard or Indian in the army; "as symmetrical and graceful as Apollo;" and of proud and princely demeanor. His mission was one of peace; and he invited De Soto, in the name of his father, to visit his residence. De Soto accordingly crossed the Tallapoosa river in canoes, and on rafts, and marching Southwest, on the third day, arrived at a small village to which Tuscaluza had advanced to meet him. The Chieftain was posted on the crest of a hill, commanding a fine view of the adjacent country. He was seated upon a rude throne, and surrounded by a hundred of his principal warriors, decorated with gay plumes and mantles. By his side stood a standard-bearer, sustaining a banner or target of dressed deer-skin, "quartered with black and white, having a rundle in the midst, and set on a small staff." This was the only military standard the Spaniards saw in their wanderings.

Tuscaluza, like his son, was of noble appearance, and of gigantic proportions, being a foot and a half taller than any of his warriors. He was said to possess Herculean strength. His countenance indicated great ferocity and pride of spirit. Upon none of the Spaniards did he bestow the least notice, save De Soto. He retained that imperturbable sternness and gravity so characteristic of "the Stoic of the woods;" until the Governor approached, and then advancing a few paces, received him with much dignity and grace.

In company with the Cacique, De Soto proceeded on his march, towards one of the principal villages of the province, called Tuscaluza. He reached it after three days' journey, of twelve miles each. It was situated on a peninsula, formed by a rapid and powerful river, said, by the Indians, to be the same that passed by Tallise.* The day after their arrival the Spaniards, with the Cacique, crossed the river upon rafts, and proceeded on their march, towards a large town called MAUVILLE.† The country, through which they passed, was very populous and fertile, and on the evening of the third day's march, they arrived within a league of the town, and encamped for the night. Tuscaluza immediately despatched one of his attendants to the town, for the purpose, he said, of causing appropriate arrangements to be made for the reception of the army. Early next morning, De Soto sent two confidential soldiers ahead, to observe the movements of the Indians, and to await his arrival. He then mustered an hundred horse and as many foot, as a vanguard, and proceeded with the Cacique, who was retained as a kind of hostage, to the village. The remainder of the army was instructed to follow as speedily as possible, under the command of Luis de Moscozo, the camp-master general.

De Soto arrived at Mauville, early on the morning

* This was the Alabama: and it is believed that Tuscaluza was situated near Evans' Landing in Wilcox County. McCullough says, "there is a ford on the Alabama, about sixty leagues above its confluence with the Tombckbee, which the Choctaws call *Tascaloussas*. Here the Army may have crossed."—*Researches, page* 525.

† This town is supposed to have stood on the north bank of the Alabama river, in Clarke County. The first Spanish settlers of Alabama found the name, *Mauville*, applied by the natives to the present

of the 18th of October. It was the capital of the kingdom of Tuscaluza; and was situated on the north bank of a magnificent river. It was completely encircled by a high wall formed of huge trunks of trees, placed in the ground, side by side, and fastened together by large vines. There were but two entrances to the town, one at the east and the other at the west. The wall was surmounted by numerous towers, and pierced at close intervals with port-holes, from which arrows might be discharged at any enemy. There were but eighty houses in the village, but they were of immense size, capable of containing one thousand persons each. They were built in the modern Indian style of council-houses, and were erected around a square in the centre of the village. De Soto had no sooner arrived in the village, than he was informed by his spies, that the Indians had collected in immense numbers, and with very hostile appearances. The spies computed the number of warriors in the village, at more than ten thousand; all well armed. The women and children were all removed. These facts convinced De Soto, that the Indians entertained hostile and treacherous intentions. He secretly ordered his men to hold themselves in readiness, and despatched a messenger to Moscozo, to hurry on with the residue of the army. Tuscaluza

---

river and bay of Mobilė. It was, in consequence, given by the Spaniards and French, to the natives themselves; whom they called *Mauville* or *Mobile* Indians. The two words are pronounced the same in the Spanish language; the letters *v* and *b* being often used indifferently for each other. See *Du Pratz*, who, most generally, observes the former orthography. The word is spelt *Mavila* by Biedma, and *Mauilla* by the Portugese.

had, in the mean time, entered one of the houses. He was sent for, and refused to return. An altercation took place between the messenger and an Indian chieftain, and the warrior was slain. The Indians now became frantic. The warhoop rang through the village. From every dwelling immense hordes of savages poured forth, and rushed upon the Spaniards, with the fury of demons. De Soto rallied his forces, and, through desperate carnage, cut his way out of the city. He was pursued by the Indians, who seized and slew some of his horses, that had been tethered outside of the walls. Fortunately at this moment the main body of the forces under Moscozo came up, and the savages were repulsed, and driven into the city. They had seized, however, the baggage and effects of the army, and carried them with them in their retreat. The Spaniards made a desperate effort to storm the walls, but were assailed with such showers of arrows and stones, from the towers and loop-holes, as to be compelled to retreat. The Indians again sallied from the ramparts, and fought like maddened tigers. Nothing but the superior armor of the Spaniards saved them from total annihilation. At length, by the aid of their battle-axes, they hewed open the gates and forced their way into the village. The battle now became more desperate and bloody. Hand to hand the steel-clad footmen fought with the naked natives. The war-club and the bow were feeble weapons in comparison with the heavy claymore and tried battle-axe. At the same time the sturdy cavaliers made frightful lanes through the ranks of the savages. Upon their trained horses they charged upon the confused hordes, trampling and hewing them down, and pursuing them from street to street. The Indians at length took refuge in their houses. But their hoped-for safety proved their entire destruction. In a moment their dwellings were wrapped in fire. Many of them continued to fight from the summits of their houses, till they fell in, and perished in the flames. The others rushed forth with dreadful yells, only to meet a no less certain doom from the infuriated Spaniards. Not one of them asked, or would accept of quarter. De Soto fought at the head of his troops, and was everywhere in the thickest of the fight. The Chieftain, Tuscaluza, perished in the flames of his dwelling—dying like a warrior; and leaving a name which deserves to be held in perpetual reverence, as that of a hero, and patriot.

The battle lasted for nine hours. As the sun set, his yellow rays fell upon the smoking ruins of the village; its houses all consumed; its walls levelled with the ground. The streets and the adjacent plains were covered with the corpses of the dead. More than five thousand Indians were slain; including those who perished in the flames. The Spanish loss was eighty-two killed. Nearly every soldier in the army was wounded,—many of them very severely. They also lost forty-two horses, and all their baggage, and effects. Thus terminated the most desperate and bloody Indian battle, that ever occurred on the soil of the United States.*

---

*The two narratives of this expedition vary in their estimates of the number of killed and wounded. De Vega says the Spaniards had

The condition of the Spaniards, after the battle of Mauville, was most deplorable. So great were their sufferings, that they became heartily sick of their enterprise, and desirous of proceeding at once to the Bay of Ochuse, or Pensacola, which they were informed, was distant about one hundred miles. The resolute cupidity and stubborn pride of De Soto would however yield to no persuasion, until he had accomplished the objects for which he had set out in the campaign. He, therefore, with the remnant of his army,—now reduced to little more than three-fourths its original number,—on the 18th of November, turned his steps to the north. He marched for five days (of eighteen miles each) through a fertile but uninhabited country, when he arrived at a village called Cabusto, in the province of Pafallaya. It was situated on a wide and deep river, with high banks.* The inhabitants at first exhibited hostile designs, but ultimately fled across the river in their canoes, taking their property and families with them. Here their main force of warriors, "to the number of eight thousand," was posted to dispute the passage. They were encamped for two leagues along the opposite bank. The Spaniards spent twelve days in constructing boats, and then passed across the river.

---

eighty-two killed; the Indians eleven thousand. The Portugese account gives eighteen Spaniards killed, and one hundred and fifty wounded: the loss of Indians, twenty-five hundred. We have adopted a medium number, as, probably, the most correct.

*This was the Black Warrior River; and it is probable that Cabusto was near the present site of Erie, in Greene County.

The Indians, after some severe skirmishing, fled before the army, which proceeded on its march.

After five days' march, through a level and fertile country, interspersed with small hamlets, in which quantities of maize and dried pulse were found, the Spaniards arrived at another river,* where the Indians were collected to dispute the passage. Their courage however soon evaporated, and the army crossed without opposition. The Spaniards were now in a province called CHICAZA, and, in a few days, arrived at the principal town, of the same name. On each side of the town flowed a small stream, bordered by groves of walnut and oak-trees. It being now the middle of December, De Soto determined to spend the winter at this place, and accordingly took possession of the village. The Indians were enraged, but remained quiet—"nursing their wrath to keep it warm." At length, one dark and windy night, when the encampment was shrouded in sleep, they deceived the sentinels and set fire to the village. And now ensued a conflict and conflagration, second only to that of Mauville. Many of the Spaniards were burned to death; others were slain. They succeeded however in repulsing the savages, after a desperate battle of several hours. The loss of their dwellings caused them to remove in a few days to a more favorable position, which they called Chicacilla. On the first of April the army proceeded to the north. They soon came to

* The Tombecbee.

a powerful fortress called ALIBAMO,* situated upon the bank of a small but rapid river, which after much hard fighting and carnage, they stormed and took. Marching northwest for several days, they came to the largest and most magnificent river they had ever seen. They consequently called it the Rio Grande. Its Indian name was Chicagua. It was the Mississippi River, and the Spaniards were the first Europeans, who beheld the Mighty Monarch of Rivers. They crossed it near the lowest Chickasaw Bluff, not far from the thirty-fifth parallel of latitude.

Beyond this point, it does not fall within our province, to trace the nomadic march of De Soto. Suffice it to say, that he continued his wanderings, for near twelve months, through the vast regions south west of the Missouri; meeting with many strange and almost incredible adventures; suffering greatly from his conflicts with the natives, and disappointed in all his endeavors to discover the precious metals. He proceeded as far west as the foot of the Rocky Mountains. At length, worn out by fatigue, and almost broken hearted, he returned to the Mississippi. Here, while making preparations to depart from the country, he was seized by a malignant fever, and on the 21st of May, 1542, died; universally lamented by his followers. He was buried in the channel of the Mississippi river; receiving, like Attila, a grave commen-

---

* This is no doubt the original of the word Alabama,—which is said to signify, in the Muscogee tongue—"*Here we rest.*" The river on which the fort was situated, is thought to be the Yazoo.

surate with his career. The surviving Spaniards made an attempt under Luis de Moscoso, whom De Soto had appointed his successor, to reach Mexico. They were foiled in all their efforts, by their ignorance of the country, and after six months' arduous wandering, were forced to return to the Mississippi. Upon it they embarked in seven rude brigantines—descended to its mouth,—proceeded along the coast,—and, after numerous perils, and sufferings, reached the Spanish settlement of Panuco, on the 10th of September, 1543,—just four years and two months after their landing at Tampa Bay. Their number was reduced to three hundred and eleven men, in an almost naked and famished condition ; their horses were all lost ; and, as for wealth and fame, they retained not even its shadow.

With this wild and romantic Expedition, we have said that the History of Alabama begins. It is however an isolated chapter in her annals. The dark curtain that covered her territory was suddenly lifted,—a brilliant but bloody panorama passed across the stage,—and then all was shrouded in primeval darkness. A sufficient glimpse was however caught, to show the condition and character of the natives, and to furnish some clue, when taken in connection with other information, by which to solve many enigmatical circumstances connected with their origin, customs, and history.

THE MASSACRE AT FORT MIMS;

WITH A HISTORICAL SKETCH OF THE FIRST WHITE SETTLEMENTS IN ALABAMA, THE BATTLE OF BURNT CORN, AND THE OTHER EVENTS THAT LED TO THE CREEK WAR OF 1813–'14.

The Muse of History has seldom been called to shed her tears over a more shocking and sanguinary event than the massacre at Fort Mims, on the Tensaw branch of the Alabama river, in the summer of 1813. For the number of its victims and the hideousness of its details, it was the most frightful tragedy ever enacted on the soil of our country, and forms the most luridly illuminated page in backwoods annals. At the time of its occurrence, it spread a thrill of horror through the Union ; and the excited fancies of the timid and exposed, along the frontiers, scarcely exaggerated the cruelties which had actually been perpetrated.

It is strange that there is no compendious and faithful narrative of this catastrophe.* The only accounts

* Pickett's "History of Alabama" has removed this reproach, since this sketch was written—in 1844.

of it are meagre and superficial, and often erroneous and contradictory. The remarkable character of the incidents, and their influential bearing upon the destiny of the Indians, and the early history of Alabama, demand that this should not continue to be the case. I shall therefore attempt to draw aside the curtain that conceals this occurrence, and let it pass, in bloody panorama, before the eye of the reader.

It is necessary in advance, to glance at the condition of the settlements in the interior of our territory; and to take a brief historical retrospect of their origin and progress.

The French, as early as 1699, had settled a colony near Mobile, and, in a few years, extended military and trading establishments along the waters of the Alabama and Tombeckbee. One of these, called Fort Toulouse, was near the junction of the Coosa and Tallapoosa, upon the recent site of Fort Jackson; another, the remains of which were not long since visible, was at the mouth of the Cahawba; and a third, called Fort Confederaicon, overlooked the Tombeckbee, at what is now Jones' Bluff, in Sumter County. Fort St. Phillipe also stood at Twenty-One Mile Bluff, on the Alabama. The purpose of these posts was mainly mercantile; though priests were present to inculcate Christianity, and soldiers to enforce submission. The sword diffused its spirit more effectually than the cross. The native tribes were kept in constant warfare with each other, or with their white neighbours, and yielded but few and trivial commodities for commercial intercourse. The French settlements were consequently never prosperous. Their entire population scarcely ever exceeded two thousand persons ; and, in 1763, they abandoned the country, which passed successively into the hands of Great Britain and Spain. These two nations made, by treaties with the natives, some slight acquisitions of soil in the interior, and, in 1788, the population of the city of Mobile, then belonging to Spain, had increased to 1468. Four years after, there was a strong Spanish post on the Tensaw, under the command of Deyveral, which instigated the Indians to hostilities against the United States. The other settlements were few and weak ; and, in a few years, the Spanish authority faded entirely from the interior.

Near the close of the last century, a considerable number of emigrants had found their way from the States of the Union, to the vicinity of Natchez, and to the rich lands upon the Tombeckbee and the Tensaw, which had been ceded as we have said, by the Indians to the British and Spanish governments, and of which our own was now the proprietary. This induced Congress to establish, by enactment of April 7th, 1798, the "Mississippi Territory." It included all the country between the Chatahoochee on the east, the Mississippi on the west, the 31st line of latitude on the south, and a parallel line drawn from the mouth of the Yazoo to the Chatahoochee, on the north. Winthrop Sargent, a native of New England, was appointed Governor, by President Adams. On the 4th of June, 1800, he, by proclamation, established "Washington County," including the settlements on the Tensaw and the Tombeckbee. In the next year, the population of these settlements was estimated at 500 whites and 250 blacks, of all ages and sexes,—" thinly scattered along the western banks of the Mobile and Tombigby, for more than seventy miles, and extending nearly twenty-five miles upon the eastern borders of the Mobile and Alabama."*

This population continued to increase in number and extent, notwithstanding the opposition of the Choctaws, who claimed the land west of the Tombeckbee and its tributaries, and of the Creeks, who asserted dominion east of those waters. A treaty was however effected in 1802, by which the Choctaws yielded all their land south of a line from Hatchatigby Bluff on the Tombeckbee, west to the Choctawhatchee. The increase of population caused the establishment, of two new counties: Baldwin, north of Washington; and Clarke, embracing the fork of the Alabama and Tombeckbee. Several villages sprang, at least nominally, into existence. The territorial legislature incorporated St. Stephens, Rodney, Wakefield, and Dumfries. The three last perished "in the bud;" St. Stephens was then the seat of the U. S. factory or trading-house under the charge of George S. Gaines, and became subsequently the Capitol of our own State. In 1804, the jurisdiction of the Federal courts was extended over the "Washington District," and Henry Toulmin, of St. Stephens, was appointed Judge.

The population of these settlements was principally

---

* American State Papers, vol. v., p. 659.

confined to the western side of the Tombeckbee; though there were some seven or eight hundred inhabitants resident upon the Tensaw and the Alabama, and in the angle made by the latter stream with its western tributary. The boundary with the Creek or Muscogee Indians was not definitely settled. The pioneers claimed so much of the land east of the Tombeckbee as had once belonged to the Choctaws. This embraced very nearly all of the present County of Clarke, and the southern borders of the Alabama, as high up as Claiborne. But the contiguous Muscogee tribe, the Alabamas, resisted this claim, and complained of the encroachments of the whites. At the treaty at Fort Wilkinson in 1802, the *Mad Wolf* said "the people of Tombigby have put over their cattle in the fork, on the Alabama hunting grounds, and have gone a great way on our lands. I want them put back. We all know they are Americans." Other chiefs reiterated complaints, and threatened to remove the intruders by force.* If there were grounds for such complaints thus early, it may well be believed that they greatly increased in the course of ten years. The only thing that reconciled the Indians to the inroads of the settlers, was the facility afforded for traffic. The spirit of trade was strong with these simple people; and, in 1809, their supplies of furs, peltries, and other produce, to the factory at St. Stephens, exceeded in value seven thousand dollars.

Mobile and the territory between the Perdido and

*Am. State Papers, v. 675.

the Mississippi, south of latitude 31°, though purchased by the United States, in 1803, as a part of Louisiana, was fraudulently held by Spain, as a portion of West Florida, until 1813. The ingenuity of Talleyrand had, by equivocal phraseology, given a color to this claim; but at length our government, wearied of juggling pretences, determined, like Brennus, to throw her sword into the scale. This was authorized by a secret Act of Congress, and, on the thirteenth of August, 1813, General Wilkinson forcibly took possession of Mobile, and placed a garrison in Fort Charlotte, formerly Fort Condé. A convenient avenue for commerce was thus opened to the interior settlements, it having been previously much restricted by the Spanish authorities at Mobile. Before this, these settlements were completely insulated. They were cut off from the white inhabitants at Natchez and in its vicinity, by a strip of Choctaw territory. To the east, the Muscogees dwelt as far as the Oakmulgee, and the nearest settlements to the north were in the bend of the Tennessee.

The character of the settlers upon the Tombeckbee, Tensaw, and Alabama, can be inferred from the circumstances which surrounded them. It is not the timid, the weak, or the luxury-loving, who make their homes in the deep wilderness and among savage tribes. The restless spirit in search of adventure; the industrious laborer anxious to repair, upon new soil and under more propitious circumstances, the fortune which had become dilapidated in his old home; the hardy hunter, whose chief delight was to pursue the bear, the beaver, or the deer; the pedlar in the wares suited to the simple taste of the children of the woods; the refugee, for whatever motive of crime, injustice, or misanthrophy, from the restrictions and associations of better regulated communities; these, and such as these, are always the constituents of our frontier settlements, and composed, in the main, the population we are now attempting to describe. They were emigrants principally from the States of South Carolina, Georgia, Virginia, and Tennessee. A small admixture of French and Spaniards from Mobile, chiefly creoles of the country, produced singular contrasts among this motley population. The names of a few of the most prominent families who had emigrated to these remote regions, from the American States, are preserved by their descendants, still in the same vicinage, or by tradition. We may enumerate the following: Upon the Tensaw,—the Halls, the Byrnes', the Linders, the Steadhams, the Hollingers, the Easlies, and the Gilcreasts: Upon the Tombeckbee,—the Bates', the McGrews, the Powells, the Calliers, the Danbys, the Lawrences, the Moungers, the Kimbills, the Barnetts, the Talleys, the Bakers, the Hockets, the Freelands, and the Wheats.* These families, and others of similar origin, were scattered over the country, at distant intervals, generally engaged in agricultural pursuits, and in hunting the valuable game that everywhere abounded.

It is not to be understood, from the general sketch-

---

* See Pickett's *History of Alabama.*

ing we have given, that the moral condition of these backwoods settlements, during the period we have in view, was either chaotic or debased. There were many men of integrity and intelligence, and many families of social worth, among the inhabitants. The laws of the territory were strictly oberved ; and even an academy "for promoting morality and virtue" among the young, was located by charter, as "Washington Academy," at the town of Rodney, then the Court House of Washington County.* But the chief characteristics of these people were the sterner virtues. They were brave, industrious, patient, generous and persevering ; and well qualified, both in moral and physical capacities, to endure the hardships and dangers of their insulated position. These capacities were soon called into requisition and tested to their utmost. We now propose to examine the causes which led to hostilities upon the part of the Muscogee, or Creek Indians, in 1813, and produced the dreadful calamity that befell the refugees at Fort Mims.

In the Spring of 1812, Tecumseh, in furtherance of his plan of uniting all the aboriginal tribes in a confederacy against the Americans, visited the Muscogee Indians. By artful operation upon their superstitions, he succeeded in enlisting the greater part of the nation, particularly the towns on the Alabama waters, in favor of his schemes. At Tuckabatchee, on the Tallapoosa, he addressed the National Council. Suspecting treachery upon the part of the principal Chief,

* Turner's Digest of Miss. Stats., 1816, p. 55.

the Big Warrior, Tecumseh, it is said, told the Council that, when he returned home, he would stamp his foot upon the ground, and shake down all the houses in Tuckabatchee. In a few weeks the great earthquakes of that year occurred, and demolished the village. The Indians immediately cried out "Tecumseh has arrived at home!" This, and similar circumstances inflamed the minds of the Indians; prophets and witches sprang up in every town; and it was impossible to restrain hostilities. Murders were committed in the nation, and upon the frontiers. A delegation, under the command of the Little Warrior, returning from a visit to Tecumseh, butchered several families in Tennessee, and took prisoner a Mrs. Crawley, "a modest, well-disposed woman," whom they carried to "a very old village," at the falls of the Black Warrior. Here it was determined to put her to death, and her grave was dug; but the squaw, in whose custody she was, informed her of the design, and the night before her intended execution, she escaped. "The chief man of the village was disposed to be peaceable, and bought her after her escape, and sent out several of his young men to hunt for her, by whom she was found, after two or three days, half-starved and half-naked."* In the meantime George S. Gaines, of St. Stephens, had heard of her captivity, and benevolently despatched Tandy Walker to her relief, by whom she was ransomed, and taken to that place, whence she returned to her friends in Tennessee.

---

* Am. State Papers, v. 814.

The Big Warrior, and other friendly chiefs attempted to punish the perpetrators of these hostilities; and several were put to death. This produced the most violent enmities among the Indians themselves. Meanwhile, the inhabitants upon the Tombeckbee and the Tensaw were in a state of terrible suspense and alarm. Abandoning their fields and residences, they fortified themselves in hastily constructed stockades; and watched the movements of the enemy. To increase their apprehensions, it became certain that British emissaries, aided by the Spanish authorities at Pensacola, were urging the Indians to hostility, and supplying them with arms and ammunition. Word was brought that a large party of warriors, under the command of Peter McQueen, an influential half-breed chief, who resided at Tuckabatchee, on the Tallapoosa, had, on their way to Pensacola for supplies, burnt the house of Joseph Cornells, the Government Interpreter, who had married a white woman, and murdered several of his family. It was determined to intercept this party, upon their return. A force, amounting to about three hundred persons, including white militia, mixed-breeds, and friendly Indians, was soon collected and organized under the command of Colonel James Caller, who was mainly instrumental in getting up these expeditions. William McGrew was chosen Lieutenant Colonel, and Zackariah Philips and Jourdan, Majors. John Wood was appointed aid-de-camp. Among the Captains, were Samuel Dale, Benjamin S. Smoot, David Cartwright, and Bailey Heard. The friendly Creeks were headed by Dixon Bailey and

David Tait, educated and gallant half-bloods. Of the Lieutenants, Patrick May, Girard W. Creagh, and William Bradberry are worthy of mention. The troops were all mounted gun-men, generally with their favorite rifles. They crossed the Alabama River at Sizemore's ferry, some distance below Claiborne, and, marching rapidly to the southeast, intercepted McQueen's command, numbering about three hundred and fifty warriors, at a ford upon Burnt Corn Creek, now in Conecuh County, "where the old furrow-path turned off to Pensacola." The returning party had, in their possession, a large number of arms. and "one hundred horse-loads of ammunition," which they had received from their British and Spanish friends. They were halted in a hill-engirdled bend of the creek, near a large spring, engaged in cooking dinner, with their pack-ponies grazing around. Caller's troops approached so cautiously, that the main body dismounted behind the hill, poured in a destructive fire, and charged, before the Indians had fairly risen from the ground. They were driven in the wildest fright and confusion across the stream, into a large swamp or reed-brake, and their horses, with their valuable loads, were at once seized by their assailants, who were greedy for pillage. This led to a disastrous reverse. The red-men rallied in the swamp, opened a heavy fire, and charged back with their tomahawks and war clubs, amid the fiercest cries for vengeance. Caller, seeing the confused and exposed condition of his men, ordered a retreat to their horses, but this produced a panic, and a general route ensued. In vain did Caller, Dale, Bailey and Smoot make desperate efforts, by rallying small parties, to turn the battle. A series of charges and retreats, irregular skirmishes and frequent close and violent encounters of individuals, and scattered squads, took place. Dale, Creagh and Bradberry were severely wounded, and, after a helter-skelter contest of three hours, the coming on of night left the tawny warriors of McQueen victors of the field, though they paid most dearly for their success, many of them being slain, and most of their ammunition and supplies destroyed or carried off, with their horses, by their fugitive foes, who had but two killed and fifteen wounded. The defeated troops fled "fast and far," all that night, in scattered bands, through the hills of Conecuh, in constant dread of pursuit. Colonel Caller and his Aid, Major Wood, escaping on foot, became lost in the wilderness, for two weeks, and nearly perished from hunger.*

This engagement, which was denominated the Battle of Burnt Corn, took place in July, 1813. It excited the Indians to instant and general hostility. The symbolic war-clubs, painted red, were at once dispatched to all parts of the nation, and old chieftains and young warriors responded to their call with as great alacrity as ever the Highland clans rallied around the cross of Clan Albin. Every friendly or hesitating warrior was compelled to join with the hostiles, or to flee from the nation. Weatherford, as will be seen, was thus forced to take up the tomahawk, and, having once embarked

* Am. State Papers, v. 849, '51.—Lewis Sewall's Poems, (Mobile, 1833.)

in the contest, his masterly and imperious spirit could hold no subordinate position. It was determined to seek signal and summary revenge for the lives of those slaughtered at Burnt Corn, and to commence at once the general warfare of extermination against the whites. For this purpose a secret expedition against the Tombeckbee settlements was planned by *Hillis-hadjo*, or Josiah Francis, and *Sinquista*, prophets; and Peter McQueen, *Hobohoithlee Micco*, Jumper, afterwards celebrated in Florida, and Weatherford, war-chiefs. The thirteen towns,—Alabama, Columa, Wewauka, Ochebofa, Waukakoya, Hoithlewaula, Foosahatchee, Ecunhutke, Savanogga, Muclausa, Hookcha-oochee, Puckuntallahassee, and Pochusa-hatchee, furnished warriors for the expedition. The towns of Oakfuskee, Tallassee, and Autossee, "formed a front of observation," towards Coweta, on the Georgia border, to conceal the movement, and keep in check the friendly Indians.

The warriors enlisted were over a thousand in number. With this force, the hostile chiefs movedstealthily to the attack on Fort Mims. This fort was selected because it was believed to contain the body of those who had been engaged in the Battle of Burnt Corn. Before we proceed to narrate the particulars of this attack, we will revert to the condition of the Settlers, and the preparations they had made to meet the hostilities of the Indians.

Immediately upon the return of the expedition from Burnt Corn, the inhabitants took every measure in their power to increase and strenghten their fortifications. Above the confluence of the rivers, in Clarke County, several picket-posts, known as Forts White, Easley, Sinquefield, and Glass, were garrisoned by the settlers from their vicinities, and white and half-breed refugées from the nation. These posts were considered, from their eastern position, as the most exposed of any, and were guarded with the utmost vigilance. The inhabitants west of the Tombeckbee felt fewer apprehensions of danger, but still sought protection at St. Stephens and Fort Stoddard. In the Tensaw settlement, the fears of the people were at first greatly excited. Though their residences were scattered for nearly eighty miles along the Alabama and the Tensaw, yet there was not a fortification, in the whole extent, which could be relied on as a secure defence against savage assault. To remedy this deficiency, Samuel Mims, an old and wealthy inhabitant, who had long traded with the Indians, erected, with the assistance of his neighbors, a stockade fortress around his residence, which was four hundred yards from "Lake Tensaw," a bay or tributary of the Alabama, that extends eastward one mile from the river. This was about two miles southeast from the "Cut-Off," and about sixty from Mobile. The site of the fortress was in a level field or "clearing," of six or eight acres, intersected by a small branch or creek, which discharges itself into the Lake. A thick growth of cane and some woods extended along this stream, and between the fort and the lake. The walls of the fortress, which were originally square, and enclosed an acre of ground, were formed in the ordinary picket-fashion of our frontiers, by the trunks of small pine trees, about fifteen feet in length, being planted in a ditch about the enclosure, and fastened together at the top by horizontal strips or braces of smaller timber. They were pierced, about breast-high, with port-holes for rifles and muskets, but with no provision for the use of artillery, as the garrison possessed none. At the southwest corner there was a rude block-house and bastion. The enclosure contained, besides Mims' frame dwelling and log out-houses, ten or twelve rude cabins and shelters, erected by the refugées and soldiers. There were two gates to the fortress, but the one on the west was permanently closed. The eastern one was eight feet wide, and formed of large and cumbrous pieces of timber. Fifty feet inside of this gate, a line of old pickets stood—the fort having been extended to the east.

Such was Fort Mims, the main defence of the settlers southeast of the Alabama ; and to it, upon the approach of danger, they fled with their families. The intestine hostilities also expelled the half-breeds and other friendly warriors from the nation, and they took refuge with their wives and children in this newly erected fortification. The number of occupants was, consequently, very considerable ; but it was still farther swelled by the addition of sixteen men, under Lieutenant Osborne, and three companies of Mississippi Volunteers, commanded respectively by Captains Middleton, Jack, and Batchelor,—comprising one hundred and seventy-five men, all under Major Daniel Beasley. The other men in the fort capable of bearing arms, including the friendly half-breeds and Indians, were seventy in number, commanded by Dixon Bailey, so distinguished at Burnt Corn. The effective military force thus amounted to two hundred and forty-five. Besides these there were three hundred women and children, making an aggregate of near five hundred and fifty souls crowded into this narrow fortification.

At the first burst of alarm, the garrison in Fort Mims were properly vigilant and cautious; but they soon became singularly inattentive to the defences of the place. The officer in command seems to have been a vain, rash, inexperienced, and over-confident soldier,—though unflinchingly brave when in the presence of the foe. In the latter part of August, General Ferdinand L. Claiborne, commanding the forces raised in Western Mississippi, visited the post, cautioned its possessors against a surprise, and advised the construction of two additional block houses. These warnings he repeated by letter even the day before the attack. But a strange fatuity appears to have befallen the garrison. They were satisfied that the Indians did not contemplate an attack upon the fort, but were directing their hostilities to the Georgia frontier. In vain did several of the most experienced and cautious of the backwoodsmen give warning of impending danger: in vain even did a hostile warrior, the very evening before, apprise some of his relatives in the fortress, of the intended attack: in vain did two negroes declare that they had seen twenty warriors painted for battle, in the vicinity of the fort: Major Beasley would listen to no remonstrance, but steadily refused to keep the gate of the fortress shut, and permitted the inmates to wander unrestrained along the banks of the Lake. He seemed to have been actuated by a spirit of vain bravado and criminal self-complacency. How forcibly does his conduct remind us of the Roman adage, "whom the gods intend to destroy, they first make mad!"

Such was the condition of things at Fort Mims, on the morning of the 30th of August. The sun rose, beautiful and with a dewy coolness, over the forests of needle-leaved pines that extended off to the east, and concealed beneath their high and shafted arcades, the grimly-painted and fast-approaching warriors of Weatherford and McQueen. In the fort all was confidence and hilarity. The women and children were scattered in idle groups around the block-houses, and in front of their tents and sheds: "the men were seated in two circles in the yard, talking what they would do if Indians should come;"* and Major Beasley, with a party of his officers, was engaged in a game of cards, and had just ordered a negro to be whipped for giving a "false alarm;" when, a little before noon, the simultaneous sounds of the rifle and war-hoop were heard, and a large body of warriors was discovered within a short distance of the fort, rushing for its entrance. A few of them passed the gate before Beasley could rally his men; but he soon collected a sufficient force to slay the intruders, and a bloody and doubtful contest ensued for the mastery of the passage. Its narrowness limited the number of the assailants, but they rushed

---

* Col. Hawkins.

desperately forward, and with their war-clubs, tomahawks and scalping-knives, grappled, hand to hand, with the defenders. The carnage was terrible on both sides. Major Beasley and his officers here almost redeemed their former criminal neglect. They resolutely bore the brunt of the conflict ; and it is worthy of emphatic remark that every officer fell fighting at the gate. Beasley was shot through the body, and died like a hero, cheering his men. A Lieutenant fell from the loss of blood, and was borne to a block-house by two women, but, reviving from his faintness, he insisted upon being carried back to the gate, which was done by the same heroines, and he died by the side of his companions. After half an hour's struggle, the garrison succeeded in shutting the gate, which, singularly enough, had remained open so long that its closure was greatly impeded by sand and rubbish.

The party thus repelled were two hundred in number, and constituted but an advance body of the Indians. The main force under Weatherford, eight hundred strong, now came up, and the attack was renewed, under the directions of that chief, with an unremitting discharge of bullets and arrows on every side of the fort. The garrison had been hurriedly formed for the defence as follows : on the eastern front, embracing the gate, Captain Middleton's command ; on the south, Captain Jack's ; on the west, Lieutenant Randon's, and on the north, Captain Dixon Bailey's. The soldiers all fought with the utmost desperation. Even the women, seizing muskets and rifles, placed themselves at the port-holes and heroically returned the fire of the assailants. The policy of the latter, however, was to carry the place by storm, and, seizing the rails from some adjacent fences, they rushed forward, stopped many of the port-holes, and commenced cutting down the pickets, with their axes. They soon broke through the outer line of pickets on the east, and then gained the mastery of most of the port-holes of the inner one, and poured their fire into the centre of the fort. The pickets now yielded at several points on the other sides, and the savages in overwhelming numbers rushed in among the defenders. Such of these, as were not slain, took refuge in the houses, and fought from the windows and through holes forced through their roofs. But the Indians had, with flaming arrows, at the outset, set these on fire, and they were soon wrapped in a general conflagration.

The scene that ensued baffles description. Notwithstanding their awful position, the besieged continued to fire their guns, through the flames, upon the savages. At length, as the roofs fell in, many rushed from the buildings, and attempted to escape or implored mercy, but were immolated without distinction of age or sex. A few negroes and some women of the half-blood were alone spared. But seventeen, of the five hundred and fifty occupants of Fort Mims, escaped to narrate the dreadful tragedy!

The loss of the Indians, during the day, was very great. Not less than fifty warriors, including five prophets, were slain in the first assault upon the gate, and more than three hundred fell in the subsequent contest.

Colonel Hawkins, the Indian agent, gives us, in his letters, some of the details of this horrible transaction, which he received from a negro taken prisoner at the time: "He said he was in Mims' house, when it was taken and destroyed. An Indian, seeing him in the corner, said, 'Come out; the Master of Breath has ordered us not to kill any but white people and half-breeds.' An Indian woman, who was in the house, was ordered out, and to go home. Dixon Bailey's sister, a half-breed, was asked what family (white or red) she was of? She answered, pointing to her brother, 'I am the sister to that great man you have murdered there:' upon which they knocked her down, cut her open, strewed her entrails around. They threw several dead bodies into the fire, and some that were wounded. . . . . There was much silver money in the houses, melted and run about, and some dollars blackened only. . . . . Among the killed are McGirth, Jones, McCarty, Sam Smith, Dixon Bailey, his two brothers, Mims and his family, Captain Melton, John Randall and all his family, except Peter Durant, and one of his daughters. . . . McGirth's wife, and Jones' wife, and all their children, except one of McGirth's, killed in the fort, were taken, with the reporter, prisoners to the nation. . . . A daughter of Mr. Cornells told him to make his escape, and tell what the Indians had done. . . . Mrs. McGirth, on her way to the nation was excessively distressed, and cried out aloud upon being threatened by some of the warriors that they would put her to death. She urged them to do it, as, in the situation of her family, she wished to die. She and

Mrs. Jones, with their families, were sent to Wewoka. . . . After the battle, the Indians encamped about a mile from the fort, until next day, twelve o'clock, during which time they were busy hunting negroes, horses and cattle, and brought off a great many."

The names of all who so miraculously escaped from this great massacre, are not now known, but the following list of most of them has been furnished me, on the authority of two of the survivors: Dr. Thomas G. Holmes, since of Baldwin County, Alabama; Lieutenant W. R. Chambliss, of the Mississippi Volunteers; Lieutenant Peter Randon, of the Tensaw militia; Jesse Steadham and his brother Edward, afterwards citizens of Baldwin County; Martin Rigdon, Josiah Fletcher, John Hoven, Joseph Perry, James Bealle, and Jones, Matthews, and Morris, whose given names are not remembered. Several others are named in Hawkins' letter just quoted. Sam Smith a half-breed, whom he names as killed, also escaped. Most of those who escaped, did so by pushing through the fallen pickets at the least exposed points, and rushing through the confused lines of the Indians, to the adjacent reed-brake, and thence to the Alabama River, which they swam, and, after innumerable hardships, reached Fort Stoddart, at Mount Vernon. Many of them were severely wounded.

Numerous anecdotes live in tradition of the heroism exhibited in the defence of this devoted fortress. The fate of the chivalrous Dixon Bailey wears a romantic hue becoming the character of the man. He was the main hope and reliance of his associates during the terrible conflict, and he cheered them by his voice and daring deeds till the very last moment. After the pickets were forced, he fought gallantly from amid the flames of Mims' house, surrounded by women and children, but as the roof fell in, he snatched up his youngest child, a boy of three or four years, leaped out of a back door, dashed unexpectedly through the foes at that quarter, and fled beyond the smoking limits of the fort. Many guns were fired at him, and, being wounded in several places, he was compelled to retreat slowly, but he kept in check three or four warriors who pursued him, by presnting towards them his formidable rifle. The Indians, flushed with victims, and more intent upon booty than solitary slaughter, did not pursue far this forest Rolla, and he succeeded in reaching the neighboring swamp, with his child.

The flight of Dixon Bailey was witnessed by another fugitive from the fort, who communicated the fact to his friends; but as nothing was heard from him, his fate remained long a subject of painful conjecture. After the lapse of several years, however, by the side of a small stream, not far from the fort, were discovered the skeletons of a man and child; and a gun firmly planted in the soft earth bore the name of DIXON BAILEY. He had died, it was supposed, of his wounds, and the child had perished of hunger, by the side of its dead father; or, perhaps, had been slain in his arms.*

* For this interesting tradition I am indebted to the MSS. of Mrs Maria Boykin, formerly the accomplished wife of Col. B. Boykin of Mobile. She had made many interesting collections as to the History of Alabama, but unfortunately died before she had finished them for publication.

We might mention other anecdotes connected with this massacre, but the reader has already "supped full of horrors," and we hasten to conclude our sketch. The bodies of the slain, on this occasion, both Indians and whites, were never buried, and long afterwards, so great had been the carnage, the fields contiguous to the fort were white with human bones, bleaching under the influence of the seasons. The disaster terminated the settlements east of the Tensaw, and they were not resumed until the conclusion of the war. Upon their return homewards, the Indians sent out a detachment of one hundred warriors, under the prophet Francis, which attacked one of the forts in the fork of the Alabama and Tombeckbee, but was repulsed with a loss of five killed. The Indians then returned to the nation, mourning in plaintive songs their warriors who had been slain, but rejoicing more loudly over the many scalps they had brought back, and the unprecedented butchery they had achieved. Well might they, in their darkened barbarism, imagine that the complete destruction, of the White Man, so positively promised by their prophets, had already been begun, and soon would be accomplished. Little did they see, in the future, the dreadful retribution to be brought upon their country, by Claiborne, and Floyd and Jackson. Their boasted massacre itself became a watchword and an impulse to devastating armies, and it was resolutely determined by each of those generals, that no warrior, whose participation in the carnage at Fort Mims could be proven, should be permitted to escape with his life. The commencement, progress, and termination of the war, viewed in this relation, develope a spirit not unlike the sullen destinies of the Greek tragedy, and partake of an interest but little subordinate to the melancholy stateliness or the Œdipus, or the Medea.

SKETCH OF WEATHERFORD,

OR THE

RED EAGLE,

THE GREAT CHIEF OF THE CREEKS IN THE WAR AGAINST GENERAL JACKSON; WITH INCIDENTAL ACCOUNTS OF MANY OF THE LEADING CHIEFS AND WARRIORS OF THE MUSCOGEE INDIANS.

"Shall not one line lament the lion race,
For us struck out from sweet creation's face?"

CHARLES SPRAGUE.

THE heroic and exalted character once generally attributed to the aborigines of our country, has come to be regarded as an overwrought fable. The singular manners and picturesque costumes which these strange people first presented to European eyes, their novel modes of life, the vast forests through which they roamed in quest of game or war, their courage, hardihood and unrestrained freedom, produced upon excited fancies an over-estimate of the happiness and virtues of their condition. Voyagers and travelers, who had seen but little of their actual character and habits, vied with each other in depicting them as a primitive people, existing in Arcadian comfort, possessing few of the vices of civilization, and retaining the traits and qualities of an almost unfallen nature. This error was extended by the virtues and romantic adventures of a few of the children of the woods, a Pocahontas or a Philip of Pokanoket, who were erroneously taken as specimens of their entire race. Poetry and fiction lent their embellishments to conceal the truth, and the pleasant fancies of Chateaubriand, Rousseau, and Campbell, were received by the world as faithful portraitures of the virtues, circumstances, and sentiments of the American Indian,—"the stoic of the woods, the man without a tear."

Observation and experience at length dissipated these errors. The American Indian was found to be what enlightened reason would expect from his circumstances. Although he possessed many of the hardier traits of character, such as we may properly call the physical virtues, yet he was entirely destitute of those excellencies of feeling and condition which give symmetry and loveliness to life. Ignorant, superstitious, cruel, bestial and obscene, the victim of strong and degraded passions, and a houseless wanderer, exposed to the inclemencies of the seasons and the trials of want, he presented, in the main, none of the better beauties of humanity, and certainly no illustration of that wild whim of the philosopher of Clarens,—the perfection of the savage state, and the moral healthfulness of barbarism! More than this, the Indian has proved himself unsusceptible of civilization, and unfitted, by the instincts of his nature, for the higher, or even the lower, degrees of intellectual and social culture.

Though such is the general character of the aborigines of this country, yet it may not be denied that, in frequent instances, there have been manifestations among them of the nobler properties of mind and heart. Some of their warriors have exhibited a military spirit and genius unsurpassed in the annals of civilized warfare. Philip of Mount Hope, and Pontiac wanted but a fair field and auspicious circumstances, to have accomplished careers as brilliant as that which extended from Austerlitz to Waterloo. Combined with this capacity, other chieftains have wielded an influence over the judgments and passions of men, by the power of their eloquence, which must ever command our admiration. Who has not felt the deep pathos of the complaint of Logan? It is difficult to award Tecumseh the higher place as an orator or a warrior; and the eloquence of Piamingo never failed of its purpose, whether urging his red followers to the battle, or censuring the white man for unjust encroachments upon the territories of the Chickasaw.

These enumerations might be extended, but we prefer passing at once to the subject of the present sketch; a chieftain, who, though comparatively little known, comprised in his character the elements of the warrior and the statesman, as fully as any other native hero, and, for the elevation and effectiveness of his eloquence, certainly surpassed all aboriginal competition. In addition to this, his career was marked by a romantic interest little inferior to the incidents of wildest fiction, and his character partook of a spirit of rude chivalry, as singular and fascinating, as the circumstances, amid which it was developed, were unpropitious and repulsive. We know no finer instance in Indian history, of genius, heroism, and eloquence united; and, about the events, which brought these qualities into action, there were a consecutiveness of arrangement and a species of retributive operation, which give to the whole an epic or dramatic semblance and coloring very rare in actual occurrences. It is true, that the character of this Muscogee Chieftain was marked by other and opposite qualities; by cruelty, superstition, and the common vices of his time and people, yet they do not diminish, but rather heighten, the effect which a faithful narrative of his life and adventures is calculated to produce.

It is exceedingly difficult, however, to procure the materials for such a narrative. Little attention has ever been given to the history of the Muscogee Indians; and he who would understand the character and career of their principal Chieftain,—a warrior whose name, forty years ago, diffused terror along the whole Southwestern frontier,—is compelled to be content with meagre and incidental allusions, in a few scattered volumes and old newspapers, or with the exaggerated and contradictory accounts of fast-fading tradition. There is not, to my knowledge, anything like a biographical sketch of Weatherford. This deficiency I propose to supply, as a subject of historic interest to all parts of our country, but especially to the Southwest. What I shall state may be relied upon as strictly true; for, in addition to having examined with all care the published histories touching the time, I have drawn my information from the statements of several individuals who were personally acquainted with Weatherford, in the last years of his life, and heard him frequently narrate the most remarkable incidents of his history. Still my account will be found, to some extent, imperfect, from an ignorance of circumstances which it has been impossible to elucidate, and from the contradictions which always exist in traditionary narratives. This obscurity, while it detracts somewhat from historic completeness, yet leaves light enough to satisfy us that we are considering one of the most remarkable men, whether savage or civilized, which the American hemisphere has produced.

WILLIAM WEATHERFORD, who was sometimes called, in his native tongue, *Lamochattee*, or the RED EAGLE, was a scion of an illustrious stock, among the Muscogee or Creek Indians, produced by the intermarriage of various white men with females of the aboriginal race. Soon after the French, from Mobile, had established, in 1714, Fort Toulouse, as a military and trading station, near the junction of the Coosa and Tallapoosa, a Captain Marchand, in command at that post, took as his wife, according to the rude rites of the wilderness, Sehoy, a Muscogee maiden of the dominant Family of the Wind. From this union was born Sehoy Marchand, who married in 1740, Lachlan McGillivray, a shrewd Scotch adventurer from South Carolina. They left three children, one of whom, Alexander McGillivray, became the great Chief, or Emperor, as he styled himself, of all the confederated

Muscogee tribes. He was a man of the highest intellectual abilities, of considerable education, and of wonderful talents for intrigue and diplomacy. This he exhibited conspicuously, through the period of the American Revolution, in baffling alike the schemes of our countrymen, both Whig and Tory, of the Spaniards in Florida, of the British at Mobile, and of the French at New Orleans, and by using them simultaneously for his own purposes of political and commercial aggrandizement. A more wily Talleyrand never trod the red war-paths of the frontiers, or quaffed the deceptive black-drink at sham councils or with deluded agents and emissaries. His Life would make a most astonishing and attractive Romance. The other children of his parents were girls, and formed distinguished alliances. One of them married Le Clere Milfort, a talented French officer, who resided twenty years in the nation, as a War Chief, and then, having lost his wife, returned to Paris, published a Memoir of his "*Sejour dans la nation Creck*," and died a General of Brigade under Napoleon. Another sister, a very gifted woman, married Benjamin Durant, a Huguenot trader from South Carolina, of wonderful athletic powers, and gave birth to several children, among whom were Lachlan Durant, still living as the head of a family in Baldwin County, Alabama, and a daughter, who married one of the half-breed Baileys, so distinguished, in the defence of Fort Mims.

By a previous marriage with a Tuckabatchee chief, the wife of Lachlan McGillivray had had another daughter, upon whom she bestowed her own favorite queenly name of Sehoy. This young princess married, in 1778, Col. Tait, a British officer at Fort Toulouse—that fortress being then a British possession, as Mobile was also during the whole period of our Revolution. David Tait, a distinguished leader, and other children were the fruits of this marriage, and they have many descendants still surviving.

But Col. Tait soon left his half-breed wife, a buxom and beautiful widow, and she formed another alliance far more important in its consequences. This was with Charles Weatherford, an enterprising Scotch pedlar and a passionate lover of horse-racing, who entered the nation from Georgia and speedily amassed a considerable fortune in negroes and horses. He was a man of good English education and of great shrewdness, though Claiborne and others have described him as sordid, treacherous and revengeful.

The residence of McGillivray was principally at Little Tallasee, upon a beautiful upland lawn called the "Apple Grove," overlooking the Coosa; but his brothers-in-law made homes and plantations for their families at different points along the Alabama River, as far, even, as its confluence with the Tombeckbee. It is perhaps proper to state here, however, that all of these "head-men" had more wives than one, the Muscogee customs allowing polygamy as freely as the most libidinous Mormon could desire. The several wives occupied different cabins, often at very remote points. Still there was always a favorite wife, of chief right and authority, and the sisters of McGillivray need fear no rivalry, as well on account of their own intrinsic rank and abilities as from the vast influence of their brother.

Charles Weatherford acquired, by his marriage, great popularity in the nation, and took an active part in the political and diplomatic dealings with the Spanish and American authorities. His residence was on the eastern bank of the Alabama River, at the first bluff below the junction of the Coosa and Tallapoosa, and opposite the Indian village of Coosawda. Here he had a good dwelling-house and store, and, near by, his favorite Race Track, a strong point of attraction to the dissipated natives. These were mainly of the Alabama tribe, a large division of the Muscogees, who populated the country along both banks of the fine stream still retaining their name, to its union with the Tombeckbee. It may also be stated, that this particular tribe appears, from old maps and records, to have been identical with the Hillabees, the Allabees, the Ullaballis, &c., as their name is variously written by the older French and English writers—thus showing that the soft word *Alabama*, whose derivation has been much disputed, is compounded of *Alaba*, the name of the tribe, and the guttural ejaculation *ma* or *me*, so commonly used by the natives in conversation.

At this residence of his father, the Race Track, William Weatherford first opened his eyes upon the scenes in which he was destined to perform so conspicuous a part. The time of his birth is not certainly known, though it must have been about the year 1780, as he was but little over thirty at the commencement of the war in 1813. Under the instruction of his father, and his uncle, General McGillivray, and of General Le Clerc Milfort, young Weatherford, though he would not learn to read or write, acquired a very accurate knowledge of the English language, which was advanced and improved by visits to Pensacola and Mobile. But the mind of the young Indian, though grasping with singular readiness the knowledge thus imparted, was subject to stronger tastes and propensities; and he indulged in all the wild pursuits and amusements of the youth of his nation, with an alacrity and spirit which won their approval and admiration. He became one of the most active, athletic, and swift-footed participants in their various games and dances, and was particularly expert and successful as a hunter, in the use of the rifle and the bow. He was also noted, even in his youth, for his reckless daring as a rider, and his graceful feats of horsemanship—which the fine stables of his father enabled him to indulge. To use the words of an old Indian woman who knew him at this period, "The squaws would quit hoeing corn, and smile and gaze upon him as he rode by the corn-patch."

As he grew to manhood, the wars of his people with the Chickasaws and Choctaws, and sanguinary excursions to the frontiers of Georgia and Tennessee, opened fields for the exercise of his talents as a warrior, and, in many perilous expeditions and adventures along the waters of the Chattahoochee and the Cumberland,—the Tombeckbee and the Tuscaloosa, the young chieftain denoted that prowess and indomitable energy of character, which laid the basis of his subsequent influence with his tribe.

But, in addition to these military qualities, Weatherford, at an early period, exhibited that more intellectual power, Eloquence, which always fascinates and sways a savage people. His familiarity with the English language gave him a range of thought and facility of utterance, uncommon with native orators. The Muscogee language, like every other aboriginal tongue, being rude and uncultivated, was necessarily deficient in terms to express abstract ideas, or spiritual conceptions; and consequently its speakers were forced, when attempting these, into circumlocutions and comparisons drawn from the physical world. Their language, so to speak, was as much a material growth, as the birds and the blossoms. They had no synonymes for such words as Peace, and Virtue—the white wing of the crane was the symbol of the one, and the clear brook, or the morning breeze, betokened the other. This accounts for the picturesque and figurative style of Indian oratory: a style admired by us, from its poetic nature, but whose beauties were not apparent to its authors and were felt as restraints and necessities. The familiarity of Weatherford with the English language enabled him, the more readily, to obviate these difficulties, and to give freer scope, in expression, to his thoughts and feelings. This will be obvious, in the specimen we shall submit, of his oratory. Early, then, he acquired influence with his people, as an orator. His stirring appeals, unsurpassed in Muscogee tradition, roused them to the fight, or guided them in their deliberations, with a judgment and perspicuity which commanded confidence and respect. It was thus that a master spirit may ever assert its superiority among an ignorant and barbarous people; and the young orator and warrior soon found himself elevated, by his own force of character, to a commanding position in the councils of his tribe.

Such was Weatherford, in the earlier years of his manhood; and, in further illustration of his character, we may here introduce a sketch given by Mr. Claiborne, in his *Notes on the War in the South.* The reader will see that this sketch is by no partial hand. It was written while the author was incensed against our hero, for the atrocities committed in the war then recently concluded,—and an unjust coloring is given to the vices of his character. But we present the narrative unbroken, with only a slight change in the arrangement of its sentences:—

"Fortune bestowed on Weatherford, genius, eloquence, and courage. The first of these qualities enabled him to conceive great designs; the last to execute them; while eloquence, bold, impressive, and figurative, furnished him with a passport to the favor of his countrymen and followers. Silent and reserved, unless when excited by some great occasion, and superior to the weakness of rendering himself cheap by the frequency of his addresses, he delivered his opinions but seldom in council; but, when he did so, he was listened to with delight and approbation. His judgment and eloquence had secured the respect of the old;

his vices made him the idol of the young and the unprincipled. . . . . With avarice, treachery, and a thirst for blood, he combines lust, gluttony, and a devotion to every species of criminal carousal. . . . . Passionately devoted to wealth, he had appropriated to himself a fine tract of land, improved and settled it; and, from the profits of his father's pack, had decorated and embellished it. To it he retired occasionally, and, relaxing from the cares of State, he indulged in pleasures which are but rarely found to afford satisfaction to the devotées of ambition and fame. . . . . In his person, he is tall, straight, and well proportioned; his eye black, lively, penetrating, and indicative of courage and enterprize; his nose prominent, thin, and elegant in its formation; while all the features of his face, harmoniously arranged, speak an active and disciplined mind. . . . . Such were the opposite and sometimes disgusting traits of character in the celebrated Weatherford, the key and corner-stone of the Creek Confederacy."

Though, we say, this portrait is somewhat too darkly shaded; yet in 1812, Weatherford began to develope those features which rendered him odious to the American people. In the spring of that year, the celebrated Tecumseh visited the Muscogee Indians, and endeavored to enlist them in his famous conspiracy. His shrewd and penetrating mind at once discovered in the young chief of the Alabamas, as he had already become, a valuable ally for his designs, and, by making him his confident and principal war agent in the nation, he succeeded in winning him to his schemes. Weatherford had never liked the American people.

He boasted that there was no Yankee blood in his veins. His uncle, Gen. McGillivray, had carefully instilled this hatred into his mind, and the Spaniards at Pensacola, had, by repeated appeals to his avarice and ambition, stimulated him to hostility. He looked upon the constant encroachments of the Americans upon the territories of his people, as foreboding the extinction of his tribe, or their reduction to slavery and want. Under all these motives, he entered heartily into the plans of Tecumseh, and began to prepare for war. Artful appeals were made to the superstitions and passions of the Indians. A chieftain, named Josiah Francis, or *Hillishadjo*, appeared as a Prophet, and claimed to have received direct revelations from the "Master of Breath," that no red-man should be hurt in the war, but that the white people should all be destroyed. As essential to this, however, the Indians were directed to abandon all the arts of civilization; to destroy their clothing, ploughs and looms; and to resume their old savage habits and modes of life. Numerous other prophets, male and female, among whom were *Monohoe*, and *Sinquista*, aided in inflaming the minds of the Indians. The substance of one of these prophecies may be gleaned from a letter of Col. Hawkins, in the American State Papers; "The Great Spirit comes down to us in the sun: he comes down right over our heads. He has given us power to make thunder, and lightning, and earthquakes, and quagmires. He can make the ground open and swallow up our enemies. He can draw circles around our houses, and no white man can come in them, without falling down dead. He can rain down fire, and make the wind cut like hatchets. Be savages, and you shall be strong as the hurricane."

With such fooleries, and by the stirring eloquence of Weatherford, most of the Indians of the "Upper Towns," those on the Alabama waters, were won to hostilities. The Indians of "the Lower Towns," upon the Chattahoochee, generally remained friendly. The hostile party became as completely free from the restrictions of civilization as the most benevolent disciple of Jean Jacques could desire.

It was the wish of Weatherford, that an outbreak should not occur until the promised return of Tecumseh from the North. As he reflected upon the magnitude of the undertaking, and the power of the white foe, and as he found that a very large part of his own nation, including many of his near relatives and friends, who were among the most influential persons in the nation, would not join in hostilities, he began to hesitate as to the course he had intended. He was now living on a fine plantation near the Holy Ground, with his family, having many negroes, horses and stock about him. Finding that the storm of hostilities could not be allayed, he secretly went down to the residence of his half-brother, David Tait, on Little River, (the present dividing line between Monroe and Baldwin Counties,) to consult him and his other relatives, among whom was his brother, Jack Weatherford, as to what course he should pursue. They advised him to fly with his family, negroes and other property, to their neighborhood ; and he started home for that purpose.

Meanwhile the hostiles, discovering Weatherford's absence, and suspecting his purpose, seized his family, negroes, horses, and movable property, and took them to the Hickory Ground, shortly above Wetumpka. Weatherford, finding this, went to the Hickory Ground, and was told by the hostiles that they intended to keep his family and negroes as hostages, and would kill them and him, if he did not join in the war. Under this necessity, Weatherford revived his old determinations, from which unavoidable embarrassments had temporarily diverted him. He consented to swim with the stream which he could not stem.

The ferocities of the two parties in the nation, and the Battle of Burnt Corn, which we elsewhere describe, led at once to the attack upon Fort Mims. The particulars of that sanguinary affair are embodied in another sketch, and it is only necessary here to remark, that the worst features of the character of Weatherford, were then developed in dreadful hideousness. He, it is perhaps true, attempted, at first, to prevent the attack, but yielded to the importunities, of his warriors, and led them in the onset with a ferocity which no excuse can palliate. That he had some motives for wishing to avert this blow, will appear from circumstances we will now relate.

Not long before the war Weatherford had sought in marriage, as a second wife, the daughter of Joseph Cornells, a white man, who had long resided among the Indians as an interpreter, and married an Indian wife, by whom he had five children. These were George, Alexander, and James, sons, and Anna and Lucy, daughters. The family was wealthy, and one of the most influential in the nation. Their residence was at Tuckabatchee, on the Tallapoosa. Alexander became a chief, and by an Indian wife was the father of Opothle Yoholo, now a distinguished chieftain of his tribe in Arkansas. Anna Cornells, shortly before the war, married a son of the Big Warrior, the principal leader of the friendly Indians. The other sons had the trading habits of their father, and acted as pedlars in different parts of the nation. The career of James was marked by some romantic incidents, which may form an interesting episode in our narrative, as showing the singular modes of life and feeling among these denizens of the wilderness.

Some years before the war, James Cornells had purchased, from one of the McGirts, a ferry on the Alabama River, not far from the present town of Claiborne. Here, on a bold bluff overlooking the river, he resided with his niece, a handsome young half-breed. A man, named Jones, came to the place, with his wife, a fine-looking woman, who had no children. Cornells employed Jones to keep the ferry, and soon fell in love with his wife. The charms of a buxom dame, with fair complexion and blue eyes, were *too much* for the half-forest Lothario. She returned his partiality, and Cornells, in a spirit of savage equity, proposed to Jones to give him his niece in exchange for his wife. The proposition was agreeable to all parties, and Cornells accordingly took the dame, and removed to Burnt

Corn, where the road from Pensacola branched off into the nation. Here he located himself, as an eligible point to deal with the Indians and pedlars trading to and from Pensacola, and with the emigrants from Georgia, who passed by this place on their way to the Tombeckbee settlements and to Mississippi.

Jones, rejoicing in his new nuptials, remained at the ferry, having agreed to pay Cornells a portion of the receipts. He was, however, dissipated and drunken, and very reckless and desperate when under the influence of liquor. The "green-eyed monster" seems also to have speedily invaded his domestic sanctuary. One day, after having been off and got drunk, he returned home and found Jim Dale, a brother of the celebrated Canoe-Fighter, of whom we speak elsewhere, in his house, talking alone with his wife. This Dale was a very powerful man, but was lame from a crooked knee, which made one leg some two or three inches shorter than the other, and forced him to walk with a hobbling gait. The sight of the suspicious intruder in the shrine where he had "garnered up his hopes," at once roused all the Othello blood in the husband's bosom, and drawing his knife, he rushed upon him. Dale, albeit brave, was unarmed, and was forced to make a hasty and limping retreat into the yard, where, seizing a large weeding hoe, he turned and struck his pursuer with great force upon the top of the head. The blade passed transversely through the skull, but did not sever the cartilage of the brain. Jones fell senseless, with the hoe sticking fast in his head. Dale continued his hobbling flight, but the injured Desdemona sprang to her fallen lord, pulled out the hoe, and nursed him as well as she could. Savage hostilities had now broken out, and concealing her husband in a cane-brake, she carefully tended him until his recovery.

After the war, Jones resumed the ferry, but refused to pay Cornells any portion of the receipts, or to recognize any title in him. The indignant owner having come to see Jones about it, he became very mad, and seizing his gun, attempted to shoot Cornells, who fled for safety. For several days he skulked about from one place to another, not having any weapon to defend himself with against his drunken and desperate pursuer. At last, he took refuge in the camp of McGirt, where he thought himself safe. But one morning he was startled by the sound of a horse's feet, and looking out, saw Jones riding rapidly up, armed with a double-barrelled shot gun. Looking around for some weapon of defence, he could find nothing but an old rusty musket, which McGirt afterwards said, he believed had not been used since sometime in the war, and certainly had been loaded more than a year. The lock was all covered with rust and dirt. With this, Cornells sprang up, and, levelling it at Jones, ordered him to stop. The latter starting to raise his gun, Cornells cocked the old musket, and, pulling the trigger, the load went off and killed Jones dead on the spot.

Cornells now got possession of the Ferry, and received back his wife from Pensacola, whither she had been taken as a prisoner by McQueen's warriors and sold, after they had destroyed her husband's residence on Burnt Corn Creek, at the commencement of the wars.

The "widow Jones" soon solaced herself for the loss of her drunken and jealous spouse, in the arms of a second husband named Oliver.

From this romantic but well-authenticated episode, we return to our main narrative. The youngest daughter of Joseph Cornells was Lucy, an extremely beautiful and spirited maiden of about seventeen or eighteen summers. With her Weatherford became passionately enamored, and his affections were reciprocated. But hostilities breaking out just at this time, Joseph Cornells fled with his family to the Tensaw settlements and took shelter in Fort Mims. The presence of these and others to whom he was related, including the Taits, the Durants, the Baileys, and the Macnacs, rendered Weatherford unwilling to permit the massacre, and it is quite certain that he apprised some of the inmates of the intended assault. Of the few who escaped destruction, Cornells was one, not being in the fort at the time of the attack, and his daughter was taken to the nation by Weatherford, with whom she remained during the war. The father took an active part on the American side, and was of essential service as a guide in our army.

After his return from Fort Mims, Weatherford was, by general consent, declared the principal chief and warrior, or Tustenuggee, of the hostile Indians, and made every arrangement in his power to meet the approaching contest. We need not detail the particulars of that war; they are a part of the permanent history of our country. In nearly all the battles that took place, Weatherford was present, and distinghished himself for his generalship, intrepidity, and endurance. But what could be expected from the feeble numbers and resources of the Indians? The invaders pressed through every part of the nation, with a celerity as astonishing as their power was irresistible. The battle of Tallashatchee was fought the third of November; Talladega, the tenth; Hillabee, the eighteenth; Autossee, the twenty-ninth; Emuckfaw, the twenty-second of January, 1814; Echanachaca, the twenty-third; Enotichopco, the twenty-fourth; Caleebe, the twenty-seventh; and Tohopeka, or the Horse-Shoe, the twenty-seventh of March. These, with numerous smaller engagements, almost exterminated the nation. Not less than four thousand warriors are believed to have fallen victims to their wild fanaticism and martyr-like courage! And is it not strange that, through all these bloody fields, the chieftain most hunted and exposed, should have passed without even a serious wound? Some Fortune does indeed protect the Brave! Let us cite a few instances, not more romantic than well authenticated.

Echanachaca, or the Holy Ground, was the residence of Weatherford. The location of this spot has been, with some, a subject of uncertainty. Eaton, in his Life of Jackson, confounds it with the *Hickory Ground*, in the fork of the Coosa and Tallapoosa, and tradition has, in part, adopted the error. The Holy Ground proper, however, was situated along the south bank of the Alabama, between Pintlala and Big Swamp Creeks, in the present county of Lowndes. It received its name from being the residence of the principal prophets of the nation, and having been by them consecrated from the intrusion of white men. Wizard circles were described around its borders, and the credulous inhabitants were assured that no enemy could tread upon its soil without being blasted. It was emphatically called the "Grave of White Men." A more fertile and beautiful track of country, especially when clothed with the vegetation of spring-time, does not exist in our State ; and it was thickly populated by the aborigines. Near the mouth of Pintlala, stood a village of eighty wigwams. The chief town, a few miles below, contained two hundred houses ; and here the council house of the Alabama tribe was situated. At the beginning of the war, the Indians had removed their families and principal property to this place ; and it was also their main depot of ammunition and provisions. As the larger village was enclosed by pickets as well as magic circles, it was considered impregnable to all assaults. But on the 23d of December, 1813, General Claiborne, at the head of the Mississippi militia, with a band of Choctaws under *Pushmataha*, their Chief, invaded the Holy Ground and destroyed its villages, after a desperate resistance, in which many were slain. The women and children barely had time to escape across the Alabama. Weatherford conducted this defence with great judgment and courage. But neither the promises of the prophets nor the example of their chief could induce his followers to withstand the superior numbers and strength of the invaders. Weatherford was the last to leave the field, and, in consequence, came near being taken prisoner. Though mounted upon a swift horse, he was so closely pursued by a body of dragoons, that the only chance of escape left him was to make his way across the river. He pressed on for this purpose, but was so hedged and encircled by his pursuers, that he was forced upon the summit of a bluff which beetles over the river with an elevation of nearly an hundred feet. Upon discovering his position, the chief checked his steed, and, gazing around, saw that his pursuers were at a short distance and approaching rapidly, with shouts of joy and derision. Quickly raising his rifle to his eye, he singled out the foremost pursuer, brought him to the ground, and then urging his horse with a sudden impulse, the noble animal, dashing down a steep ravine for about half the distance, leaped over the bluff, and the two were borne with dreadful rapidity to the water. The horse retained his upright position, and the rider his seat, until they were within a short distance of the stream; they then seperated; the horse sank to rise no more; but the gallant Indian, unhurt by the fall, swam across the river, and escaped from his wondering and baffled pursuers.

The battle of Tohopeka put an end to the hopes of Weatherford. This village was situated on a peninsula, within the "horse-shoe bend" of the Tallapoosa. Here twelve hundred warriors, from the towns of Oakfuskee, Hillabee, New Yauka, and Eufaula, had fortified themselves for a desperate struggle, assured by their prophets that the Master of Breath would now interpose in their favor. Across the neck of land, three hundred and fifty yards wide, that leads into the peninsula, they had constructed powerful breastworks of hewn logs, eight or ten feet high, and pierced with double rows of port-holes, from which they could fire with perfect security. The selection of this spot and the character of its defences did great credit to the military genius of Weatherford—and his eloquence, more than usually persuasive and inspiriting, filled his devoted followers with a courage strangely compounded of fanaticism and despair. At an early hour in the morning, General Coffee's command having crossed the river and encircled the bend so as to cut off all escape, General Jackson opened his artillery upon the breastworks, and having but in part demolished them, ordered forward the thirty-ninth regiment to carry the place by storm. The van was gallantly led by Colonel Williams, Colonel Bunch, Lieutenant-Colonel Benton, and Major Montgomery. Amidst a most destructive fire, they pressed to the breastworks, and desperately struggled for the command of the port-holes. But Major Montgomery, impatient at the delay, cried out to his men to follow him, and leaped upon the wall in face of the deadliest fire. For an instant he waved his sword over his head in triumph, but the next fell lifeless to the ground, shot through the head by a rifle ball. A more gallant spirit never achieved a nobler death, and the name of the young Tennesseean is preserved as a proud designation, by one of the richest counties, as well as by one of the most flourishing cities, in the State whose soil was baptized by his blood!

The breastworks having been carried by storm, the Indians fell back among the trees, brush and timber of the peninsula, and kept up a spirited contest. But, in the meantime, a portion of Coffee's command, and some of the friendly warriors under their distinguished chieftain, *McIntosh*, had swam across the river, fired the village of Tohopeka, and carried off the canoes of the enemy. The followers of Weatherford now became desperate, and from the banks, hollows and other fastnesses of the place, fought with fury, refusing all offers of quarter. The fight continued in severity for five hours; and the going down of the sun was hailed by the survivors as furnishing them some chance of escape. But the hope was, in the main, deceptive. Already five hundred and fifty-seven lay dead upon the battle-field, and a great number now perished in the river. Not more than twenty warriors are believed to have escaped, under cover of the night.. Among these, strange enough, was the chieftain whose appellation, "the Murderer of Fort Mims," had formed the watchword and war-cry of his enemies in this very engagement. Favored by the thick darkness, he floated down the river with his horse, until below the American lines, and then, reaching the shore, made his way in safety to the highlands south of the Tallapoosa. The principal prophets of the nation perished in this engagement. In wild and fantastic decorations,—their heads and shoulders adorned with the plumage of the peacock and the flamingo, and with many jingling bells that kept music to their wizard contortions and dances, they had howled forth their incantations during the day; but perished with their deluded followers. Monohoe, one of the principal, was struck by a cannon ball in the mouth, while in the very act of giving utterance to a burst of pretended inspiration. Is it wonderful that the simple and superstitious savages regarded this as a signal and punishment of his impiety and falsehood?

After this battle, the hostile Indians generally came in and surrendered to General Jackson. A few, among whom were Francis, the prophet, and Peter McQueen, succeeded in escaping to Florida. The position of Weatherford was painful in the extreme. He knew that he was an object of special vengeance and retaliation with the American commander, for the cruelties perpetrated at Fort Mims. He felt that he was properly regarded as the head and front of the whole offending. A talk of Gen. Jackson to the Hillabee tribe, at the beginning of the war, had come to his ears, in which that officer said, that "the instigators of the war, and the murderers of our citizens, must be surrendered; the latter must and will be made to feel the force of our resentment. Long shall they remember Fort Mims in bitterness and tears." Weatherford could not consent to fly from the nation; he felt that he owed it, as a duty to his people, not to abandon them until peace was restored. In this state of mind he was apprised that the American commander had set a price upon his head, and refused peace to the other chiefs, unless they should bring him either dead, or in confinement, to the American camp, now at Fort Jackson, near the junction of the rivers. His determination was at once taken in the same spirit of heroism that always marked his conduct. Accordingly, mounting his horse, he made his way across the country, and soon appeared at the lines of the encampment. At his request, a sentinel conducted him to the presence of the commander-in-chief, who was seated in his marquee, in consultation with several of his principal officers. The stately and noble appearance of the warrior, at once excited the attention and surprise of the General, and he demanded of the Chief, his name and the purpose of his visit.

In calm and deliberate tones, the chieftain said: "I am Weatherford. I have come to ask peace for myself and for my people."

The mild dignity with which these words were uttered, no less than their import, struck the American commander with surprise. After a moment he expressed his astonishment that one whose conduct at Fort Mims was so well known, and who must be conscious that he deserved to die, should venture to appear in his presence. "I had directed you to be brought to me confined. Had you appeared in that way, I should have known how to have treated you."

Weatherford, his brow becoming slightly clouded, and his voice deep but not tremulous, immediately answered: "I am in your power. Do with me as you please. I am a soldier. I have done the white people all the harm I could. I have fought them, and fought them bravely. If I yet had an army, I would fight and contend to the last. But I have none. My people are all gone. I can now do no more than weep over the misfortunes of my nation."

The bold, dignified, and firm tone of this reply struck a sympathetic key in the commander's bosom. By intuitive perception the forest orator had discovered the only mode of address which, perhaps, could have softened the iron rigor of his conqueror's feelings: and the latter answered, in substance, that, while the only terms upon which the nation could be saved, were unconditional submission, yet, he said,—"as for yourself, if you do not like the terms, no advantage shall be taken of your present surrender: you are at liberty to depart, and resume hostilities when you please. But, if you are taken then, your life shall pay the forfeit of your crimes."

This answer appeared to Weatherford, at first, as a little ungenerous; and, calmly folding his arms upon his bosom, he replied: "I desire peace for no selfish reasons, but that my nation may be relieved from their sufferings; for, independent of the other consequences of the war, their cattle are destroyed, and their women and children destitute of provisions. But," he exclaimed, "I may well be addressed in such language now! There was a time when I had a choice, and could have answered you. I have none now. Even hope has ended. Once I could animate my warriors to battle. But I cannot animate the dead. My warriors can no longer hear my voice. Their bones are at Talladega, Tallashatchee, Emuckfaw, and Tohopeka. I have not surrendered myself thoughtlessly. While there were chances of success, I never left my post, nor supplicated peace. But my people are gone, and I now ask peace for my nation and myself. On the miseries and misfortunes brought upon my country, I look back with the deepest sorrow, and wish to avert still greater calamities. If I had been left to contend with the Georgia army, I would have raised my corn on one bank of the river, and fought them on the other. But your people have destroyed my nation. General Jackson, you are a brave man: I am another. I do not fear to die. But I rely upon your generosity. You will exact no terms of a conquered and helpless people, but those to which they should accede. Whatever they may be, it would now be folly and madness to oppose them. If they are opposed, you shall find me among the sternest enforcers of obedience. Those, who would still hold out, can only be influenced by a mean spirit of revenge. To this they must not, and *shall not*, sacrifice the last remnant of their country. You have told us what we may do and be safe. Yours is a good talk, and my nation ought to listen to it. They *shall* listen to it!"

This speech, pronounced with a calm, impressive voice, an erect attitude, and but little gesticulation, would have moved feelings less generous than those of Gen. Jackson. He at once acceded to the demands of Weatherford, and assured him of peace and safety for himself and people. As a specimen of oratory we know nothing finer than this address. It even surpasses the admired speech of Caractacus, the Briton, when led captive to Rome, and displays a spirit which would have done credit to Napoleon, under similar circumstances, after the Battle of Waterloo. In the ordinary characteristics of Indian eloquence, profuse imagery, it is wanting. There is not a metaphor, simile, or superfluous phrase in the speech. But in this consists its excellence. Deep feeling ever utters itself in the plainest language, and does not stop to cull the flowers of rhetoric and fancy. Had Weatherford dealt in these, would he not undoubtedly have failed in securing deliverance from his perilous position?

Though the American commander was thus conciliated, there were many friendly chiefs in the encampment who did not readily acquiesce in the pardon of Weatherford. Even during the delivery of the first part of his speech several guns were presented at him, and *Tustenuggee Thlucco*, the Big Warrior, went so far as to attempt his life, being with difficulty restrained by Gen. Jackson. Weatherford never forgave this conduct of his old enemy, but, long after, spoke of it as proceeding from cowardice and malevolence. The friendly Indians generally, however, treated the fallen chieftain, during his stay in camp, with the utmost deference. They seldom came in his presence, and, when any did, they were observed to quail before his eye, and tremble with fear.

From this time, until the treaty of peace and cession, on the ninth of August, 1814, Weatherford was actively engaged in inducing his friends and followers to accept the terms of submission offered by the American General. After some weeks, he visited his relatives upon Little River, near Fort Mims, and endeavored to collect together his negroes and cattle, at his plantation, in that quarter. But his life was in constant danger from the Steadhams and other survivors of the massacre, and he went to Fort Claiborne, and received the protection of Col. Russell, the commander. Even here, however, the avengers were upon his track, and the commander thought it best to send him to the main army under Gen. Jackson. Accordingly, one dark, stormy night, he was secretly conducted by Captain Laval, beyond the lines; was mounted on a fine horse, and started off rapidly for the American Head-Quarters. Here he remained, under the immediate protection of General Jackson, until the conclusion of the treaty of peace and cession. In that treaty, so marked by its stern and dictatorial tone, the Creeks were forced to yield all their territory west of the Coosa and south of the Alabama. This had been the country, principally, of the hostile party, and was demanded as the price of the war. Thus, the cruelties perpetrated at Fort Mims, and the mad policy of the fanatical chiefs and prophets, lost to the nation all the fine domains which subsequently became the State of Alabama. Truly does the gentle and sympathetic Bryant sing:—

> "And we have built our homes upon
> Fields where their generations sleep!"

In this treaty it was stipulated that a township of land should be reserved in the ceded territory, to each of the heads of the Indian families, who had been friendly during the war. By this provision, the Taits, the Cornells, the Sizemores, and Jack Weatherford, the brother of the chieftain, and many others were secured in their possessions. They also took charge of the property of their distinguished but unfortunate relative, in this quarter.

The war being over, General Jackson returned to Tennessee, taking with him several of the leading Indians. Among these, was his gallant and eloquent antagonist—Weatherford. The safety of the chief was the object of this act, and his presence was sedulously concealed. At the Hermitage he remained for nearly a year, (until after the seizure of Pensacola by Jackson,) and then returned to his relatives upon Little River. He brought with him two fine horses,—one of them a splendid blooded animal,—which had been presented to him by General Jackson. His relatives soon restored to him his property, and generously granted to him portions of their reservations, for a plantation. Such of his negroes, horses and cattle as had not been destroyed, were now brought from the interior of the nation, and served to re-instate the chief in somewhat of his ancient wealth. His home, to which his family repaired, was located in a fine live-oak grove upon the banks of Little River.

Here, almost within sight of the scene of his greatest cruelties, the chief of many a hard-fought field, pursued the peaceful occupations of a farmer. Gradually the country about him filled up with that race against whom his hand had been lifted with so much violence: but we know not that his quiet or repose was ever disturbed by unfriendliness or intrusion, except on one or two occasions, by the still revengeful Steadhams, who were eventually propitiated by the explanations of the chief and his friends. The character of the man seemed to have been changed by the war. He was no longer cruel, vindictive, idle, intemperate, or fond of display. But, surrounded by his family, he preserved a dignified and retiring demeanor; was industrious, sober, and economical; and was a kind and indulgent master to his servants, of whom he had many. A gentleman, who had favorable opportunities of judging, says of him, that "in his intercourse with the whites, his bearing was marked by nobleness of purpose, and his conduct was always honorable. No man was more fastidious in complying with his engagements. His word was by him held to be more sacred than the most binding legal obligation. Art and dissimulation formed no part of his character. Ever frank and guileless, no one had the more entire confidence of those among whom he lived." Another gentleman, who knew Weatherford intimately for a number of years, informs me that "he possessed remarkable intellectual powers: that his perceptions were quick almost to intuition, his memory tenacious, his imagination vivid, his judgment strong and accurate, and his language copious, fluent and expressive. In short," he says, "Weatherford possessed naturally one of the finest minds our country has produced."

These traits of character, exhibited for a number of years, won for their possessor, the esteem and respect of those who knew him, notwithstanding the circumstances of his earlier life. Indeed, those circumstances threw around the man a romance of character, which made him the more attractive. After the bitterness, which the war engenered, had subsided, his narratives were listened to with interest and curiosity. Though unwilling, generally, to speak of his adventures, he would, when his confidence was obtained, describe them with a graphic particularity and coloring, which gave an insight into conditions of life and phases of character, of which we can now only see the outside. He always extenuated his conduct at Fort Mims and during the war, under the plea that the first transgressions were committted by the white people, and that he was fighting for the liberties of his nation. He also asserted that he was reluctantly forced into the war, as has been described.

There are many characteristic anecdotes of Weatherford, in the last years of his life. We can preserve but one. A desperado named Callier, had committed a murder at Claiborne, and being armed, refused to be taken by the sheriff, and swore he would kill any man who approached him. The *posse* had been summoned, but were deterred by the threats of the criminal. At last, it was suggested that Weatherford was in the village, and if summoned would take him. The sheriff sought the chief, and, informing him of the circumstances, asked if he would make the attempt? "If you order me, I will do my duty," was the reply. "Then I order you to take him, dead or alive,"—said the sheriff, and the two proceeded to the ground. Callier was standing in an open square, with a drawn butcher-knife in his hand. Weatherford, loosening a knife which he wore in his girdle, immediately approached him, and ordered him to surrender. He replied only in a husky voice, "Keep off!" Nothing daunted,

Weatherford marched immediately up to him; he dropped the point of his knife; it was wrested from his hand; and he was delivered, a prisoner, to the officers of the law. Weatherford, being asked of his design in case of resistance, replied: "I fixed my eye upon his as I approached, and, if he had moved a muscle to strike, I should have dodged his blow, and cut his throat before he recovered." There is no doubt the chief understood the business he was about.

Weatherford continued to reside at his plantation until the spring of 1824. In that year, we find the following notice in a Mobile paper, with which we may draw our sketch to a close:

"William Weatherford, the celebrated savage warrior, is, at length, vanquished,—the destroyer is conquered,—the hand, which so profusely dealt death and desolation among the whites, is now paralyzed,—it is motionless. He died at his late residence near Montpelier, in this State, on the 9th of March instant. His deeds of war are well known to the early settlers in South Alabama, and will be remembered by them while they live, and be talked of, with horror, by generations yet unborn. But his dauntless spirit has taken its flight: he is gone to the land of his fathers."

Weatherford left behind him, a large family of children. They have now grown to years of maturity; have intermarried with our own population, and are highly respected for many excellent traits of character. A grand-nephew of his is now the United States' Consul at Cadiz, in Spain. No monument marks the spot where the remains of the distinguished chieftain were deposited,* but yet no unfit inscription for his grave might be found in the words which Wordsworth has applied to Rob Roy :—

> "And thou, although with some wild thoughts,
> Wild chieftain of a savage clan,
> Hads't this to boast, that thou didst love
> *The liberty of man!*"

---

* Recently, arrangements have been made by the descendants of Weatherford, to erect a monument to his memory, with suitable inscriptions.

THE CANOE FIGHT;

WITH A SKETCH OF THE FIRST AMERICAN SETTLEMENTS IN THE INTERIOR OF ALABAMA, AND OF MANY ROMANTIC AND SANGUINARY INCIDENTS IN THE CREEK WAR. ALSO, BIOGRAPHIES OF GENERAL SAM. DALE, JERE. AUSTILL, AND JAMES SMITH, THE HEROES OF THAT FIGHT.

"——The aged crone
Recounts the scenes of strife and daring gone:
Tells how the Indian scalped the helpless child,
And bore the shrieking mother to the wild,—
Butchered the father hastening to his home,
Seeking his cottage, finding but a tomb."

J. G. C. BRAINARD.

THERE has seldom occurred in border warfare, a more romantic incident than the one known in Alabama tradition, as the Canoe Fight. History has almost overlooked it, as too minute in its details for her stately "philosophy." Yet, for singularity of event, novelty of position, boldness of design, and effective personal fortitude and prowess, it is unsurpassed, if equalled, by anything in backwoods chronicles, however replete these may be with the adventures of pioneers, the sufferings of settlers, and the achievements of that class who seem almost to have combined the life and manners of the freebooter with the better virtues of social man. A detailed account will illustrate somewhat of this, and show, partially at least, the characteristics of the first white settlers, along the Alabama and Tombeckbee, and the difficulties they encountered and overcame.

The Canoe Fight was one of the early consequences of the massacre at Fort Mims. The friends and relatives of the sufferers in that sanguinary affair were roused to almost savage indignation and hostility. They were men well calculated, both by nature and habits of life, to meet such an emergency. With no dependence but the axe and the rifle, they had brought their families through the wilderness, and made them homes upon the table-plains and rich alluvial bottoms of our two principal streams. The character and habits of the Indians, they understood well; their stratagems in warfare, their guile and cunning. With a flexibility of nature, that still retained its superiority, they accommodated themselves to these, and were prepared, as far as their limited numbers would go, for the necessities of either peace or war. To a spectator, the strange buckskin garb, the hunting-shirt, leggings and moccasins, the long and heavy rifle, the large knife swinging by the shot-bag, the proud, erect deportment, but cautious tread, and the keen, far-seeing, but apparently passive eye, of the settler in the fork of the Alabama and Tombeckbee, upon the Tensaw, or about

Fort St. Stephens, would have spoken much of the moral energies and purposes of the man. Of such an order were most of those who determined to avenge the butchery of their neighbors, by Weatherford, at Fort Mims.

But before proceeding to narrate the particulars of the Canoe Fight, we will look at the situation of the settlements in the interior of Alabama, more immediately connected with that event, and narrate some of the more interesting incidents in their history, which led to the singular and sanguinary occurrence. They are in themselves sufficiently romantic to attract and repay perusal.

The extensive delta, forming Clarke County, was originally obtained from the Choctaws, by the British, under a treaty made at Mobile, the 26th of March, 1765. The boundary of the entire British acquisitions in West Florida was then designated as follows: "by a line extended from Grosse Point, in the island of Mon Louis, by the course of the western coast of Mobile Bay, to the mouth of the eastern branch of Tombeckbee River, and north, by the course of the said river, to the confluence of Alebamont and Tombeckbee Rivers, and afterwards along the western bank of Alebamont River to the mouth of Chickasaw River, and from the confluence of Chickasaw and Alebamont Rivers, a straight line to the confluence of Bance and Tombeckbee Rivers; from thence, by a line along the western bank of Bance River, till its confluence with the Tallotkpe River; from thence, by a straight line, to Tombeckbee River, opposite to Alchalickpe; and from Alchalickpe, by a straight line, to the most northerly part of Buckatanne River, and down the course of Buckatanne River to its confluence to the River Pascagoula, and down by the course of the River Pascagoula, within twelve leagues of the sea coast; and thence, by a due west line, as far as the Choctaw nation have a right to grant."

This treaty was signed by George Johnstone, Governor of West Florida, John Stewart, Superintendent of the Southern District, and twenty-nine Kings and Chiefs of Indians.* It is now mainly interesting as preserving the names by which several of our principal rivers were aboriginally known. The Alabama below the junction was called the Tombeckbee; the Cahaba was styled the Chickasaw, and the Black Warrior the Bance. The Choctaws, also, claimed much farther to the east than was then or subsequently recognized by the Creeks.

But few white men penetrated into this region during the British and Spanish times, and when the Americans began to take possession, about the commencement of the present century, they had to determine a new line with the conflicting Indian claimants. This was done in a treaty, made by Silas Dinsmoor and James Robertson, U. S. Commissioners, at Mount Dexter, in November, 1805. The new boundary of the white possessions was a line running north from Nanahubba, or the Cut-Off Island, along the dividing ridge between the Alabama and Tombeckbee waters, to the "Choctaw Corner," and thence westwardly to the mouth of Fluctabunna Creek on the Tombeckbee.

---

* American State Papers, Public Lands, v. 314.

Within the diminished area, thus acquired, emigrants, from South Carolina, Georgia, and Tennessee, poured rapidly for the first twelve years of the present century. These were the people destined to encounter the savage hostilities of the Creeks, after the Fall of Fort Mims, and whose characteristics have been described. Those nearest the border speedily erected stockade defences, and took refuge in them, with their families, servants, and moveable chattels and effects. Fort Sinquefield was erected a short distance north-east of Grove Hill, the present Court House of Clarke county; Fort White, some miles west of it; and Fort Glass, fifteen miles to the south, upon the dividing ridge between Cedar and Bassett's Creeks, and about three miles south from the present village of Suggsville. They received their names from the settlers upon whose premises they were established, and were densely crowded by the terrified inhabitants.

Around these border forts or stations, the hostile Indians were continually prowling,—burning and laying waste the farms, killing the cattle, and murdering every white person they could meet. The utmost terror and insecurity prevailed.

To give protection to these settlements, General Floyd, of Georgia, then in command of the South-western forces of the United States, ordered General Claiborne, in July, 1813, to march his command of Mississippi Twelve-months' Volunteers, to Fort Stoddart, and thence to yield assistance to the most exposed points to the east. At the close of that month, he arrived with seven hundred men, and sent two hundred of them under Col. Joseph E. Carson, a gallant volunteer, who lived near Mount Vernon, to the relief of Fort Glass, which he rebuilt near by and called Fort Madison in honor of the President. The refugée settlers in this station were under the command of Captain Evan Austill, a native of North Carolina, who had emigrated to this section, the year before, and located on a farm three miles from the fort.

Within two days after the massacre at Fort Mims, a large body of warriors, under Francis, the Prophet, appeared in the vicinity of Fort Sinquefield, the most exposed station, and massacred twelve members of the families of Abner James and Ransom Kimball, who rashly remained at the residence of the latter, two miles from the fort. Five persons escaped, one of whom was Isham Kimball, then a boy of sixteen, afterwards Clerk of the Circuit Court of Clarke County, where he still resides. Another was Mrs. Sarah Merrill, a married daughter of Abner James, who was destined to have a romantic history. She was knocked down by the Indians, scalped and left for dead. In the night, she revived, and, groping among the corpses, found her infant son, not a year old, who was also scalped, and apparently lifeless. With the utmost exertion, she made her way to the Fort, where she and her infant were gradually restored to health. Her husband was at this time absent, with the troops under Claiborne, and, on the march to the Holy Ground, heard that his wife and children were both slain. In the Battle at that place, he was severely wounded and reported as dead; but recovering, made his way to Tennessee.

Each party thus believing the other dead, Mrs. Merrill, some years after, married, and became the mother of a large family, residing in Clarke County, near the Choctaw Corner. She was happy, and some of her children had grown to maturity, when one evening a traveler with his family, a matronly wife and several children, stopped at the house of Mrs. Merrill. Great was her astonishment and consternation to find in the stranger her first husband; and his, none the less, to recognize his former wife. An explanation ensued, and, to the satisfaction of all parties, it was agreed that matters should remain as they had been providentially disposed. The traveler went on his way to Texas, and Mrs. Merrill continues to reside in Clarke, esteemed and respected by all who know her.

The news of the massacre of these families, reaching Fort Madison, a detachment of ten men, among whom were James Smith, John Wood, and Isaac Haden, were sent to the spot. They found the bodies of the dead, and took them to Sinquefield for burial. While the whole garrison of that little station, including the women and children, were outside of the fort, engaged in this ceremony, Francis and his warriors suddenly rushed down towards them from behind a neighboring hill. All escaped in safety to the fort, except a few women who had gone some distance to a spring. Seeing the Indians about to intercept these, Haden, who happened to be on horse-back, with a large pack of dogs, which he kept for hunting, immediately dashed forward, and cheered his dogs, with many others from the fort, numbering in all about sixty, to an assault upon the savages. Never did a pack of English hounds leap more furiously upon a captured fox, than did these wild curs upon the naked Indians. The necessity of defence against their strange foes, checked the savage onset, and all the women, but one, a Mrs. Phillips, who was overtaken and scalped, escaped with Haden into the fort. His horse was killed under him, and he had five bullets through his clothes, but received no wound.

The incensed Francis and his followers now made a furious attack upon the fort, but were repulsed with a considerable loss. Only one man and a boy of the defenders were slain. The Indians, having drawn off, the occupants of Sinquefield that night stealthily abandoned the place and fled to Fort Madison.

Meanwhile, Col. Carson had despatched Jerry Austill, a youth of nineteen, to Gen. Claiborne, at Fort Stoddart, for aid to drive away the Indians, who had killed one of his men, named Stewart, within five hundred yards of the gate. The youthful emissary traveled through the woods all night, and reached the General at day-break, greatly to his surprise and admiration. No assistance, however, could be sent, and Austill bore back an order to Carson to evacuate his defences and retire, with the inhabitants, to St. Stephens.

This order produced the greatest dissatisfaction, and Captain Evan Austill, the father of our young hero, and fifty other men, with their families, determined to remain. Four hundred persons left with Carson's command, amid a scene of great distress and lamentation at the separation of friends and relatives, who never expected to meet again. The little garrison remaining behind, protected themselves with the utmost vigilance, until at length Clairborne again despatched Carson's command to re-possess the fort.

During the occupation of Fort Madison, frequent parties of the more adventurous woodsmen made scouting excursions into the surrounding country, to watch the proceedings of the Indians. One of these advanced across the Alabama, as far as the destroyed residence of Cornells on Burnt Corn Creek, at the crossing of the Pensacola road. This party consisted of Tandy Walker, formerly the Government blacksmith at St. Stephens, but a most experienced and daring backwoodsman; George Foster, an expert hunter; and a bold quadroon mulatto, named Evans. When near the place, Evans dismounted, and, leaving his horse with his companions, stealthily approached to make observations. In a field, he saw an Indian, at a short distance, digging potatoes. He at once shot him, and, after some minutes, not seeing any other Indians, he entered the field and took the scalp of his victim. Returning to his companions, they examined the premises and found, on the opposite side of the field, the camp and baggage of a considerable party of Indians who had fled at the sound of Evans' gun. With this booty, the three adventurers now hastened towards the Alabama. At Sizemore's deserted old place, near the river, they found a field of corn nearly ripe, with a plenty of fine grass. Though they saw many fresh moccasin tracks and other signs of Indians, they determined to stop here to feed their horses and to pass the night. They accordingly went a short distance into the field, and, as it was a cool November evening, kindled a small fire and laid down to sleep. In the night, Foster had a strange and alarming dream, or "vision," as he termed it, which awoke him and filled him with apprehension. Arousing his comrades, and telling his dream, he urged them to leave the spot, as he felt they were in danger there from the Indians. They made light of his fears, and lapsed back into slumber. He however arose, and going still farther into the field, threw himself down in the high grass, and went to sleep. At the dawn of day, he was roused by a volley of guns fired upon his companions, and fled with all haste into a neighboring cane-brake, through which he made his way to the river, and swimming it, safely reached the fort.

After two days Tandy Walker came in, severely wounded,—his arm being broken by several balls, and his side badly bruised by a ball which struck a butcher-knife in his belt. It appeared that the Indians had waited until the first faint light of day to make their attack. They then fired some five or six guns and rushed forward with their knives. Evans was killed; but Walker, though wounded, sprang from the ground, and ran through the corn and high grass. Being very swift of foot, he outstripped his pursuers, and soon got into the cane-brake, where he lay concealed till night, suffering greatly from his wounds. Then he proceeded to the river, and making a raft of canes, to which he hung by his well arm, swam across the river. He was so feeble from the loss of blood and from pain, that it took him all that night and the next day to reach Fort Madison.

Shortly before this occurrence, Col. Willian McGrew, with twenty-five mounted men, had fought a battle with a party of Indians, on Tallahatta or Barshi Creek, near the northern boundary, in which he with three of his company was killed; and Gen. Claiborne, with a small command of Mississippi volunteers, under Major Hinds, had traversed the country as far as Baker's Bluff, on the Alabama, losing in a skirmish Capt. William Bradberry, a young lawyer, who had distinguished himself at Burnt Corn.

The inmates of Fort Madison, incensed at these sanguinary events, and satisfied that the body of the hostile Indians was now south of the Alabama, extending their depredations upon the plantations along that river, determined to make an expedition against them. This was at once organized; consisting of thirty "Mississippi twelve-months' yauger men," commanded by Capt. Richard Jones, from near Natchez, where he now resides, and forty-two volunteers, from the "settlers" themselves, commanded by Capt. Samuel Dale, who also had command of the expedition. A bolder or a finer set of men, for such a service, never swung their shot-bags by their sides, or grasped their long and trusty rifles. It may be well to look particularly at the character of three, who were destined to act the most conspicuous part in the events that are to follow.

SAMUEL DALE.

Was there ever a more Herculean figure than SAMUEL DALE, then in the noon and fulness of manhood? He stood a giant among his fellows,—already distinguished by feats of prowess, daring and enterprise, that had made his name known throughout the frontiers, and caused him to be dreaded more than any other white man by the Indians. They called him, in their simple tongue, *Sam Thlucco*, or Big Sam. Descended from Irish lineage, he was born in Rockbridge County, Virginia, in 1772. Twelve years after, his parents removed to Green County, Georgia, then on the border of the hostile Creeks. Here, among continued troubles and bloody forays, he grew to manhood, the eldest of eight children, left orphans by the death of both their parents. In 1794, he joined Capt. Fosh's troop stationed at Fort Matthews on the Oconee, and distinguished himself, in several encounters, for his courage, enterprise, and masterly knowledge of Indian character. On one occasion, when out as a solitary scout, at a great distance from the fort, he stopped at a spring to drink, and, as he knelt down for that purpose, two Muscogee warriors leaped from behind a log and sprung upon him, with their knives and tomahawks. Throwing one of them over his head, he grappled with the other, and plunged his knife in his body. Both of them now closed, but Dale, by his great strength and dexterity, in a few seconds laid them dead at his feet. Though wounded himself in five places, he retraced their trail nine miles, to their camp, where he saw three warriors asleep, with a white female prisoner. Rushing suddenly upon them he slew them all, and turning, had just cut the thongs of the woman, when a fourth warrior sprang from behind a tree, knife in hand, upon the bent body of the wounded and exhausted Dale, and brought him to the ground. With a wild scream of vengeance, the savage swung aloft his knife to give the deadly blow, when the woman, who had seized a tomahawk, dashed it into his head, and he fell lifeless upon the body of her preserver. They then safely proceeded to Fort Matthews.

Elected Colonel, Dale was advanced to the command of a frontier post on the Apalachy, where he made himself the terror of the Red Men, and the shield of the settlements, till McGillivray concluded peace with Washington at New York.

Frontier tastes and aptitudes now converted the young soldier into an Indian trader, and we find him among the Cherokees and Creeks, exchanging calicoes, gewgaws, ammunition, fire-waters, &c., brought from Savannah and Augusta, for peltries and ponies. The profits of this trade were exorbitant, and would have enriched Dale, but he was as thriftless as he was adventurous and brave.

Desirous of becoming acquainted with the settlements upon the Tombeckbee, Big Sam made his way thither about the year 1808, accompanied by a party of emigrants, among whom was his younger brother,

James Dale, like himself a bold and powerful man, but who had been unfortunately wounded in one of the knees, so that a contraction of the muscle took place, making one leg two or three inches shorter than the other.

A series of expeditions to and from Georgia, in which he acted as guide for travelers and emigrating parties, with occasional protracted loiterings in the Indian villages, taking part in their athletic sports and games, and surpassing their swiftest and most powerful champions, now engaged our hero for a number of years. He also acted as a spy for our government, upon the operations of the Spaniards at Pensacola and Mobile, who, at the instigation of the British, were constantly exciting the Indians to hostility. In this capacity, he was greatly useful in counteracting the schemes of a notorious English emissary named Elliott, who was most energetic in fomenting discord. He also encountered Tecumseh, in the Tuckabatchee towns on the Tallapoosa, and first apprised the incredulous Hawkins, the United States agent, of the schemes of that bold and ambitious chieftain.

Dale was at the house of Colonel Joseph Phillips, at Jackson, on the Tombeckbee, in July, 1813, when James Cornells, mounted on a fast-flying grey horse, brought the intelligence that a large body of hostile warriors from the towns on the Tallapoosa, had burnt his house and corn-cribs, at a creek, afterwards called Burnt Corn, from that event, and taken his wife prisoner to Pensacola, where they had gone to receive arms and ammunition from the Spaniards and British. The startled settlements at once sprung to arms, and marched under Col. James Callier, to cut off the Indians on their return. In this expedition, Dale was Captain of the company from Clarke county. The unfortunate result of the battle is narrated elsewhere. But Dale performed miracles of valor, and was one of the last to leave the field, which he did not do until he received a severe wound in the breast, from a rifle ball, which glanced around a rib and came out at his back. For several weeks he suffered greatly from this wound, but at length fully recovered so as to take part in the expedition we are proceeding to describe.

JAMES SMITH.

In Dale's command was a private soldier, who already had a high reputation as an expert, daring, and powerful Indian fighter. Born in Georgia, in 1787, this scion of the universal Smith family was now a very stout, finely proportioned man, five feet eight inches high, weighing one hundred and sixty pounds. Residing near Fort Madison, he took refuge there at the outbreak of the war. His fearless and adventurous character may be indicated by an incident. One day he determined to visit his farm, about eight miles distant, to see what injury the Indians had done. Proceeding cautiously, he came to a house in which he heard a noise, and, stealing up to the door, he found two Indians engaged in bundling up tools and other articles, to carry them off. Leveling his gun at them, he made them come out of the house, and march before him towards the Fort. In a thicket of woods, the Indians suddenly separated, one on each hand, and ran. Smith fired at one of them and killed him, and, dropping his rifle, pursued the other, and, catching him, knocked him down with a light wood-knot, and beat out his brains. Recovering his gun, he went on to the Fort, and announced the adventure, which a party, who were sent out, discovered to be true.

This, and similar deeds of daring and prowess, gave James Smith a high position among his frontier friends and neighbors, as he took his place, rifle in hand, with buckskin garb, in the ranks of Captain Dale's adventurous volunteers.

JEREMIAH AUSTILL.

That tall, slender, sinewy youth of nineteen, six feet two inches high, erect and spirited in port, dark complexioned, eagle-eyed, is the son of a gallant sire, who, even since hostilities commenced, had made his way back from Georgia, through the heart of the Creek nation, swimming the streams, and stealing through the woods, to his family, in Fort Madison, there to as-assume, by election, the temporary command. Such was Evan Austill, a native of North Carolina, and the son was worthy of the sire. "Jerry" was born in Pendleton District, South Carolina, the 10th of August, 1794. Four years after, his father went as a gunsmith, with Silas Dinsmore, the agent to the Cherokees, to reside in the nation. In 1813, the family removed to the vicinity of Fort Madison. Driven from their residence by the Indians, during the absence of his father, young Austill returned to the spot, put up the fences, and kept a close guard, lying at night in the grass, or thick undergrowth near the farm, to protect the growing crop from the depredations of straggling Indians.

We have seen how he was sent, soon after, for assistance to General Claiborne, and how gallantly he performed that hazardous service. On one occasion he was dispatched with a party of five, to guard a wagon to a mill for meal. On their return, a fire was opened on a party of Indians, from the opposite side of the fort, at which all of the guard, save Austill, immediately fled from the wagon. With characteristic firmness and fidelity, he remained, and no assault being made, drove the wagon, with its precious contents, in safety to the fort, amidst the applause of the garrison, who derided his timid companions.

"Jerry," was now very little more than a boy in age, but his skill as a marksman, his swiftness of foot, his dauntless courage, and his deep knowledge of Indian schemes and cunning, acquired among the Cherokees, render him one of the most useful and manly of the frontier defenders. We have said that he was slender, but look at his muscular limbs, as revealed through his hunting shirt closely girdled around his waist, and his tight leather leggings, and you may appreciate that his frame, weighing as it did one hundred and seventy pounds, is possessed of all those powers which are most serviceable in the hardships and encounters of backwoods warfare.

These three, Dale, Smith and Austill, were the leading spirits in the expedition, fitted out under the command of Dale, for the exploration of the country along the Alabama River. The party left Fort Madison on the 11th of November, 1813. It proceeded southeasterly, under the guidance of Tandy Walker and George Foster, of whom we have spoken, to a point on the river, two miles below "Bailey's Shoals," and about eighteen miles below the present town of Claiborne. Here they found two canoes, carefully concealed in the inlet of a small creek, in which the entire party crossed to the eastern bank, and passed the night in concealment and under arms, no one being allowed to sleep. They were at this point within thirty miles of the ruins of Fort Mims.

The next morning the party ascended the river; Austill with six men in the canoes; and Dale, with the remainder, through the woods upon the eastern bank. No signs of Indians were discovered until their arrival at "Peggy Bailey's Bluff," three miles above. Pursuing these, which led up the river, Dale, being in advance of his men, soon came upon a party of ten Indians, who were, with all imaginary security, partaking of a bountiful breakfast. His unfailing rifle dismissed them without a benediction; the chief, a noted warrior, being slain, and his followers, in their hurried flight, leaving their well-stored pack of provisions behind them.

One mile higher up the stream Dale's party came to a field known as Randon's farm. This was a few miles below Claiborne and one hundred and five miles, by the course of the river, above Mobile. Here, upon consultation with Austill, it was concluded that the main party should re-cross the river to its western bank. For this pnrpose the canoes were put in requisition, and the men were cautiously and with as much swiftness as possible conveyed across the stream.

The river, at this point, was about four hundred yards wide. Its banks were irregular, somewhat precipitous, and covered with beech, pine, and sycamore trees, with a thick undergrowth of cane, vines, and luxuriant shrubbery. The eastern shore, which the party were now gradually leaving, sloped away into two embankments, one rising above the other with considerable abruptness, and then spreading out into the field of which we have spoken.

While the conveyance of the men across the river was progressing, Dale, with Austill, James Smith, G. W. Creagh, and a few others, determined to partake of the provisions they had found in the Indian pack. In the old field, on the second bank, they kindled a fire for the purpose of cooking these, and were about, in the language of Dale himself, "to make use of the *briled* bones, and hot ash-cake," when they were startled by the discharge of several rifles, and the sudden war-whoops of some twenty-five or thirty Indians, who came rushing towards them from three sides of the field. Dale's party immediately seizing their rifles, and being too few to oppose the force of the enemy, dashed down the second or upper bank of the river, and took post among the trees, whence they kept in check the approach of the savages.

By this time the canoes had conveyed all but twelve of the entire force to the opposite side of the river, and one canoe alone had returned for the residue. This was the first thought of the little party, who were now hemmed by the Indians. But simultaneously with the attack by land, a large canoe, containing eleven warriors, had issued from a bend in the river above, and descended rapidly with the evident design of intercepting communication with the opposite shore. They now attempted to approach the shore, and join in the attack, but were kept at a distance by the well-directed fire of a few of Dale's men. Two of their number however leaped into the river, and swam, with their rifles above their heads, for the bank, just above the mouth of a little creek, near the northern corner of the field. One of these, as he approached the shore, was shot by Smith; but Austill, in attempting to intercept the other, was thrown by the under-wood, and rolled into the water within a few feet of his antagonist. The Indian reached the shore, and ran up the bank. Austill, in pursuing him, through the cane, was fired at, in mistake for an Indian, by Creagh, and narrowly escaped.

During this bye-scene, Dale and the other eight of his valiant companions were interchanging hot fires with the enemy. Those in the canoe sheltered themselves by lying in its bottom, and firing over the sides. The party on shore were deterred from pressing closely by an ignorance of the number of Dale's forces. This cause alone saved them from certain destruction. But the circumstances were now growing more critical.

Soon the Indians must discover the weakness of their opponents, and rush forward with irresistible superiority. A more perilous position can scarcely be imagined: and yet there was one in this contest!

Dale, seeing the superiority of the enemy, called out to his comrades on the opposite shore for assistance. They had remained, thus far, inefficient, but excited spectators of the scene. But now eight of their number leaped into their canoe, and bore out towards the enemy. Upon approaching near enough, however, to discover the number of the Indians, the man in the bow, becoming alarmed at the superiority of the foe, ordered the paddles to "back water," and they returned to land! Dale, indignant at this cowardice, demanded of his men, who would join him in an attack upon the Indian canoe? Austill and Smith immediately volunteered; and with a negro, as steersman, named Cæsar, the little party embarked for the dreadful encounter. As they approached, one of the Indians fired without effect. When within thirty feet, Smith fired and probably wounded an Indian, whose shoulder was visible above the canoe. Dale and Austill attempted to fire, but their priming having been wet, their guns could not be discharged. Fortunately the Indians had exhausted their powder. The white party now bore down, in silence, upon the foe. As the boats came in contact at the bows, the Indians all leaped to their feet. Austill was in front, and bore for a moment the brunt of the battle. But, by the order of Dale, the negro swayed round the canoe, and "Big Sam" leaped into the enemy's boat, giving more room to Smith and Austill, and pressing together the Indians, who were already too crowded. The negro occupied his time in holding the canoes together. The rifles of both parties were now used as clubs ; and dreadful were the blows both given and taken ; for three stouter or more gallant men than these assailants never took part in a crowded *melee*. The details of the struggle can scarcely be given. Dale's second blow broke the barrel of his gun, which he then exchanged for Smith's, and so fought till the end of the scene. Austill was, at one time, prostrated by a blow from a war-club ; fell into the Indian canoe, between two of the enemy, and was about being slain by his assailant, when the latter was fortunately put to death by Smith. Austill rose, grappling with an Indian, wrested his war club from him, struck him over the skull, and he fell dead in the river. The last surviving Indian had been before the war, a particular friend of Dale's. They had hunted together long and familiarly, and were alike distinguished for their excellence in those vigorous sports, so much prized by the man of the woods. The young Muscogee was regarded as one of the most chivalrous warriors of his tribe. Dale would always say, when, long subsequently, he narrated these circumstances, and he never did so without weeping,—that he "loved that Indian like a brother, and wanted to save him from the fate of the others." But the eye of the young warrior was filled with fire ; he leaped before his opponent with a proud fury ; cried out, in Muscogee, "Sam Thlucco, you're a man, and I am another ! Now for it !"—and grappled in deadly conflict. The white man proved the victor. With one blow of his rifle he crushed the skull of the Indian. The young brave, still holding his gun firmly in his hands, fell backwards into the water; and the Canoe fight was over.

The victors now employed themselves in clearing the canoes of the dead bodies of the Indians. The only weapons left, of either party, were a war-club and rifle. The Indians upon the shore had, during the progress of the fight, kept up a constant fire with the party on land. They now directed many shots at the canoes, as they approached the shore. One ball passed between Smith and Austill, and another struck one of the canoes. But, in spite of this firing, Dale and his colleagues returned to the shore, took off their friends in safety, and passed across the river triumphantly. Notwithstanding the dangers they had encountered, the whole party had not lost one man, and the only injuries they had suffered, were some severe bruises received by the combatants on the water. Austill had a severe contusion on the top of the head, which left a permanent dint in the skull. It was subsequently ascertained that the entire Indian force, on land and water, was two hundred and eighty.

Such, in its details, was the Canoe Fight,—certainly the most remarkable of our *naval* engagements. Neither Porter at Valparaiso, nor Perry on Lake Erie, displayed more reckless courage, or indomitable fortitude, than did these backwoodsmen of Alabama. The difference, as far as personal achievement, is all in favor of the latter. The statements made may be relied on as strictly true. They are collated from accounts given by the actors themselves; and the events were witnessed by many who are still living to attest their truth.

Brightly shone the eyes of the anxious occupants of Fort Madison, when, on the very evening of this bloody engagement, Dale and his gallant comrades, by a forced march of twelve miles, returned to that place. Loud were the plaudits of all, and aged gossip and prattling child learned to utter the names of the Heroes of the Canoe Fight with admiration and pride.

The war went on, with many stirring adventures and bloody incidents; but these we cannot now enumerate, except casually, in connection with the biographies of Dale, Smith, and Austill. They each marched with Gen. Claiborne in his expedition to the Holy Ground, and acted conspicuous parts in the battle there fought, on the 23d of December, 1813. Austill, in particular, distinguished himself, by crossing the river in a canoe, with Pushmataha, the great Choctaw chief, and six warriors, in front of the enemy's fire, putting a large party to flight, and capturing a considerable quantity of baggage and provisions.

The army having returned to Fort Claiborne, the volunteers and militia were disbanded, as their time of service had expired, and returned home, leaving only a small force of regulars under Col. Gilbert C. Russell, at that place. The troops, however, from along the Tombeckbee, and the fork of the rivers, were not willing to leave the frontiers thus poorly defended, and they accordingly formed a force of volunteers, under Colonel Joseph E. Carson, with Reuben Saffold, Charles Devereaux, John Wells, and —— McFarland, as Captains; Smith and Austill were Sergeants in this command, which acted as rangers from Claiborne to the Gulf, and frequently encountered parties of Indians, and killed many of them.

After the conclusion of the war, Dale became an agent of Gen. Jackson and the other American officers in command at Forts Claiborne and Montgomery and at Mobile, to watch the proceedings of the British and Spaniards at Pensacola, performing many hazardous enterprises, and mainly communicating the intelligence which led to the seizure of that post—bearing himself a part in its assault and capture.

Smith and Austill lapsed back into private life,—resuming agricultural pursuits in Clarke County, which they had so gallantly defended. Smith, in a few years, removed to eastern Mississippi and there died, respected for his sterling qualities of character.

Austill removed to Mobile, and engaged in commercial pursuits, greatly esteemed for his intelligence, integrity, and energy of character. For one session he has served in the State Legislature. At the present time (1857) he partly divides his time with agricultural pursuits in Clarke, and is in the enjoyment of vigorous health, looking many years younger than he really is.

The career of Samuel Dale was more conspicuous than that of his two associates in the Canoe Fight. In 1817, the people of Monroe, then a rich and flourishing county, chose him Tax Collector; but, by a fire, he lost a portion of the funds in his hands, and became a defaulter, in the sum of three hundred dollars. This the Legislature in 1821, by an Act, exonerated him from paying. His misfortunes drew attention to his services, and at the same session an Act was passed "expressing the gratitude of the State of Alabama, for the services rendered by Samuel Dale." It recapitulated, in a laudatory preamble, his preeminent services during the war, and stated that he had "exposed himself to privations, hardships and difficulties that have impaired his constitution and reduced him to indigence:" also, that from a want of sufficient vouchers, he had never received any compensation from the General Government. It, *therefore*, enacted that "the Treasurer be and he is hereby required to pay to the said Col. Samuel Dale, half the pay now allowed by the General Government to Colonels in the army of the United States. And that he is hereby declared a Brevet Brigadier General, in the militia of this State, and shall rank as such whenever called into the service of this State. And the Governor is hereby required to commission him accordingly; and that the Treasurer is authorized and required to pay to said Brevet Brigadier General Samuel Dale, on the first day of January, in each and every year, the half-pay as aforesaid for and during his life, out of any monies in the Treasury not otherwise appropriated."

This act, so creditable to the gratitude of our people, was permitted to operate for two years, when, upon some constitutional scruple, it was repealed, and a memorial pressing Gen. Dale's claims on the General Government was sent to Congress in the name of the State. It is an eloquent vindication of his right to remuneration, and says, among other things, that "during the war he frequently went on express with dispatches from the armies in this country, to the State of Georgia, through a hostile country of Indians, of nearly three hundred miles, and almost every foot of the journey, through the woods, and thereby rendering services to our armies which no body else could be found who would undertake or who would perform. Compensation in money, or by grant of lands in this State, is earnestly besought."

To this appeal of the State of Alabama in behalf of an old and indigent soldier, who, it was said, had, "at the head of small parties, waged a gallant partisan war, surpassed probably in no age or country, and which will some day form an interesting page in American History,"—Congress continued to turn a deaf ear, and, it is believed, he never received any assistance from the Federal Government. He made several ineffectual visits to Washington City for that purpose. His fellow-citizens of Monroe County were, however, more kind and considerate. Besides ministering to his pecuniary wants, they elected him on several occasions a member of the General Assembly. The State also showed her honors for him by establishing a county with his name, in December, 1824. After a short residence in Perry County, Gen. Dale, in 1835, removed to Lauderdale County, Mississippi, and the next year was elected to the Legislature of that State. He, however, had little taste for public life, and passed his time chiefly on his farm, which was a favorite resort of white visitors who loved to hear the old warrior recount his adventures, and of a neighbouring band of Choctaws, still lingering in the State, who also gazed with curiosity and admiration on "Big Sam," and partook of his bounty always liberally bestowed.

On the twenty-third day of May, 1841, this old hero, pioneer and guide closed his many fights,—passing through the last struggle with more calmness and serenity than he had ever exhibited before. He died, says a friend, with the fortitude of a soldier, and the resignation of a christian. The day had been one of cloud and tempest, but ended with a golden sunset: no unfit type of a career of struggle and suffering, brightened at the close by the purest consolations of humanity. A Choctaw warrior stood, the next evening, by his grave, and exclaimed in his rude vernacular: "Sleep here, Big Sam, but your spirit is now a Brave and a Chieftain in the hunting-grounds of the sky!"

This rambling record here must end. We have shown the condition and character of our earliest Anglo-American population; the Red Sea of trials and sufferings through which they had to pass; the fragile bark that floated in triumph through the perils of the tide; and the heroic performances of the three master spirits of the period. From such rude and troublous beginnings, the present prosperous population of Alabama, acquired the right to say, "Here we rest!"

THE FAWN OF PASCAGOULA;

OR, THE

"CHUMPA" GIRL OF MOBILE.

SHALL I tell you a story of real life as romantic and *ffecting* as any you will find in fiction? Well—lis-en! Every citizen of Mobile is familiar with the sight f the Indian girls who are in our streets in the winter. With their little bundles of lightwood upon their backs, hey mark the advent of cold weather as regularly as he mocking-bird and the cardinal chronicle the ap-roach of Spring. They peddle their small parcels of ine from door to door, and all are familiar with the oft, quick, petitionary voice in which they exclaim "*chumpa*," as they offer their cheap burdens for sale.

These Indian girls, it is well known, belong to cer-ain Choctaw families, who refused to emigrate with heir tribe beyond the Mississippi, and yet linger upon heir aboriginal hunting-grounds on the waters of the Pearl and Pascagoula. Though they thus exhibit an nconquerable attachment to their native soil, they ave yet refused to adopt the habits, language or pursuits of the whites by whom they are surrounded, and are perversely indifferent to all the inducements of civilization. They persist in leading a species of savage *gipsy* life—the men sustaining themselves by hunting, and the women, by vending whortle-berries, and other wild fruits in the summer, and bundles of pine in the winter. With these simple productions, they visit Mobile semi-annually, and for the time reside in the vicinity, in small huts or camps, constructed of bark, boards, or the limbs of trees. This has been their custom from time immemorial, and it yet continues.

These Indians are generally a miserable and ignorant race, but with all their degradation, they possess some of the virtues in a singular degree. The women are proverbially chaste and modest, and, of all the young girls that annually visit our city, none have been known to depart from the paths of rectitude. A strong interest therefore surrounds these simple daughters of the woods, who resist all the blandishments of their station, and pass unharmed through the streets of our city. Many of them are quite handsome, and possess, beneath their rustic garbs—the calico gown and the red blanket—considerable graces of manner and appearance. As they invariably refuse to talk English, very little conversation can be had with them, and that only in reference to the small bargains which they desire to make. "*Chumpa,*" and "*picayune,*" are almost the only words which they employ in their intercourse with our inhabitants. Still, they are not reserved in their movements where they wish to make a bargain, and enter the different houses of the city, stores, dwellings, and offices, without ceremony, hesitation or announcement. Who has not been startled many a morning, by a voice, at the chamber-door, exclaiming "Chumpa?"

The stoical demeanor of these Choctaw maidens has often led to the impression that they are destitute of the natural sensibilities and sentiments of their sex. They have bright, flashing eyes, well developed, symmetrical and flexile forms, beautiful small hands and feet, and show, in their love for brilliant articles of dress, rings, beads, and other personal decorations, the taste and vanity of their civilized sisters; is it possible that they are destitute of those delicate sympathies and tender affections which have marked woman in all other classes and conditions of life? This question has doubtless suggested itself to many, as an interesting problem of character. In one instance, at least, an attempt—perhaps a heartless one—was made to solve it, and it is to that the story which I have to tell refers. It came to my knowledge in all its details, but I will attempt to narrate it in such a manner as not to detain the reader with particulars which he can imagine for himself.

Among the Choctaw gipsies, who visited Mobile in the winter of 1846, was one of unusual beauty and attractiveness. Although scarcely developed into womanhood—not more than seventeen "suns" having kissed the rich bronze of her cheek—she was yet tall, round-limbed, straight and graceful—a very model of feminine form. Her features, more prominent and regular than is usual with her tribe, were delicately sculptured, and the erect attitude of her head, with her large fawn-like eyes, and abundant coal-black hair, always neatly plaited in massive folds, gave to her appearance an air of superiority such as the youthful Pocahontas is said to have possessed. Her dress was extremely neat, though with a large number of silver and wampum ornaments, and her small feet, which any of the fair promenaders on Dauphin might have envied, were invariably dressed in moccasins, ornamented in the most fanciful style with many colored beads. As she walked about the streets of Mobile, arrayed in this way, with her parcel of pine swung across her shoulders, she attracted the attention of all spectators, for her beauty, though she would hold converse with none except in the few words, by which she endeavored to dispose of her burden.

Much interest was naturally felt in this young girl, and many efforts were made to learn something of her character and history. Nothing further could be gleaned, (and this was told by "Captain Billy," a drunken Choctaw, frequently seen, in garrulous moods, in our streets,) than that she was the daughter of an Indian Chief of much note, who died many years before, leaving her, an only child, with her mother, in their cabin on the Pascagoula. Her singular beauty had made her quite a belle with the young Choctaw warriors, but she was very shy, and was called in the Indian tongue, The Wild Fawn of Pascagoula. She supported her mother, who was very old, and herself, by her traffic in berries and "lightwood." Her personal charms made her one of the most successful dealers in these articles, and every one, particularly the young men of Mobile, were glad to give the preference in their patronage to this young and attractive creature. Many were the efforts made to gain her smiles, and enlist her in conversation, but they were all in vain. She would go her daily round, and enter with perfect unreserve, the rooms or offices of her patrons, deposit her little load of pine, receive her dime, and then quickly retire with, *the sticks in her hands*, to procure another parcel.

Things glided on in this way for some months, during the winter of which I speak. At last an event occurred, which tested the stoicism and character of the young Fawn of Pascagoula. Among those whom she daily supplied with lightwood, was a young lawyer, residing in an office in the second story of a building on one of our principal streets. Admiring the beauty of this timid visitor, and feeling a strong interest in her, he determined to see if he could not, by kindness of manner, deferential notice, and elegant presents, win the heart of this simple child of the woods. Though his motive was mainly curiosity, his purposes were not bad, and he had no idea of doing any injury to the object of his experiment—by paying her those attentions which had been found potent to enchain the admiration, and win the love of more enlightened and accomplished maidens. He was a man of uncommon personal beauty, and singularly fascinating manners, and all these he brought to bear, as well as he could, to effect his innocent, and, as he thought, harmless *flirtation*.

It is needless to detail the arts resorted to by Henry Howard to win the heart of the Fawn of Pascagoula. He began in the most modest and deferential manner; he purchased from her, much more frequently than he needed, supplies of fuel, paid her larger sums than she asked, and made her presents of trinkets, pictures, and little ornaments of dress, and accomodated himself in every way to her apparent wishes. These things continued for some weeks, and at last began to have obvious effects. The Fawn tarried longer in her visits at his office than elsewhere; she always came there first, and took an evident interest in his attentions. At length she began to answer his remarks in such few words of English as she could command, and to look upon his handsome and fascinating countenance with pleased smiles and earnest continued attention. The spell evidently began to work! Henry Howard understood the secrets of woman's heart well; but here he had to deal with an untutored Indian girl, timid as a bird, and whose springs of emotion and sympathy could not be determined by the ordinary standards of feeling.

Do not think that I am depicting those subtle arts of fascination by which the rattle-snake lures and captivates the humming-bird. There was no purpose of evil in the heart of the young attorney. He was but practising, with a simple savage heart, those tricks and elegancies of intercourse, which are recognized as legitimate in civilized society. He wished to see if the same affections could be developed in the beaded beauty of the forest, as are to be found with the polished belle of the ball-room and the *boudoir*. The probabilities were, that the experiment would not succeed—a casuist would therefore think it harmless.

Months had passed in this way, and Henry Howard at last determined to make a more obvious demonstration of his love, to the Fawn of Pascagoula. One cold morning in February, just as he had finished his toilet, he heard a light step at the door, and a well-known voice, as the speaker entered, playfully exclaiming "*chumpa, chumpa!*" Arrayed in her most beautiful dress, with a band of silver around her hair, and long necklaces of beads falling from her graceful neck, the Fawn stood before him. She threw her armful of pine upon the hearth, and looked smiling into his face. In his most graceful manner he approached her and took her hand in his. Suddenly he encircled her waist with his arm, and, drawing her to him he imprinted upon her lips, a long and fervent kiss. Modestly she looked into his face, with a slight expression of surprise, but not dissatisfaction; and then he poured forth to her warm and urgent words of love. Neither were these coldly spoken, for the young and ardent admirer had been no little interested in the object of his attentions. As he was about, however, to repeat his kisses, the now startled Fawn, by a quick movement, unloosed herself from his embraces, and glided across the room.

"Stand off, Mr. Howard," she exclaimed in better English than he had ever heard her speak before, "Me good friend to kind gentleman—but no love! The Fawn must marry her own people. She love young warrior up on Pascagoula! He have heart and skin the same color! Mobile man not good for Choctaw girl. Me go to my home—to Choctaw Chief's cabin—to morrow. Good-by! Me love you much,—you so kind,—but no wife!"

As she said this, she drew her red blanket as proudly about her, as ever a fashionable belle donned her mantilla at a ball, and glided from the door. Struck as motionless as a statue, the elegant Henry Howard, the Mobile dandy, stood gazing at the door through which the young Choctaw girl had vanished! His lips were slightly parted, his eyes widely open,—a look of wonder and doubt upon his handsome face!

"By heavens!" he exclaimed, "Is it possible! Caught in my own trap! Jilted by an Indian! Well! it's a good joke, and all right! But, by Tecumseh and Pushmataha! I must take care that the belles of Mobile do not find out the story. Let who will hereafter experiment upon Choctaw character, to discover whether these Chumpa-girls have not like affections with other people, I, for one, am satisfied. This Fawn of Pascagoula has for months taken all my presents and delicate attentions with the timid gentleness of a nun, and now has given me the *sack* as completely as it could have been done by any fashionable coquette in a gilded saloon, by the light of a chandelier. Well, that's something rich! Bravo! Henry Howard! Recollect hereafter, as Tom Moore says:

'What'er her lot, she'll have her will,
And Woman, will be Woman still.'"

THE END.

www.ingramcontent.com/pod-product-compliance
Lightning Source LLC
LaVergne TN
LVHW020212110826
845151LV00003B/685

9781425534738